Flexibility and Pedagogy in Higher Education

Flexibility and Pedagogy in Higher Education

Delivering Flexibility in Learning through Online Learning Communities

Edited by

Chris Dennis, Stuart Abbott,
Ruth Matheson and Sue Tangney

BRILL
SENSE

LEIDEN | BOSTON

All chapters in this book have undergone peer review.

Library of Congress Cataloging-in-Publication Data

Names: Dennis, Chris, editor. | Abbott, Stuart (Stuart G.), editor. | Matheson, Ruth, editor. | Tangney, Sue, editor.
Title: Flexibility and pedagogy in higher education : delivering flexibility in learning through online learning communities / edited by Chris Dennis, Stuart Abbott, Ruth Matheson and Sue Tangney.
Description: Leiden ; Boston : Brill | Sense, 2020. | Includes bibliographical references and index.
Identifiers: LCCN 2020031601 (print) | LCCN 2020031602 (ebook) | ISBN 9789004438095 (paperback) | ISBN 9789004438101 (hardback) | ISBN 9789004438118 (ebook)
Subjects: LCSH: Internet in higher education. | Web-based instruction. | Education, Higher--Effect of technological innovations on. | Distance education.
Classification: LCC LB2395.7 .F59 2020 (print) | LCC LB2395.7 (ebook) | DDC 378.1/7344678--dc23
LC record available at https://lccn.loc.gov/2020031601
LC ebook record available at https://lccn.loc.gov/2020031602

ISBN 978-90-04-43809-5 (paperback)
ISBN 978-90-04-43810-1 (hardback)
ISBN 978-90-04-43811-8 (e-book)

Copyright 2020 by Koninklijke Brill NV, Leiden, The Netherlands.
Koninklijke Brill NV incorporates the imprints Brill, Brill Hes & De Graaf, Brill Nijhoff, Brill Rodopi, Brill Sense, Hotei Publishing, mentis Verlag, Verlag Ferdinand Schöningh and Wilhelm Fink Verlag.
All rights reserved. No part of this publication may be reproduced, translated, stored in a retrieval system, or transmitted in any form or by any means, electronic, mechanical, photocopying, recording or otherwise, without prior written permission from the publisher. Requests for re-use and/or translations must be addressed to Koninklijke Brill NV via brill.com or copyright.com.

This book is printed on acid-free paper and produced in a sustainable manner.

CONTENTS

	List of Figures and Tables	vii
	Notes on Contributors	ix
	Introduction *Chris Dennis, Ruth Matheson and Sue Tangney*	1
1.	Bend Me, Shape Me: Flexible Pedagogies to Widen Participation and Deliver on Social Justice *John Butcher and Liz Marr*	11
2.	Promoting Flexible Learning through Embedded, Online Study Skills Support *Leila Griffiths*	23
3.	Greater Than the Sum of Its Parts: Coalescing Digital and Physical Learning Spaces in Temporary Online Learning Communities *Chris Little and Matthew Street*	39
4.	Enhancing the Student Experience: Examples of Joint Student-Staff Partnerships to Create and Embed Online Peer Networks within Programmes of Study *Nicola Poole and Sophie Leslie*	53
5.	A Classroom without Walls: Academic and Student Nurses Co-Curating Twitter in Partnership *Moira McLoughlin and Wendy Sinclair*	65
6.	Shadow Modules and Student-Led Online Learning Communities: Supporting Learning, Engagement, and Student Empowerment within, and across, Institutions in Higher Education *Sheila L. Amici-Dargan, Amber M. Moorcroft and Stephen M. Rutherford*	79
7.	Youth Justice Live! Flexible Pedagogies in an Online/Offline Community of Practice *Sue Bond-Taylor and Ceryl Teleri Davies*	97
8.	Opening the Door to the Virtual School: Enhancing Student Engagement through Online Learning Communities *Sharon Smith and Ruth Hewston*	109

CONTENTS

9. Academic Support Online: Developing an Integrated Academic Support Environment at the University of the Arts London   123
   Graham Barton and Alex Lumley

10. Commonplace: A Student-Led Survival Guide to Support Transitions and Belonging at University of the Arts London   145
    Siobhan Clay and Paul Tabak

11. Flexibility, Socialisation and the Use of Twitter by a University Library: Building Community through Social Media in Co-Curricular Settings   163
    Chris Dennis, Stuart Abbott and Rob Sell

12. The Student Hub Live: The Open University's Solution to Facilitating the Development of an Academic Community in Distance Learning through Collaborative Online Interaction   179
    Karen Foley

13. Online Learning Communities and Flexibility in Learning   193
    Chris Dennis

Index   199

FIGURES AND TABLES

FIGURES

6.1.	The shadow module	82
6.2.	Interactions between shadow module constituencies	83
6.3.	Potential benefits of shadow modules on key stakeholders	89
6.4.	Summary of the key motivations and barriers to student engagement in online communities specifically for supporting shadow modules	90
9.1.	Key features of *Academic Support Online*; resources sit under nine topic areas	126
9.2.	Each menu-based topic area ('writing' has been selected in this example) has a range of resources organised under 'getting started', 'developing skills' or 'exploring further'	127
9.3.	Each individual resource has an introductory page, which is tagged, and shows links to related workshops, tutorials or other events; a click on the image opens the resource	127
9.4.	Further resources related to the one selected appear under each resource descriptor, extending the visibility of the offer	128
9.5.	Workshop description, with additional screenshot illustrating the one-click registration functionality, and integration of face-to-face and online offer	128
9.6.	Enhanced search functionality and integrated tagging. This example page shows search returns for the term 'essay' – illustrating the ability to search and then browse via ASO content type (event, FAQ, resource, tutorial, viewpoint) and theme	129
9.7.	Relational tagging, termed 'themes' – users can navigate the site through themed hyperlinks	129
9.8.	A 'Viewpoints' resource within the media channel, illustrating the simplified contextual information	130
9.9.	Summary analytics data for *Academic Support Online* – year 1	131
10.1.	Screen capture of Commonplace homepage	146
10.2.	Content posted by type 2011–2017	152
10.3.	Screen capture of 'If only someone had told me'	153
10.4.	Screen captures of 'Jargon Buster'	154
10.5.	Page from 'Student Guide to Elephant & Castle 2017'	155
10.6.	Screen capture of 'Cai eats London' article	156
10.7.	User sessions and unique page views 2011–2017	159

FIGURES AND TABLES

TABLES

1.1.	YXM130 learning outcomes	16
2.1.	Content and learning outcomes	28
2.2.	Assessment criterion, per assessment method	31
3.1.	Example *Mentimeter* question scheme	47
3.2.	Selected responses to 'what did you find most useful about this workshop and why?'	48
6.1.	Evaluation of the benefits and limitations of online platforms for creating online learning communities based on our own experiences	85
6.2.	Comparison of the benefits and limitations of true-, near-, and far-peer teaching	91
11.1.	Division of tweets by category	171
11.2.	Percentage of total tweets in the 'Engagement' and 'Interactive' categories next to number of new followers	171
11.3.	'Engagement' and 'Interactive' tweets set against tweet impressions, profile visits, mentions and number of new followers	172
11.4.	December 2015: most popular tweets, ranked according to total number of tweet impressions	173

NOTES ON CONTRIBUTORS

Stuart Abbott is Course Leader of the PgCLTHE at the University of South Wales and is as such responsible for supporting early career academics from across the institution in transitioning into learning and teaching roles within HE. Stemming from his academic background as a social scientist of religious thought and practice, Stuart is interested in the social contexts in which learning occurs and the influences they have on processes of individual self-development and identity. He is interested in a range of pedagogical approaches that can engender transformative learning experiences among participants including authentic learning and assessment, values based education and reflective practice. He is currently writing a book for students on academic practice, *Excelling at University*, with Chris Dennis having previously worked as an Educational Developer and Academic Skill Specialist at Cardiff Metropolitan University. Stuart has also researched and published in the field of South Asian religious traditions, having lectured in Religious Studies at Cardiff University and the former University of Wales, Newport.

Sheila L. Amici-Dargan is an Associate Professor in the School of Biological Sciences at the University of Bristol (UK). She was awarded her BSc honours degree in Biological Sciences and PhD in Biophysics from the University of East Anglia (UK). After spending many years undertaking postdoctoral scientific laboratory-based research, at the University of California, Irvine (USA) and at the Centre for Synaptic Plasticity (Bristol, UK), Sheila realised that her passion was rooted in Education. She has worked as an Educational Projects Manager for the Biochemical Society (UK), was awarded a Postgraduate Certificate in Higher Education from the University of Bristol (UK) and is an active Fellow of the HEA/Advance HE. Sheila was promoted to Reader/Associate Professor in 2019 in recognition of her contributions to Teaching and Scholarship over 10 years working at Cardiff University (Wales, UK). Sheila currently teaches Neuroscience and Physiology to undergraduate Biology students at the University of Bristol, and is an Education and Teaching Theme Lead for the Physiological Society (UK). Sheila's educational research projects include developing effective and sustainable 'communities of practice' in higher education, enhancing student-led collaborative and social learning within and beyond the classroom, working with students as 'co-creators' in curriculum development, and innovations in assessment and feedback.

Graham Barton is an academic coordinator at the University of the Arts London. Following an early career in commercial property as a Chartered Surveyor, Graham switched to parallel careers in performing arts, as a musician, sound designer and producer, and then in higher education, in which he specialises in Learning

NOTES ON CONTRIBUTORS

Development. His educational interests have emerged from these personal and professional changes, and from finding ways to draw on educational theories as vehicles to help learners engage with transformative learning, particularly in group settings. Areas of research interest include academic study as creative practice, contemplative practices for self-enquiry in learning, sound arts practice, threshold concepts and practices, disciplinary discourses, three-dimensional conceptual mapping and other creative methodologies for developing epistemic-, systemic- and meta-cognition.

Sue Bond-Taylor is Senior Lecturer in Criminology in the University of Lincoln's School of Social & Political Sciences, where she has worked since 1998 after completing her LLB and MA at the University of Hull. She contributes to the Criminology, Social Policy and Sociology degree programmes, leading modules relating to youth justice and youth culture. Sue's research explores the connections between social care provision, crime prevention and youth justice. In particular, her doctoral thesis evaluated the use of family intervention services in supporting families with complex needs, in the context of the UK's controversial Troubled Families Programme. Since then, she has developed an interest in how early help and diversionary approaches can be used to support young people in conflict with the criminal justice system, as well as exploring the potential of 'child friendly' community-based strategies for improving the opportunities, wellbeing and outcomes for vulnerable children and young people. Her research is underpinned by feminist theory, with an emphasis on intersectionality and the ethics of care, and these approaches also influence her work with students.

John Butcher is Director, Access, Open and Cross-curricular Innovation at the Open University (UK). He re-joined the OU in 2012 after senior roles in Learning and Teaching at Derby, Northampton and Falmouth universities. His interest in widening participation began early in his teaching career when heading up progression to higher education in a sixth form, and subsequently in tutoring and teacher training roles for the OU. His research interests are in the areas of part-time and adult higher education, Access programmes, inclusive assessment and mentoring. His most recent works include national reports published by the Higher Education Policy Institute (adult learners), the Office for Fair Access (adult outreach) and the HEA/ Advance HE (part-time learners), and journal articles on the language of assessment and progression from Access modules.

Siobhan Clay is an Educational Developer in the Teaching and Learning Exchange at University of the Arts London (UAL). Her role is focused on student experience and attainment agendas, working with academics to support inclusive pedagogies and curriculum development. Siobhan holds an MA in Social Justice and Education from University College London, IOE (UK) and a BA in Fine Art. She has taught on the Postgraduate Certificate in Teaching and Learning (PG Cert) for staff and supervised colleagues undertaking diversity and inclusion research projects. She is a Senior Fellow of the HEA/Advance HE.

Ceryl Teleri Davies is a qualified Solicitor and Social Worker, with an MA degree in both work areas, a postgraduate diploma in Community and Criminal Justice, and qualifications in Mental Health. Ceryl has extensive practice-based experience across social care, criminal justice and learning disability services, including work on a multi-agency basis to support children, young people and vulnerable adults at practitioner, middle and senior management level. Ceryl's research interests are focused on exploring the nature of young people's intimate relationships, domestic abuse, healthy relationships and also learning disabilities. Ceryl has taught at undergraduate and postgraduate levels on Education, Law, Criminology and Social Work degrees. Ceryl is currently working as a Social Work Lecturer at Bangor University, North Wales.

Chris Dennis is an Academic Skills Specialist at Cardiff Metropolitan University. In this role, Chris is responsible for the development of provision in the area of academic practice; in addition, he works closely with academic staff in embedding this provision within curriculum-based teaching. He is particularly interested in the links between this provision and student transition, as well as its contribution to the development of 'graduateness' and graduate identity. He is currently writing a book for students on academic practice, *Excelling at University*, with Stuart Abbott, for Palgrave Macmillan. Chris received a PhD in medieval history from Cardiff University in 2012. Prior to working in learning development, he taught history in several departments at the same institution. He is research active in this area, having recently published several book chapters and edited two essay collections; he is currently completing a monograph on the history of the church in eleventh-century Normandy, to be published by Brepols. He is a Senior Fellow of the HEA/Advance HE.

Karen Foley is a lecturer in cross-curricular innovation at the Open University (OU) and is responsible for developing and delivering Student Hub Live, the OU's platform of live, online interactive events that facilitate academic community. With an academic background in Theatre and Film, English and Psychology, Karen chairs Y032, People Work and Society, the OU's Access module for Social Science, Psychology, Health Studies, Education and Business and Law. Karen is an Associate Lecturer for the OU, teaching in the Social Sciences and Psychology.

Leila Griffiths is a Study Adviser at Bangor University. She holds an MPhil and a PhD in Welsh traditional music from the School of Music at Bangor University, where she also graduated in Welsh and Music. During her period of research, she delivered multiple conference papers and published her findings. Currently, she is working as part of a team aiming to support undergraduate and postgraduate students during the period of transitioning to university-level studies and proceeding through them. She works closely with academic schools, offering consultancy to academic staff regarding curriculum design and workshop planning, and collaborating with colleagues to embed provision. She reviews HEA/Advance HE applications, provides staff development workshops as well as online resources for the Coleg Cymraeg Cenedlaethol, and has been awarded SFHEA/Advance HE status.

Ruth Hewston is Professor and Head of Department for the Centre for Lifelong Learning at the University of Warwick. She has worked in both teaching and research led higher education institutions for over twenty years, including as a former Principal Lecturer and Head of the Department for Education and Inclusion at the University of Worcester. She has led and contributed to a number of national and international projects in inclusive education, giftedness and supporting learners with additional educational needs. Between 2012–2015, Ruth was involved with the GUIDE project, funded by the European Commission under the Lifelong Learning Programme, which developed a professional training package for teachers across Europe working with learners with additional needs in mainstream settings. Ruth is a Senior Fellow of the HEA/Advance HE (SFHEA) and a Fellow of the Royal Society for the Encouragement of the Arts, Manufactures and Commerce (FRSA). She is also an Associate Fellow (AFBPsS) and Chartered Psychologist (CPsychol) with the British Psychological Society.

Sophie Leslie is a Student Partnership and Feedback Development Officer within the Student Partnership and Engagement Services team at Swansea University, and is a Senior Fellow of the HEA/Advance HE. Her work examines student experience and quality enhancement within the university, student engagement and student partnership. Previous research has focused on students as partners, online learning communities and peer learning, and the development of staff attributes and their importance within the student experience.

Chris Little first studied in the areas of Cultural Studies and Youth Studies, gaining a PhD focused on youth subcultures and social exclusion in 2011. Chris has lectured extensively in both higher education and further education, teaching cultural studies, youth studies and psychology before focusing on the scholarship of teaching and learning when he moved to Keele University in 2013. Since then, Chris has published research in the areas of learning development, technology-enhanced learning, academic reading and writing, and undergraduate research. Chris has also remained a committed student of education, gaining a Masters of Education degree in 2017. Chris has been accredited as a Senior Fellow of the HEA/Advance HE, a Certified Member of the Association of Learning Technologists, and a Certified Leading Practitioner of the Association of Learning Development in Higher Education.

NOTES ON CONTRIBUTORS

Alex Lumley was Associate Dean of Academic Support at University of the Arts London. In this role, she led on delivering the ambitions articulated in UAL's strategy for academic support, centred on improving retention, attainment and student success. Prior to taking on this role, she was Associate Dean of Learning, Teaching and Enhancement at Central Saint Martins. She is an experienced arts and design practitioner, teacher and manager.

Liz Marr is Pro-Vice-Chancellor (Students) at The Open University (OU) in the UK. She has responsibility for all student facing development and enhancement, including student success (retention, progression and attainment) and satisfaction, student voice and engagement, widening access and success, employability and quality monitoring and enhancement. She is also Chair of the OU's Equality, Diversity and Inclusion Steering Group. Liz has over twenty years' experience in UK higher education and is co-author of *Identity Crisis: Working in Higher Education in the 21st Century*, former managing editor of the journal *Widening Participation and Lifelong Learning*, an editorial board member of *Learning and Teaching in the International Social Sciences* (LATTISS) and a regular reviewer for *Open Learning and EURODL*. She is also President of the European Association of Distance Teaching Universities.

Ruth Matheson is Head of Learning, Teaching and Student Experience for the Faculty of Life Sciences and Education at the University of South Wales. In 2012 she was awarded a National Teaching Fellowship following a University of Wales Teaching Fellowship in 2010. Starting working life as an Occupational Therapist (OT) and then as a OT lecturer at Cardiff University she is still driven by her OT Philosophy of person-centredness, holism and the importance of activity. In 2008 she took up a post in the Learning and Teaching Development Unit (Cardiff Metropolitan University). She has co-edited three books and contributed chapters, case studies and articles to many publications focusing on teaching and learning in higher education. She has a keen interest in curriculum design and in particular the active engagement of students in the design process. Her research interests focus around student as partners, belonging, problem-based learning, creativity, transition and pedagogy. Her most recent publication explores teaching excellence and the difficulty of measuring excellence.

Moira McLoughlin entered nurse education in 1996 as a lecturer, becoming a Senior Lecturer in 2003 at the University of Salford and latterly Head of Children and Young People's Nursing (CYP). Her Masters dissertation was in education where she explored the role of the facilitator in a problem-based learning curriculum. She instigated the first PBL Special Interest Group (SIG) in 1999 which became part of the HEA/Advance HE theme groups. Prior to entering the University, she worked in children's nursing clinical practice for 15 years and set up one of the first job share Sister roles in 1988. She became the Student Experience Lead in January 2008 at the University of Salford joining the School executive team the following year. This role focused more specifically on the student journey from pre-induction through to completion of the programme and she planned and organised student welcome weeks, the National Student Survey (NSS) and student consultation meetings. She has been a reviewer for Nurse Education journals, a member of numerous conference committees and since 1997 linked internationally with universities in Sweden to support students with Erasmus exchange, namely Linkoping and Mälardalens. In 2013 she set up the @nursingSUni School Twitter with Wendy Sinclair, working in partnership with students and colleagues to enhance the role of social media in education and to support students. This initiative received the JISC award of most influential on social media in 2014.

Amber M. Moorcroft is a Junior Doctor working at The University Hospital of Wales, Cardiff. She studied BSc Biomedical Sciences and MBBCh at Cardiff University, the former of which fuelled her interest in collaborative learning. Since completing her dissertation on computer-supported collaborative learning, she has worked with Cardiff University Biosciences and School of Medicine to develop innovations for student learning.

Nicola Poole is currently Head of Quality Assurance and Enhancement at the University of South Wales. Here, she is responsible for the maintenance of quality and standards at the University and the implementation of Regulations and Quality Processes that support this, with an aim to enhance the student experience. She is the Chair of the Welsh Quality Network, an Advance HE fellow and academic associate. Prior to this, she worked at Cardiff Metropolitan University for nearly twenty years as a lecturer, project lead, senior quality enhancement officer in the Learning and Teaching Development Unit, and finally as Deputy Head of the Academic Standards and Quality Unit. She has a particular interest in the area of Students as Partners and has worked on a number of national projects in this area.

Stephen M. Rutherford is a National Teaching Fellow, and Professor of Bioscience Education, Head of the Education Division, and Director of Undergraduate Education in the School of Biosciences, Cardiff University, UK. Stephen gained his BSc and PhD in the Biosciences at the University of York, followed by post-doctoral research in the USA, and the University of Oxford. Stephen joined the faculty of the School of Biosciences at Cardiff University in 2005. Stephen gained an MA(Ed) in 2009, and an EdD in 2019. Stephen's pedagogic research interests focus around four themes: (i) Self-regulated learning and the development of student study skills; (ii) student identity and the transition from school to university; (iii) collaborative learning and the formation of student learning communities outside of the classroom; and (iv) the use of Web 2.0 tools in assessment, collaborative learning and teaching.

NOTES ON CONTRIBUTORS

Rob Sell is the Social Media Lead for the University Library Service at Cardiff University. He has worked for libraries in both the public and academic sectors since 2005 after completing a BSc in Geography at the University of Birmingham. He was nominated and shortlisted for an Enriching Student Life award by the student body for his authorship of the library's social media account in 2015 and 2016.

Wendy Sinclair is Senior Lecturer in Children's Nursing at the University of Central Lancashire. She has been a registered nurse (RN child) since 1998. After working as a staff nurse and sister in a busy children's hospital, a career in nurse education followed. She became a practice educator before joining higher education in 2007 as a lecturer in children's nursing. Wendy has worked with pre-registration student nurses and post-registration nurses, in addition to students on new apprenticeship programmes. Wendy has a real interest in using social media to engage with students and develop digital professionalism and is currently exploring this through a professional doctorate.

Sharon Smith is a Senior Lecturer at the University of Worcester. Prior to her role at the University of Worcester the majority of her teaching has been within further education. Her expertise has been in the area of special educational need and the use of virtual learning environments. She has also been involved in teaching a range of adult learners including those with learning difficulties and disabilities (and learners with Acquired Brain Injury). Sharon has worked closely with the University of Worcester for some years delivering Foundation Degrees and engaging in research within the University through funded seconded projects. Sharon has been involved with European Union Comenius-funded Projects and is currently engaged with the Student-Centred Adult Learning Engagement in Higher Education (SCALE) project aimed at supporting lecturers delivering degree-level courses in universities, colleges and other educational providers through online resources.

Matthew Street holds a Masters in Online and Distance Education and is a Senior Fellow of the HEA/Advance HE. To date his career has encompassed many different aspects of education. He currently leads the Educational Technology unit at Keele University. He co-ordinated the successful implementation of a Jisc funded project, Technology Supporting Assessment and Feedback (STAF, 2010–2012), creating a step change in assessment and feedback processes by building capacity and sharing practice across the University. Building on this experience, he has led a number of institutional projects in relation to educational technology. Instrumental to his approach is a strong educational foundation, institutional perspective and a commitment to continually learning and developing. These strands coalesce around thirteen years' experience collaborating with and influencing people to develop their practice, eight years' experience designing, developing and delivering professional development opportunities for staff, and five years' experience co-leading a PGCert in Teaching and Learning with Technology (TaLwT).

NOTES ON CONTRIBUTORS

Paul Tabak is a Frontend Designer/Developer for Digital Learning at the University of the Arts London. His particular interest lies in improving the usability and accessibility of the various platforms that underpin his University's virtual learning environment. Paul was once resident at the "Rijksakademie van Beeldende Kunsten" in Amsterdam and practiced and exhibited as a painter and mixed-media artist for many years. He was awarded a number of grants by the "Fonds voor beeldende kunsten, vormgeving en bouwkunst" and took part in solo and group exhibitions in the Netherlands and Germany. Upon moving to London, he worked in the commercial sector as a designer for both print and digital media before taking up his post at UAL. Paul is currently studying part-time for an MSc in Digital Humanities at UCL.

Sue Tangney is a Principal Lecturer at Cardiff Metropolitan University in the UK where she works in a central Quality Enhancement Directorate. The Directorate is responsible for all quality assurance and enhancement activities in the University, and Sue's role is currently as programme director for two Advance HE accredited postgraduate programmes aimed at academic and professional staff teaching students. She is also leading a programme to develop more pedagogic research across the University, and to build networks amongst pedagogic researchers. She has an MA in Education (2004) and a Doctorate in Education (2012) from The Open University in the UK. Her most recent publications include: *Developing Mid-career Academic Staff in a Changing University Environment* (AISHE, 2019, with Flay-Petty), and *How Internationalised Is Your Curriculum?* (IHE, 2019, with Leslie & Newman-Ford). She was also a co-editor of the book *Transition in, through and out of Higher Education; International Case Studies and Best Practice* (Routledge, 2018, with Matheson & Sutcliffe).

CHRIS DENNIS, RUTH MATHESON AND SUE TANGNEY

INTRODUCTION

The word 'flexibility', whether used as a noun or in its adjectival form ('flexible'), has appeared with greater frequency in recent years in discourse surrounding a variety of topics associated with higher education. Despite its broad applicability, it has proved a difficult concept to define. At its heart lie the related principles of pace, place and mode of learning: the notion that learning should be designed in such a way as to allow learners to participate in it flexibly, when, where and how they would prefer (AdvanceHE, 2019). Yet it tends to be interpreted in different ways by different people and, as a result, is often seen as an ambiguous term (Evans & Smith, 2011). When seen from the perspective of students, for example, flexibility is very much about the learning experience and the amount of control they might exercise over it, not only in the sense of when and where they might engage with learning, but even in terms of the content of such learning. For teaching staff, on the other hand, flexibility is grounded in the process of learning design and the decisions involved in creating a learning experience that affords more of this control to students. From the viewpoint of professional services staff supporting academic schools, flexibility may represent a complicating factor affecting systems, processes and procedures, which may require their adaptation as course structures change and academic calendars become less rigid. This collection looks at the application of flexibility in learning, specifically its relationship to online learning communities. In focusing on this context, the essays found within will inevitably consider the student perspective of flexibility. Yet in explicitly addressing learning design, several contributions include consideration of the way flexibility is conceived by teaching staff, whilst its meaning at an institutional level is touched upon at different points in the collection. The context has been chosen for several reasons, not least that it allows for the consideration of multiple viewpoints. By focusing on online communities, the relationship between flexibility and technology-enhanced learning might be looked at in more detail. This is timely, since the greater sophistication of digital learning tools available today has made it easier than ever to 'add in' flexibility by adapting more traditional, classroom-based approaches to teaching. Furthermore, by providing examples of what flexibility in learning might look like in practice, the collection attempts to fill a gap in the literature that hitherto has been more focused on abstract or theoretical discussions of the idea, with less consideration of its practical application (Latcham & Moran, 1998, as cited in Willems, 2011).

Flexibility, as it might be applied in a higher education context, is not a new concept. Over the last thirty years, it has been discussed in relation to a variety of issues. For example, in the context of the financial uncertainty in the early 1980s, Mortimer, Bagshaw and Masland (1985) examined the application of flexible strategies to academic staffing at universities in the US, such as the use of fixed-term contracts, as a way of alleviating the financial burden of tenure-track positions. Bligh (1982) addressed similar issues as part of a broader set of recommendations on the need for greater professionalism amongst university teachers and for more flexibility in learning. In considering the former, he anticipated some of the key features of flexible pedagogies: the importance of courses being student-centred, for example, and the role of the teacher in empowering students to take greater responsibility for their learning. In relation to the latter, he recognised the potential influence of flexibility on teaching in catering for the needs of a more diverse student body, as well as making university education more accessible in general. In the context of curriculum design, Goodlad, Pippard and Bligh (1982) explored the role of flexibility in redesigning the structure of academic courses, reducing the number of years of study, for example, and considered the need to revise institutional procedures in order to promote innovation within the curriculum. The essays edited by Diana Thomas (1995a) followed a similar path by looking at the application of more innovative approaches to learning, particularly those that make use of technology-enhanced elements. For Thomas (1995b), flexible learning is about meeting the needs of a specific cohort of students by arranging course elements in such a way for that learning to be effective. However, it is in relation to distance learning that it has most often been discussed, as universities have sought to identify new ways of heightening the accessibility of higher education (Van den Brande, 1993; Burge, 2011). Much of this discussion has been focused on time flexibility and place flexibility (e.g. Goodyear, 2008). Focusing on these elements has had the effect of opening up the complexity of flexibility, for in order to provide a flexible learning experience that gives each student the choice over when and where to engage with learning, a variety of operational activities that support such an experience also need to be shaped with flexibility in mind. Collis and Margaryan (2007), for example, have distinguished between pedagogical flexibility and its logistical counterpart, with the former referring to the decision-making required by students in flexible-learning scenarios and the latter to the changes to institutional systems and processes needed in order to deliver such learning effectively. However, this model perhaps does not go far enough, as will be noted below, for flexibility, ideally, requires coherent guidance or even a policy if it is to be implemented at an institutional level.

Flexibility in learning, as noted above, is about providing students with greater choice as to the way in which they might engage in learning. For example, adopting a blended learning approach in which classroom-based teaching is complemented by online learning resources hosted on a virtual learning environment immediately provides learners with greater choice. At a basic level, through the online resources, such an approach gives to students greater freedom over when and where they participate in learning activities, since these resources are accessible at any time of the day and in any location, as long as the learner has access to the internet. In other scenarios, learners might even be given choice over the content of a programme of study through the opportunity to select which modules to study. Decisions such as these are difficult for students to make; since flexible learning requires learners to act with greater autonomy, actively participating in such learning can represent a significant challenge. Yet by encouraging students to assume greater responsibility for their learning, flexible learning has the potential to impact more broadly on the personal development of learners. Flexibility and a willingness to adapt to new situations as they are experienced form an important element of graduate identity, while the pedagogies associated with flexible learning have the potential to foster the development of other graduate attributes. Social learning, for example, might facilitate the development of networking skills and effective communication, just as learner empowerment might help students to develop entrepreneurial skills and the ability to think more creatively and find innovative solutions to problems (Barrie, 2004). Flexibility, in this way, may be considered as a personal attribute of learners (Collis & Moonen, 2001; Ryan & Tilbury, 2013) and a significant element in lifelong learning. It is thus a necessary characteristic of learners if they are to participate actively and meaningfully in a learning community. In presenting flexibility in these terms, Collis and Moonen were echoing the thoughts of Charles Wedemeyer (1981; Burge, 2011), writing in a distance learning context, who highlighted the characteristics and behaviours of students engaged in flexible learning when he spoke of self-directed learners, working at their own pace, in their own time and place, and in doing so moulding their learning experience around other work and life commitments.

In more recent years, there has been broader acknowledgement within the sector of the ubiquity of the concept of flexibility, its complexity, and the potentially negative impact of that 'foggy mélange' surrounding its application (Evans & Smith, 2011, p. 231). The HEA project, 'Flexible pedagogies: Preparing for the future', for example, led by Professor Ron Barnett, tackled these issues by recognising, quite rightly, that whilst the concept itself was not new, the changed circumstances within the sector meant that the application of flexibility had entered 'a new era' (Barnett, 2014, p. 22). These circumstances included, notably, the increased significance of technology-enhanced learning and its potential for providing for students a truly 'flexible' learning experience, the marketisation of higher education and the impact on student expectations of the related notion of 'students-as-consumers' (Barnett, 2014), as well as the greater diversity of the student population and the demands such diversity places on institutions to meet such a varied body of learning needs. In arguing that flexibility is a 'highly fluid, not to mention ambiguous, concept', Barnett (2014) brought sharper definition to the some of the existing ideas surrounding flexibility by setting out what he described as the facets of flexibility: he defined four levels of flexibility – sector, institutional, pedagogical and learner – as well as three concepts relating to the orientation of flexibility – flexibility as flexing, as enterprising, and as responding to situations in the world empathetically and appropriately – and two dimensions – space and time – in which it might be applied. Such a scheme captured much of the existing thought on flexibility and its application in higher education settings whilst at the same time pushed it further in directions determined by the new context in which the sector found itself. Barnett's report was complemented by the publication of four related studies that collectively made up the work stream, with each one examining a particular topic relevant to the theme of 'flexibility': Neil Gordon (2013) looked at *Technology-enhanced learning*; Alex Ryan and Daniella Tilbury (2013) considered *New pedagogical ideas*; Jane Kettle (2013) focused on *Employer engagement and work-based learning*; while Michael McLinden (2013) examined *Part-time learners and learning in higher education*. These five publications have together provided the immediate scholarly context for the essays collected here, but it is the work of Barnett, Gordon, and Ryan and Tilbury that have proved to be most influential in shaping the content of this collection.

Indeed, this collection has been inspired in large part by the new direction in which these works have taken the discussion. As a context in which flexibility might be examined, technology-enhanced learning has much to recommend it. It is perhaps inevitable that flexible learning and technology-enhanced learning have often been seen as one and the same thing, but, in Gordon's (2013) words, they should be seen as 'natural partners' (p. 4) rather than as identical ideas. As Gordon (2013) pointed out, technology-enhanced learning promotes flexible learning by empowering the learner to take greater control over and responsibility for their studies; at the same time, when used effectively to enhance the learning experience, it acts as a powerful tool for the delivery of flexible learning and assessment. However, its use presents a number of challenges. In the context of the learning itself, staff, for example, may require further training in order to use this technology effectively. More broadly, at an institutional level, adaptability in systems, processes and operational activities is needed in order to support the greater flexibility in learning offered by the adoption of this technology (Gordon, 2013). Its principal advantage is that it presents opportunities to enrich traditional approaches to learning, notably via blended learning. When coupled with the 'new pedagogical ideas' presented by Ryan and Tilbury (2013), devised 'with a focus on building the capacity of learners to anticipate and engage with the future and to navigate through complexity, uncertainty and change' (p. 4), the potential impact of technology-enhanced learning as a means of not only delivering flexible learning but of fostering the development of the characteristics associated with it, which have been discussed above, is greatly enhanced. Indeed, it is for this reason that the relationship between flexibility and online learning communities has been chosen as the context for the essays presented in this collection.

Technology might be used to enrich learning by creating either an entirely online learning experience, in which students participate in education via an internet connection, as opposed to attending classes in person, or a blended one, in which technology and digital media is integrated into traditional, instructor-led classroom activities (Anderson, 2008; Garrison & Vaughan, 2008). In online learning, it is the activities of the learner that provide the focus of the programme of study; teaching, in this context, serves as a means of supporting learners as they participate in these activities. By challenging the learner to own, manage and schedule their learning, online learning is therefore active in nature; it is also student-centred, in that it is the learners who are ultimately responsible for constructing cognition and competencies (Anderson, 2008). Indeed, with tutors fulfilling a supportive role, online learning should also be interactive and collaborative. These peer interactions allow for asynchronous learning to take place, in which learners deepen their knowledge and understanding by discussing insights and viewpoints with each other outside formally arranged teaching time. Similarly, as technology has evolved in more recent years, opportunities to engage learners in synchronous learning, when learners participate in learning in real time, in online learning contexts have increased (Bach, Haynes, & Smith, 2007). However, regardless of whether learning is asynchronous or synchronous, its quality is largely determined by the usability of the virtual environment in which it is situated. In a blended learning experience, a learner might benefit from the face-to-face contact with a tutor offered by classroom-based teaching as well as the virtual interactions with peers associated with online learning (Juwah, 2006). Whilst the online elements of a blended approach shifts some control over the pace and place of learning to the learner, online learning, detached as it is from any physical setting, has the potential to provide learners with much greater control over when and where they participate in learning.

The collection begins with a discussion by John Butcher and Liz Marr of the potential role flexibility might play in widening participation in higher education and assisting in the progression of students through a programme of study. The focus of their essay is a case study of an 'Open Box' module – 'Making your learning count' – delivered digitally, via a VLE, at the Open University, which sits within its Open Degree programme structure. By encouraging reflection on prior learning experiences, the module empowers new students to take greater control of their learning. Butcher and Marr observe that flexibility, if it is to inform truly innovative pedagogies, needs to be 'designed-in', rather than tagged on to existing modules. Furthermore, they argue that approaches to teaching that encourage greater student participation are needed in order to enhance learner autonomy. Finally, if the use of flexible pedagogies is to be effective, it requires the development of greater 'systems flexibility' or flexibility in institutional structures and operational processes.

Leila Griffiths builds on aspects of this discussion – notably the need for models of teaching that encourage greater participation in learning – by looking more closely at the design of an academic skills module sitting within a certificate in higher education qualification offered by the universities of Bangor and Aberystwyth. The context itself is quite unique, since the module caters for Welsh-speaking students studying in Wales and in other Welsh-speaking areas, such as Patagonia. Griffiths considers the potential value of technology-enhanced learning in allowing the use of modes of teaching underpinned by Ryan and Tilbury's 'new pedagogical ideas', in particular, learner empowerment. This was achieved by exploiting Web 2.0 technologies (e.g. discussion boards) for promoting collaboration amongst the students driven by peer and social learning, even in formative assessment contexts. The participatory environment such interactions created, as in the case study discussed by Butcher and Marr, was well suited to the process of acculturating students into the practices of higher education. In this way, Griffiths' example highlights the potential impact of flexible pedagogies in integrating students into an online academic community.

A similar point is made in a case study discussed by Chris Little and Matthew Street. By allowing a cohort of international students to share reflections on prior experiences of learning and their concerns as they begin degree-level courses via the SRS software *Mentimeter*, a temporary online learning community is created, one that provides a safe environment in which students are empowered through technology-enhanced learning to interact with one another. The empowerment afforded to these students may also be found in the second case study discussed by Little and Street, though in a different guise. In this example, students on a postgraduate certificate in teaching and learning with technology engage in an online debate focused on a topical issue related to education. The empowerment occurs as students assume particular character roles in the debate (e.g. student, teacher or employer), an approach that enables participants to consider this issue from multiple perspectives, not just their own. The online debate is followed by face-to-face sessions in which the participants reflect on the experience of taking part. In both examples, as Little and Street point out, such blended approaches are future-facing in that they can re-shape the relationship between educators and learners, and promote the development of flexibility as an attribute in both teaching staff and students.

In the following chapter, Sophie Leslie and Nicola Poole demonstrate how an online community can act as a vehicle for implementing flexible pedagogies through a discussion of three case studies. The difference here, however, is that they approach the subject from the perspective of learning developers working in collaboration with students and academic staff in order to improve NSS scores on certain programmes. The case studies discussed – an online journal club for Speech and Language Therapy students, a student-led redevelopment of a personal and professional development module for Health and Social Care students, and the student-led creation of guidance documents on using technical software for architectural design and technology students – are all driven by the notion of students acting in partnership with staff, a collaborative approach facilitated by learning developers, with the result that students co-created programme content. In this sense, as Leslie and Poole highlight, students were empowered through their participation in an online community and encouraged to take greater ownership of the learning in which they were taking part.

The principle of students acting as partners in the learning process may also be seen in the example of student nurses co-curating a Twitter account with staff at the University of Salford, discussed by Moira McLoughlin and Wendy Sinclair. Academic staff in the school set up a Twitter account with the dual intention of engaging students with social media from the very start of their university careers and thereby cultivating a sense of digital professionalism, and enhancing communication more broadly. The act of curating the account represented a future-facing learning activity because of its transformative nature. Since its objective was to heighten student awareness of and competency in digital professionalism – or, as the authors note, make the students 'fit for practice' – the act of curating went beyond knowledge acquisition, working towards the development of what Ryan and Tilbury (2013) describe as 'agency and competence' (p. 5).

Three contributions follow that look in more detail at how online communities might be used as a means of delivering flexible pedagogies. In the first, Sheila Amici-Dargan, Amber Moorcroft and Stephen Rutherford examine the role of a shadow module – one that runs in parallel with a taught counterpart – in creating a student-led, collaborative community that supports and enhances learning taking place in curriculum-based teaching. It achieves this by facilitating social learning and by empowering students to take greater control of their learning. The learning that takes place through the interactions and activities associated with the shadow module is at a deeper level than that achieved by more traditional, didactic approaches. In a similar way, *Youth Justice Live!*, an educational development project discussed by Sue Bond-Taylor and Ceryl Teleri Davies, highlights the potential of an online community for providing a framework for developing flexible pedagogies. The community created here brought together teaching staff, students and local youth justice professionals to work collaboratively on the design and delivery of a module. By encouraging collaboration between these groups and thereby challenging traditional hierarchies of power in higher education, the module had a transformative impact on student learning, since working with the youth justice professionals in particular afforded them better preparation for their subsequent careers in the field. A similar effect can be seen in the third of these contributions, by Sharon Smith and Ruth Hewston, which considers the role of problem-based learning in developing learner empowerment amongst students on a foundation degree in learning support. In this case, a virtual school was created within a VLE, which provided an authentic context in which students might be challenged by a variety of problem-based scenarios. The experience of participating in such an exercise not only encouraged students to act with greater autonomy; it had a transformative effect, as in the *Youth Justice Live!* project, and the use of Twitter by student nurses, for the learning sat very clearly in the context of professional practice.

Graham Barton and Alex Lumley, followed by Siobhan Clay and Paul Tabak, explore the relationship between flexibility and online communities in co-curricular settings at the University of the Arts, London by reflecting on two complementary projects. In the first, Barton and Lumley discuss the creation of *Academic Support Online*, an online tool providing a virtual space for students to discuss with each other a variety of issues related to academic support. As the authors demonstrate, through participation, an online community emerges, one that crosses boundaries, in the sense that it is not anchored to a particular discipline, and promotes transformative learning. The latter is rooted in the decision-making involved in such participation, and in this way, *Academic Support Online* highlights the potential role technology-enhanced learning might play in achieving greater personalisation in student learning and thus a more flexible learning experience. The purpose of *Commonplace*, discussed by Clay and Tabak, is to facilitate the transition of new students into university life by providing practical advice on a diverse range of issues, from finding accommodation in central London, to explaining elements of assessment. Since the guidance is provided by other students, working with staff in professional services, *Commonplace* is driven by co-creation and social learning. In this way, its success illustrates how co-curricular activities and the work of professional services can contribute to the development of a flexible learning experience.

The final two contributions consider in more detail the role of Web 2.0 technologies in building a sense of community amongst students which might, when done effectively, empower students to achieve even greater academic success. Karen Foley, in the first of these chapters, looks at this issue in a distance learning context provided by the Open University. Her contribution is focused on the *Student Hub Live* initiative, an online and interactive platform created in order to welcome new students to the university and the experience of studying in higher education. This is achieved by building a dialogue between students and academic members of staff, interactions that help to build up the confidence of student. Chris Dennis, Stuart Abbott and Rob Sell, writing about the use of Twitter by a university library to develop a similar sense of community amongst its users, make a similar observation. Here, by encouraging students to engage with library staff and their peers about a wide range of topics, not simply those related to library resources or academic study, an online community is created, one that promotes participation and proactive approaches to learning, and which ultimately helps to enrich the learning experience in which the library sits.

REFERENCES

AdvanceHE. (2019). *Flexibility in higher education.* Retrieved from https://www.advance-he.ac.uk/guidance/teaching-and-learning/flexible-learning

Anderson, T. (2008). Toward a theory of online learning. In T. Anderson (Ed.), *The theory and practice of online learning* (2nd ed., pp. 45–74). AU Press.

Bach, S., Haynes, P., & Smith, J. L. (2007). *Online learning and teaching.* Open University Press.

Barnett, R. (2014). *Conditions of flexibility.* HEA.

Barrie, S. (2004). A research-based approach to generic graduate attributes policy. *Higher Education Research & Development, 23*(3), 261–275.

Bligh, D. (1982). Recommendations for learning. In D. Bligh (Ed.), *Professionalism and flexibility in learning* (pp. 11–30). SRHE.

Burge, E. (2011). Why look at flexibility? In E. Burge, C. Campbell Gibson, & T. Gibson (Eds.), *Flexible pedagogy, flexible practice* (pp. 1–13). AU Press.

Collis, B., & Moonen, J. (2001). *Flexible learning in a digital world.* Kogan Page.

Evans, T., & Smith, P. (2011). The fog of flexibility: The riskiness of flexible, post-secondary education in Australia. In E. Burge, C. Campbell Gibson, & T. Gibson (Eds.), *Flexible pedagogy, flexible practice* (pp. 231–241). AU Press.

Garrison, D. R., & Vaughan, N. D. (2008). *Blended learning in higher education: Framework, principles and guidelines*. Jossey-Bass.

Goodlad, S., Pippard, B. with Bligh, D. (1982). The curriculum of higher education. In D. Bligh (Ed.), *Professionalism and flexibility in learning* (pp. 68–105). SRHE.

Goodyear, P. (2008). Flexible learning and the architecture of learning places. In M. Spector, D. Merrill, J. van Merrienboer, & M. Driscoll (Eds.), *Handbook of research on educational communications and technology* (3rd ed., pp. 215–257). Taylor & Francis.

Gordon, N. (2014). *Flexible pedagogies: Technology-enhanced learning*. HEA.

Juwah, C. (2006). Interactions in online peer learning. In C. Juwah (Ed.), *Interactions in online education: Implications for theory and practice* (pp. 171–190). Routledge.

Kettle, J. (2013). *Flexible pedagogies: Employer engagement and work-based learning*. HEA.

McLinden, M. (2013). *Flexible pedagogies: Part-time learners and learning in higher education*. HEA.

Mortimer, K., Bagshaw, M., & Masland, A. (1985) *Flexibility in academic staffing*. ASHE.

Ryan, A., & Tilbury, D. (2013). *Flexible pedagogies: New pedagogical ideas*. HEA.

Thomas, D. (Ed.). (1995a). *Flexible learning strategies in higher and further education*. Cassell.

Thomas, D. (1995b). Learning to be flexible. In D. Thomas (Ed.), *Flexible learning strategies in higher and further education* (pp. 1–11). Cassell.

Van den Brande, L. (1993). *Flexible and distance learning*. Wiley.

Wedemeyer, C. A. (1981). *Learning at the back door: Reflections on non-traditional learning in the lifespan*. University of Wisconsin.

Willems, J. (2011). Students' perceptions: flexing pedagogy and practice. In E. Burge, C. Campbell Gibson, & T. Gibson (Eds.), *Flexible pedagogy, flexible practice* (pp. 29–40). AU Press.

JOHN BUTCHER AND LIZ MARR

1. BEND ME, SHAPE ME

Flexible Pedagogies to Widen Participation and Deliver on Social Justice

INTRODUCTION

Ryan and Tilbury (2013) challenge the sector to explore how 'flexibility' could inform the future of HE pedagogy, identifying flexibility as an attribute developed in learners through democratic and emancipatory approaches to technology-enhanced teaching and learning. We might argue universities need to be far more flexible themselves in considering the what, where, when and how questions (HEA, 2015) which remain fundamental to developing flexible pedagogies. However, in this chapter, we pick up on a crucial contextualising factor in their report.

We want to explore the pedagogic implications around the fact that HE is engaging with a far more diversified student body as a result of participation rising. This is of course true in England, and in many other countries, but we suggest that, in relating flexibility and pedagogy to modes of participation in HE, learner engagement needs to be reimagined as learner empowerment. In this chapter we will explore the application of pedagogic ideas around learner empowerment through a case study of a module developed at the Open University to award credit for the learning students bring with them from previous (less-formal) study. This undergraduate module was designed with the needs of students who had begun their learning outside 'traditional' HE settings, places or modes in mind, thus seeking to provide opportunities to widen participation by providing a bridge to aid progression, and to meet the needs of a more diverse range of learners. In this instance, flexibility had to inform every pedagogic decision made, especially around assessment, because we were not imposing the content of students' learning from above – students brought learning with them, into the open box module.

WIDENING ACCESS, DIVERSITY AND THE NEED FOR FLEXIBLE PEDAGOGIES

Within the UK, successive policies and funding schemes have, since the publication of the Dearing Report (1997) sought to diversify the student body. As a result, participation for 18-year-old school leavers in full-time, campus-based HE has risen (HESA, 2017), albeit with students from the most advantaged backgrounds far more likely to gain places at the most selective universities. However, retention data reveals a persistence problem (the withdrawal/non-completion rate) as a consequence of the more diverse student body, and achievement data reveals a gap in the proportion of an advantaged, as opposed to a disadvantaged, demographic, achieving a 'good' degree outcome. This achievement gap has been, and remains, stubbornly difficult to close across the sector. Students from groups traditionally under-represented in HE, including learners from specific black and minority ethnicity backgrounds, those entering HE with low or alternative prior qualifications, those in the lowest quintiles of social deprivation and those declaring a disability, remain less likely to succeed (HEFCE, 2014; UCAS, 2016) in current pedagogic paradigms.

The HE sector continues to be challenged to widen participation in order to contribute to government social mobility targets and societal needs (OFFA, 2017). Yet the UK is entering a decade when the proportion of 18-year olds will be in decline, just as the number of mature/adult students, and those studying part-time has been falling dramatically. A 61% drop in adult part-time learners between 2006 and 2017 (HESA, 2017) represents a critical missed opportunity to widen participation, since those older learners, often most in need of greater flexibility, are disproportionately likely to come from a disadvantaged background.

New pedagogical ideas can make a significant contribution to addressing this conundrum of diversity/achievement, not least by embedding an inclusive approach which affirms the knowledge that, for example, adult learners or students from marginalised groups bring to their HE learning. However, for too long, doors have been opened (a little) in terms of participation, but pedagogy has, in most cases, remained rooted in exclusive and inflexible teaching models, a reality premised upon face-to-face, full-time attendance on a campus and high-stakes summative assessment. This situation warrants, as Ryan and Tilbury (2013) remind us, moving beyond a *tabula rasa* (p. 16) approach which treats learners as 'cultural dopes' (Garfinkel, 1967), into a far more participatory environment in which a flexible learning situation (Barnett, 2014) enables learner autonomy within a framework of support.

Students from 'non-traditional' backgrounds have always had to fit in with, and conform to, traditional pedagogies, bending themselves to align with taken-for-granted assumptions about prior knowledge and behaviours and the rules of the assessment game. This is premised on particular assumptions about what makes HE 'higher', but in a more diverse world of mass HE participation, this is not sustainable, and, we would argue, appears increasingly immoral. At the Open University we are regularly reminded that students from so-called 'non-traditional' backgrounds bring with them valuable life experiences (both personal and professional) which are reflected upon and often galvanise learning. Such 'non-traditional' learners are also likely to be highly engaged with learning (seizing a 'second chance') and acutely aware of the impact their previous education had on their life chances. They expect to be active participants, and once confidence has been developed, seize opportunities to co-construct a personalised and transformative learning journey.

We argue HE ought to be flexible enough to address the needs of a far higher proportion of the whole population, and the possibilities afforded by digital developments around learning should enable a far wider range of student needs to be met. Flexible digital learning can also offer a challenge to the apparent ghettoisation of some non-traditional students in particular subject areas, which remains a severe obstacle to social mobility. Examples might include the disproportionate numbers of students from disadvantaged backgrounds on social care or early years' qualifications, rather than medicine or other subjects which lead directly to 'elite' professions.

The very fact that the HE student body is now more diverse, encompassing an increasingly varied set of learner backgrounds, needs and learning styles, should be pressurising institutions to exploit flexible study modes and the affordances of IT to introduce greater inclusivity in novel learning spaces. Potentially, this would change the pedagogy experienced by all learners, bringing 'interpersonal flexibility' into what Bradwell (2009, as cited in Barnett, 2014, p. 46) terms the 'edgeless' or 'liquid' or borderless module. It could also enable a shift to a more personalised and open notion of learning to be developed, in which learner empowerment can be envisioned through transformative pedagogies.

However, as yet, relatively few HEIs offer an explicitly personalised digital learning experience, whether through accelerated degree routes (DFE, 2017), extensive recognition of prior learning (ibid.), genuinely flexible part-time routes (Butcher, 2015), remote study opportunities or bridging routes (Butcher, 2017), all of which may better meet the needs of a diverse student body than current pedagogic models.

Open and Distance Universities have been attempting to address these challenges in innovative ways for the last forty years and, as technology-enhanced learning has become increasingly ubiquitous across the HE sector, there is much which can be shared with face-to-face institutions in terms of innovative approaches to blended learning. However, implementation of flexible pedagogies is not easy when teaching approaches are policy-driven rather than pedagogy-driven, and even distance universities have struggled to offer a viable teaching and learner support approach which encompasses the needs of students who may be working, who may have demanding personal responsibilities, and who may come from backgrounds lacking the social, educational and cultural capital to succeed in HE. There is a big difference, not always acknowledged, between policies encouraging participation, and pedagogies supporting flexible learning and inclusive notions of success.

Learner empowerment (Ryan & Tilbury, 2013) is signalled as the key, unifying theme in defining flexible pedagogy in HE. While in some HE settings the notion of delivering learner empowerment through co-creation, in order to challenge conventional learning relationships, could be considered radical, in adult education empowerment is an accepted underpinning to notions of andragogy (Knowles, 1984). In theories of adult education learner empowerment informs transformative learning, such that the facilitation of learning is not bounded by knowledge and understanding, but encourages learner agency. It is this latter approach which underpins the Open University's social justice mission to be 'open to all'.

If flexible pedagogies are conceptualised as transformative, in taking students beyond knowledge and understanding, it is in the application of their learning that success might be measured. Students need support (and regular feedback) to develop confidence in applying acquired skills to familiar or unfamiliar circumstances. This transformative approach is more common in community and adult education settings (through lifelong learning), and in alternative modes of study (in life-wide learning). This aspect of flexible pedagogy crucially depends upon the use of critical reflection, encompassing affective as well as cognitive capabilities. With adult learners, teaching is likely to be participatory, resulting in so-called 'third-order learning' (Ryan & Tilbury, 2013, p. 22) through which students engage with the world differently. The challenge for traditional HE is that in conventional academic systems, including at the OU, the structural division of the curriculum into separate disciplines, and the consequent flow of resources, presents barriers to introducing this kind of flexibility. As a consequence, aspirations for students to become critical agents, 'learning to be' (Sen, 1992), may be difficult to roll out across the sector without related fundamental changes to the ways in which HEIs organise themselves.

The Open University has, since 1969, pioneered innovative pedagogies at scale, in response to societal needs, reimagining what a university can do. Initially this was via distance learning in which teaching was delivered through written and increasingly audio and visual course materials, supported by engagement with a tutor at optional face-to-face tutorials. From the 1990s this evolved into blended online learning in which computer-mediated conferences enabled students and tutors to interact asynchronously. More recently, Web 2.0 possibilities have enabled interactive media-rich resources to become ubiquitous in OU teaching, supported by synchronous online video meetings to engage groups of students regardless of location.

Nonetheless, the flexibility which such innovations promise has always been limited, and possibly illusory. Learners must still follow a pre-determined curriculum in fixed study patterns with pre-set assessment points. Learning design specialists support academic staff in developing modules, with due regard paid to accessibility, for example, but the products themselves are still quite 'static' and, it could be argued, are sometimes heavily influenced by the subjective experience of the academic authors.

DESIGNING-IN FLEXIBILITY – A CASE STUDY

This chapter focuses on a case study exemplifying an attempt to 'design-in' flexibility, driven by a desire to empower learners. This offers a transformative pedagogy which is both future-facing and consciously crossing boundaries (Ryan & Tilbury, 2013) connecting different forms of learning, particularly the journey from informal or non-formal to formal learning. Our example illustrates the potential for designing-in flexibility, rather than falling into the sector trap (again) of patching and mending (Barber et al., 2013).

The development of an 'Open Box' module *Making Your Learning Count* (YXM130) at the Open University is premised on the idea that it is possible to assess digital learning flexibly against generic learning outcomes, with students bringing their learning from outside the formal HE curriculum. This model sits within the OU's Open Degree programme structure, which allows students to personalise their own learning journey through relatively unrestricted module choice. The module's innovation is in recognising the kind of informal learning currently excluded from most conventional HE. The module deliberately transcends those disciplinary specialisms in a manner beyond what Ryan and Tilbury (2013) identify as 'crossing boundaries' (p. 24) and positions students rather as 'brave learners' (Cooke et al., 2018, p. 146). Critically, the drive behind the module's instigation was that studying single disciplines is perceived as inadequately serving the complexities of twenty-first century, real-world scenarios. Students taking the open box module learn in a post-disciplinary landscape in which learners connect their own and others' experiences of learning through guided activities and reflection. Applied pedagogies and discovery-based learning enable soft skills and personal approaches to learning to be recognised and developed. By recognising the varied contexts in which learning takes place, the learning space is extended. This Open University module is delivered online, but we believe the approach could be negotiated just as effectively in a face-to-face teaching situation.

Making your learning count, is a 30 credit Open Box module at OU L1 (FHQ L4/SFHQ L7) which assesses the prior HE learning that students bring with them. Initially, in the pilot presentation of the module, it drew on MOOCs and Open Educational resources, but it is envisaged subsequent presentations will accommodate Work-based Learning, Level 0 Access modules, the Recognition of Prior Learning, and partly-completed courses from other HEIs. Crucially, the Open Degree within which the module sits was produced by academics committed to the value of interdisciplinary learning in what is manifestly a flexible qualification with the empowerment of student choice in mind. In the Open Degree structure, students can personalise their individual learning pathways, following a mix of cognate or wildly divergent disciplines, subject only to pre-requisite study rules. The Open degree focuses on cross- and interdisciplinary learning, and the open box module is intended as an entry point into the qualification for students who began their HE journey in less formal settings. The module uses structured digital reflection and remote peer learning – with very little new content – to bridge informal and formal learning as flexibly as possible.

If assessment drives pedagogy (Serrano et al., 2017), any innovative steps towards genuinely flexible pedagogy depends on transformation in conventional assessment practice as part of a re-imagined learning infrastructure. Acknowledging that much traditional assessment practice was an obstacle to innovation, the module was designed as a flexible enabler to meet the needs of a more diverse range of learners in HE. In producing the Open Box, module authors focused on assessment *for* learning rather than *of* learning: in other words, rather than limiting students to measurements of attainment or achievement mirroring an increasingly dominant performative culture in HE, the articulation of learners' needs were embedded in a more participative and democratic learning culture. Reflection on personal learning was foregrounded at the expense of the 'tyranny of micro-outcomes' (Ryan & Tilbury, 2013, p. 30). Pedagogy was thus envisaged to be more holistic and inclusive, engaging students and ultimately empowering them in terms of owning their learning.

In distance education, although assessment is much espoused as the starting point in module design, too often we have observed assessment as the final focus of a module development team, often rushed at the last moment as the priority has been with producing new content. *Making Your Learning Count*, the open box module, deliberately began with assessment, by framing the module around a flexible set of learning outcomes. These were developed from our Level 0 Access programme (which has an explicit focus on skills development), and proved a crucial starting point to producing a flexible learning experience (see Table 1.1).

The alignment with ideas of a future-facing pedagogy can be seen in the embedded personalisation, in which a learner's critical and creative skills are supported to envision their own individual learning future – thus becoming agents in their own adult learning journey. The module team had to understand how to support the 'conversion' of informal to formal learners, and provide a rationale to bring highly individualised learners into a developing community.

Table 1.1. YXM130 learning outcomes

Students will be able to:

Knowledge and understanding

1. understand and appreciate the difference between multi- and interdisciplinary study.

Cognitive skills

2. demonstrate effective distance learning skills.
3. effectively use assessment to develop learning.
4. actively reflect as a way to improve learning.

Key skills

5. demonstrate effective communication skills.
6. apply different subject approaches or views to different contexts.

Practical/professional skills

7. use digital tools for learning and working.
8. demonstrate insight into personal goals, preferences and aptitudes.
9. develop the self-study skills required to continue OU level 1 study.
10. develop the employability skills relevant to level 1 study.

In seeking to empower students, we drew on existing marketing insights which established that OU distance learners, commencing their Open Programme studies, did want skills as well as knowledge, and just as crucially, that they knew that was what they wanted. This challenged the module team to scaffold learning activities at the right level to prompt students from highly varied learning backgrounds to understand their learning needs at HE level, and to reflect accordingly, all through a digital learning environment. To be effective, students had to feel that the reflection they were prompted to engage in was useful and relevant to their skills development.

The module team were also highly conscious that, in designing the module, it was vital to embed the development of study skills, and make the related activities as interesting as possible. At the same time they were aware of the need to balance 'online-ness' (e.g. utilising a range of different media/content) in order to ensure engagement was sustained and progress through the module was effective. Additionally, the tone of materials had to be sufficiently inclusive to meet the needs of a diverse student cohort.

ASSESSMENT, DELIVERY AND SUPPORT

In that there is inevitably a wide variety of ways in which learners might demonstrate the achievement of learning outcomes in what is effectively a co-created curriculum on YXM130, the module assessment strategy is of necessity flexible, but also needs to be meaningful to individual learners. In the context of flexible pedagogy, there was far greater weight given to consideration of what our students would be bringing with them, rather than conceptualising them as empty vessels to be filled. The team had learned from previous module production that the scheduling of assessment was crucial in supporting the retention of distance learners. All too often, we refer to our provision as flexible when in fact assessment deadlines are fixed and unauthorised late submission is penalised. To address this the majority of assessment activities have been designed as negotiable with a tutor and formative online feedback is provided. Only the initial needs analysis and summative end of module task received a formal grade. We also faced the challenge of inevitable disciplinary assessment differences, given the openness of what learning could bring to their open box. For example, there was a danger that a lack of shared topic/language between tutors and students would impede learning. This was surfaced in tutor briefing and through online discussions in the forums.

It is well-established that some distance learners can experience student isolation (Goldrick & O'Higgins, 2012), and the module team were aware this effect could be amplified in a context in which each learner brought their unique personal content with them. Therefore, one consideration which became even more important than on traditional modules, was the extent to which the module could be made digitally engaging and interesting in order to sustain students' interests and stimulate a sense of community. Material on the VLE had to be carefully paced to meet student expectation, guidance around the particularities of formal distance learning had to be embedded in the preparatory induction materials, and peer engagement had to be encouraged through discussion forums.

Calculating workload balance for learners manifested itself as more of an art than a science, but it was essential to ensure expectations of tutor support in this highly flexible online learning world were manageable and proportionate. That being so, identifying the online support necessary for such an inevitably disparate range of learners to thrive, became critical. This was manifest in the development of the online tutor's role, and in structuring the workload they might encounter to prevent overload. In recruiting tutors, they not only had to demonstrate a breadth of knowledge to meaningfully support students with interests in different disciplines, but to have the digital empathy to provide appropriate support to all types of learners. Defining the tutor's role in a content-free module was not without its challenges – conceptually, the role was to personalise the learning, and feedback accordingly to support progression.

DISCUSSION

The 'open box' approach we describe here deliberately deconstructs the dominant pedagogical frames (Ryan & Tilbury, 2013) traditional in HE. The module team were open in rising to the challenge of producing an innovative learning experience. In so doing, they operated in spite of conventional production norms at the Open University, innovating in (minimal) content and speed to market (agility enabled the drag factor of traditional time-frames to be by-passed). By being transparent about the need to avoid exploitative relationships and knowledge hegemonies, a highly student-centred structure was put in place. This included a more transparent approach to where 'learning objectives' came from (and indeed, recognition that they could be flexible and personalised), and where the module fitted within existing HE quality frameworks. By situating the learner in a more inclusive environment, the result is a particular application of Freire's (1970) 'conscientization', through which students are taking a far more active role in their own learning, and making authentic decisions about the direction they want their learning to take – and to what end.

For flexible pedagogy to become a powerful change agent, we argue that the inflexibilities inherent in the current complex organisation of HE and of HEIs need to be addressed. This is the kind of systems flexibility at an institutional level advocated by Barnett (2014). We were lucky, in that, for the development of the open box module we found ourselves with the right idea to pilot at the right time. At the micro-level, our key instigator/lone pioneer happened to be a hugely influential (and well-networked) Professor, Director of our cross-institutional Open Degree programme, who was sufficiently experienced in OU systems to pre-empt obstacles, avoid faculty politics and sidestep institutional barriers. At the meso-level, we developed a module team of academics and production staff who were, by inclination, innovative and creative and who were delighted to be given the permission to work with greater agility and with greater freedom. At the macro-level, the module was created in the context of a new PVC's portfolio, which happened to be titled 'Learning and Teaching Innovation'. The timing coincided with a period of university volatility, when new ideas which could be quickly brought to students were valued. Thus innovative ideas were encouraged from the top, and the passage through complicated and time consuming governance structures was smoothed.

An interim evaluation of YXM130 was conducted six weeks in, to inform OU decisions about whether the pilot presentation would be extended. Real-time student feedback questions were built into the study planner in the module VLE. Initial feedback from tutors suggested good peer engagement in the online community, with acknowledgment that (given the small, for the OU, student cohort) tutors were using the module forum website to contact students, with group emails developing a tutor group identity. Tutors (all experienced teaching on other OU modules) perceived the YXM130 forums as more active than others they knew, and they believed students new to the OU were being given a very positive first experience of online learning communities. It was the students who were happiest to express their enthusiasm for learning (rather than those who had studied online before) who engaged most online. Tutors were impressed with the level of peer support and guidance students were offering one another through the online forums.

However, tutors also noted that for some students, studying in an online community was a new experience, and for those with limited IT experience, personalised support had to be given to help learners navigate the YXM130 website/VLE, and to find their module forums. In addition, students needed support to find the wide-range of freely available learning materials on the *OpenLearn* platform which enabled students to further explore their areas of professional interest.

One key decision that did appear validated was that tutors reported students appeared to value the opportunity to try out different subjects before making a decision about what to study in the future. This aligned YXM130 with the student-centred flexibility inherent in the OU's Open Programme, and meant that those students from Widening Participation backgrounds who might not be confident about which discipline to study can benefit from the flexibility afforded by the 'open box' approach.

In light of our experience and thinking around the production of an 'Open Box' module, we suggest that a fundamental and radical reconceptualising of pedagogy could stimulate a more inclusive student journey. In this way, universities can open up opportunities for more potential learners to be successful in HE by providing the appropriate scaffolding for those from a more diverse array of backgrounds. In relation to the affordances offered by online learning communities, we argue flexible digital pedagogies for a diverse and vibrant learning experience need to encompass three key elements:

- supported transitions;
- inclusive approaches to teaching;
- learner-centred approaches to assessment.

Together, these could improve the student experience, rendering it flexible of itself and supporting the development of flexible learner attributes, as well as fostering much-needed inclusivity between learners and educators. YXM130 'shapes' student learning by legitimising what adult learners bring with them – it does not 'bend' students to the exclusive paradigms of traditional HE. Early tutor evaluations of YXM130 do signal a potential irony though, in that the flexibilities inherent in an 'open box' approach may inadvertently raise expectations about learning subsequently, when more traditional pedagogies dominate on conventional modules.

However, we question whether, given the narrow policy drivers around traditional notions of graduate employability impacting many institutions, there are systems flexible enough and open enough to support this laudable aim of learner empowerment. Such concerns extend to whether the culture of HE will allow for a more open conception of the purpose of higher level learning, whether that be for employment or self-actualisation.

According to Barnett (2014)

> In a fluid, dynamic and global world, higher education systems cannot but exhibit flexibility and it is right that they should do so. (p. 7)

But flexibility can manifest in a range of ways, some good, some not so. Do flexible pedagogies, in themselves, inevitably deliver on widening participation and social justice? There is a balance to be reached between student choice and what is needed to validate higher level learning but this decision sits with the institution and its regulatory context and needs to reflect the student's learning goals. If universities are serious about widening the participation of non-traditional learners, flexible pedagogies have to be embedded alongside a whole range of flexible 'conditions' (Barnett, 2014, p. 68).

REFERENCES

Barber, M., Donnelly, K., & Rizvi, S. (2013). *An avalanche is coming.* Retrieved from https://www.ippr.org/files/images/media/files/publication/2013/04/avalanche-is-coming_Mar2013_10432.pdf

Barnett, R. (2014). *Conditions of flexibility: Securing a more responsive higher education system.* HEA.

Butcher, J. (2015). *'Shoe-horned and side-lined'? Challenges for part-time learners in the new HE landscape.* Retrieved from https://www.heacademy.ac.uk/resource/shoe-horned-and-side-lined-challenges-part-time-learners-new-he-landscape

Butcher, J. (2017). *Understanding the impact of outreach on access to higher education for disadvantaged adult learners.* Retrieved from https://www.offa.org.uk/wp-content/uploads/2017/07/Final-Report-Understanding-the-impact-of-outreach-on-access-to-higher-education-for-disadvantaged-adult-learners-docx.pdf

Cooke, H., Lane, A., & Taylor, P. (2018). Open by degrees: A case of flexibility or personalization? In C. Stevenson (Ed.), *Enhancing education through open degree programs and prior learning assessment* (pp. 128–148). IGI Global.

Dearing, R. (1997). *The Dearing report: Higher education in the learning society.* HMSO.

Department for Education. (2017). *Higher education and research act, 2017* (c. 29). HMSO.

Freire, P. (1970). *Pedagogy of the oppressed.* Penguin.

Garfinkel, H. (1967). *Studies in ethnomethodology: Social and political theory.* Prentice Hall.

Goldrick, M., & O'Higgins, N. (2012). Reducing academic isolation in favour of learning relationships through a virtual classroom. *Journal of Learning Development in Higher Education, 4.* Retrieved from http://www.aldinhe.ac.uk/ojs/index.php?journal=jldhe

HEFCE. (2014). *Difference in degree outcomes: Key findings.* Retrieved from http://www.hefce.ac.uk/pubs/year/2014/201403/

HESA. (2017). *Higher education student enrolments and qualifications obtained at higher education providers in the United Kingdom 2015/16.* Retrieved from https://www.hesa.ac.uk/news/12-01-2017/sfr242-student-enrolments-and-qualifications

Higher Education Academy (HEA). (2015). *Framework for flexible learning in higher education.* HEA. http://www.flexiblelearninguk.co.uk/framework-for-flexible-learning-in-higher-education-higher-education-academy.html

Knowles, M. (1984). *Andragogy in action: Applying modern principles of adult learning.* Jossey-Bass.

OFFA. (2017). *Strategic guidance: Developing your 2018/19 access agreement.*

Ryan, A., & Tilbury, D. (2013). *Flexible pedagogies: New pedagogical ideas.* HEA.

Sen, A. (1992). *Inequality re-examined.* Clarendon Press.

Serrano, M., O'Brien, M., Roberts, K., & Whyte, D. (2017). Critical Pedagogy and assessment in higher education: The ideal of 'authenticity' in learning. *Active Learning in Higher Education,* 1–13.

UCAS. (2016). *End of cycle report 2016.* Retrieved from https://www.ucas.com/file/86661/download?token=Ls6kLU5-

LEILA GRIFFITHS

2. PROMOTING FLEXIBLE LEARNING THROUGH EMBEDDED, ONLINE STUDY SKILLS SUPPORT

The learner experience and the student-centred learning environment are at the forefront of HEIs' underpinning pedagogies. These require innovative and effective planning and teaching strategies when developing and delivering online content (Palloff & Pratt, 1999; Gordon, 2014). Learning characteristics have adapted significantly with the rise of technology (Palloff & Pratt, 2007), which in turn has affected and transformed students' needs. For example, students' expectations are higher regarding the way in which lecturers communicate and deliver course content, and how students are expected to engage with it. This might be one of the reasons for the shift from the conventional learning medium of the lecture theatre to the more interactive learning experience of online platforms (Mason & Rennie, 2008). The growing number of online distance-learning courses available to students is indicative of this trend, and the *Coleg Cymraeg Cenedlaethol* (an initiative set up by the Welsh Government in 2011 to promote Welsh language provision at universities; henceforth, CCC) proposes to deliver its provision to Patagonia and Welsh speakers everywhere with a view to building on this development.

The two part-time, Welsh medium distance-learning Certificates in Higher Education (Humanities, Social Sciences), offered jointly between Bangor University and Aberystwyth University by the CCC in the 2015/16 academic year, were the first of their kind, providing a Welsh medium curriculum to online communities. Within these two discipline-specific courses students were required to complete a skills component for each Certificate. The CCC approached the Study Skills Centre (SSC) at Bangor University to develop a core 10-credit skills module for the Certificate in Higher Education in the Social Sciences, entitled 'Studying Social Sciences'. Welsh medium skills provision and resources at HE level are relatively rare, with only certain degree programmes offering Welsh medium support to students to discuss and explore the strategies and processes surrounding writing, reading and researching at university. Therefore, the aim of this core skills module was to bring about a shift in cultural behaviour regarding embedding skills provision within the curriculum and thereby make a significant contribution to this ever-changing learning environment. It not only offered opportunities to provide more developed online learning experiences and content but also possibilities for modes of teaching, driven by some of Ryan and Tilbury's (2013) 'new pedagogical ideas', through various design and delivery processes, as well as the reimagining of learning relationships and spaces. This essay explores the considerations taken during the module design stages and the systematic approach behind building online course content, drawing on some of Ryan and Tilbury's (2013) ideas, influences derived from the literature surrounding online communities and learning development, and the author's own experience as an online distance learner.

Background

The SSC took into account four main considerations relating to the philosophy behind the content and framework for this module. Firstly, the SSC saw the blank canvas provided as an opportunity to involve students in developing their own learning. This consequently enhanced student participation and engagement, as 'learning is a social process, conducted [...] with other humans' (Clair, 2015, p. 29) and highlights how personal relationships are at the heart of learning (Macmurray, 2012). This is emphasised further by Ryan and Tilbury (2013), who described such participation as 'learner empowerment', an idea consisting of 'actively involving students in learning development and processes of "co-creation"' (p. 5). Secondly, underlying assumptions regarding disciplinary discourses, cultures and backgrounds, which can occur on the sides of both student and tutor, were considered (Young, 2005). By acknowledging that these factors play an integral part in how students navigate their courses, as explored by Gordon (2014), a more informed yet flexible approach to the design process was created. This module therefore sought to embed key aspects of studying at university into the wider course content, to ensure cross-disciplinary learning and to address certain key stages of academic study, with a view to raising awareness of academic expectations. The third consideration was the use of virtual spaces, conceived broadly as not only the natural platform offered by the online distance-learning medium but also the opportunities presented to participate in less formal digital environments and to engage across learning spaces. These complementary spaces ensured that learning was facilitated on a social level, a concept explored further by Ryan and Tilbury (2013). The fourth consideration was the prospect of 'decolonising education' by creating 'inclusive learning environments' (Ryan & Tilbury, 2013, p. 20). The very nature of this module challenged, or at least attempted to moderate, the impact of dominant cultural interests, by providing support for those wishing to engage and express their learning through the medium of Welsh. Consequently, Welsh speaking communities were immersed in a learning experience that advocated 'cross-cultural socialising' and therefore addressed current issues of equal opportunities, to 'extend inter-cultural understanding' within the HE setting (Ryan & Tilbury, 2013, pp. 5 and 20).

These key principles held during the planning and designing stages stemmed from many established methods and practices surrounding learning development, namely the pedagogical background addressed by Lea and Street (1998) and the practical approaches to implementing this background introduced by Burns and Sinfield (2004), among others. For example, by drawing on the background surrounding 'academic socialisation' and 'academic literacies' (Lea & Street, 1998; Lillis & Scott, 2007; Lillis et al., 2015) the module's focus deviated away from the micro elements of writing, reading and studying (when study skills is 'normative') to consider higher order concerns (Severino, 2004; Gillespie & Lerner, 2004). Rather, it was directed more towards evaluating how students go about 'doing' (Lillis, 2006), therefore becoming 'transformative' (Warren, 2002). As part of an online distance-learning course, the module itself offered the opportunity to develop teaching in a transformative and flexible way through the evaluation of students' academic 'voice', students' responsibility for their learning, and how learning development relates to the discipline.

Using E-Learning to Assist Transition into HE

The aims and objectives of this core 'Studying Social Sciences' module were to help students during the period of transitioning to university-level study by raising awareness regarding academic expectations and enabling students to develop the strategies and processes that will assist them to benefit fully from those studies. The module also aimed to help students reflect on and develop their methods of dealing with key fields of academic study in order to help them grow into independent, confident learners. These aims, identified as key needs among e-learners, mirror many other learning development centre objectives, including those introduced by Clair (2015). For example, regarding students who study discipline-specific subjects online, a national survey conducted by Honey et al. (2000) shed light on students' learning patterns and preferences by showing that

> despite the well-educated nature of the sample [which includes formal and informal e-learning] and the fact that they have participated in e-learning recently, e-learners clearly feel a need for learning support. Only 4% do not want support with their e-learning. (p. 3)

Learning support in this context is explained further as 'personal learning support rather than technical or electronic support' (p. 7), which indicates the need for online courses to include, and ideally embed, study support within the curriculum, especially since 'the majority are interested in e-learning (85%), and feel e-learning has been useful to them (90%)' (p. 8). The knowledge that learning development provision helps support students at a much deeper level when it is embedded and directly relevant to their discipline-specific assessments has been an established realisation since the 1990s (Hicks, 1999, as cited in Stefani, 2003; Baillie, 2003).

Furthermore, 'e-learning compares well with traditional learning approaches: six in ten individuals think it is possible to learn as effectively through e-learning as other means' (Honey et al., 2000, p. 4). However, the negative aspects are apparent and seem to relate to the learning environment: 'it is impersonal [30%], lonely [16%] and frustrating [29%]'. The most frequently used positive adjectives which came out of this study was 'convenient' (56%), 'fast access to information' (50%) and 'working at my own pace' (42%), while the positive comments (86%) outweigh the negative (57%) (p. 8). To ensure e-learning convenience and to allow e-learners the flexibility to work at their own speed requires effective communication and flexible teaching and learning methods. Communication is of paramount importance when students study at a distance, and fully involving students in their own learning by facilitating the development of learning environments and allowing them to 'choose aspects of their study' (Gordon, 2014, p. 4) is central to effective online course design. As a module designed for first year undergraduates, facilitating transition to university-level study and clarifying academic expectations at the outset can alleviate uncertainties and promote creative learning relationships. Palloff and Pratt (2007) explore these ideas in relation to building a sense of community within an online setting, by 'promoting collaborative learning' (p. xvi) and stressing the importance of implementing an 'interaction and feedback' (p. 16) loop to ensure students gain understanding and knowledge.

Another area highlighted by this study is the level of learning undertaken by the individual during formal e-learning. Although only 12% felt they had learned 'a great deal', 60% 'a fair amount', 23% 'a little', 2% 'not very much', 0% 'nothing at all' and 3% stating 'don't know', students 'still feel it is a method through which they can learn successfully' (Honey et al., 2000, p. 6). Consequently, it is important that courses are implemented with greater transparency so that students are made aware of what they are learning and why. Fostering this transparent approach may allow the employment of a 'constructive alignment' method (Gibbs & Tang, 2011), to help communicate the links between each course element and wider learning or any particular assignment (Clair, 2015). As a result, students are made aware of what is expected of them (Burns & Sinfield, 2004) and are therefore seen as partners within the learning process (Healey et al., 2014). For example, detailing learning outcomes can demonstrate this, as can mirroring these outcomes in the questions posed to students in feedback sheets and aligning these with formative assessment methods (Ellington & Race, 1993; Hogg & Doig, 2012). Healey et al. (2014) also highlight the importance of connecting learning and teaching methods with assessment to foster co-learning and co-developing within learning communities. This is an essential step in the critical skills development stage, 'by which disciplines define, explore and solve problems, and communicate and evaluate knowledge' (Warren, 2002, p. 94). Palloff and Pratt (1999) suggest other ways of ensuring 'buy-in from everyone', which include the creation of 'shared goals' and 'focused outcomes' (p. 17). Ensuring a more flexible learning process helps facilitate teamwork and encourages collaborative learning (Palloff & Pratt, 2007), some of the characteristics that form the foundation for developing and facilitating online content.

Module Content and Learning Outcomes

The 12-week 'Studying Social Sciences' module was structured around a systematic approach to any given assignment. It supported students with other discipline-specific needs by being embedded within the Social Sciences Certificate in Higher Education, consequently ensuring student involvement and a more holistic, transferable outlook on learning. To achieve the module's aims and purposes and to identify student need in order to build module content, a central consideration at the outset was the necessity to involve academic staff in the initial developmental stages. They were then responsible for the discipline-specific modules that made up the rest of the course. As with student-facing support, adopting an exploratory approach when discussing student needs with academic staff initiates a collaborative process without assuming tacit knowledge (Wisker, 2003). This approach enables the collaboration to match student needs to achievable outcomes.

Another model which demonstrates how implementing a transparent and flexible approach to collaboration between learning development teams and academic staff, further helping the development of provision, is the SOL Standard developed at Southampton Solent University, which ensures 'a new way of engaging with academics' (Hogg & Doig, 2012, p. 9). Academic staff and the Flexible Delivery Development and Support Team (FDDST) at Southampton Solent University have moved away from groups of staff working independently of each other when developing learning support, towards a more collaborative model. This involves both FDDST and academic staff in the materials development and delivery stages. By encouraging participation from multiple directions, learning from others to reach shared interpretations relating to teaching and learning, and instigating an approach to steer away from established biases and assumptions, such inter-departmental collaboration positively informs teaching and the module design process as a whole.

As part of this process, an exchange was undertaken of sample student scripts (ranging from D to A grades) from within particular disciplines, together with their corresponding tutor feedback comments, which were subsequently analysed and used as materials for the skills module. By listening to discipline discourses instead of accepting cultural assumptions, teaching and learning attitudes can be open to new approaches and ways of thinking (Young, 2005). Consequently, the weekly content and learning outcomes seen in Table 1 emerged out of these discussions on student needs.

Embedded Provision

Learning outcome number 13 (seen in Table 2.1) makes explicit the embedding of learning development within the wider course context. The disciplines represented within this Certificate in Higher Education in the Social Sciences are Geography and Earth Sciences (Aberystwyth), Law (Aberystwyth), Education and Childhood Studies (Aberystwyth), English, Communication and Philosophy (Cardiff University), Social Sciences (Bangor University) and Business (Bangor University), and were taught by eight lecturers. Since this skills module proposed to raise students' awareness of academic expectations and develop their approach to dealing with key fields of academic study at an inter-disciplinary level, it was

Table 2.1. Content and learning outcomes

Weeks	Content	Learning outcomes
1	Introduction to the module (and the wider course context, as well as assessment methods and guidelines on using *Y Porth*)	LO 1 – Use *Y Porth* effectively as a study resource and post comments to the discussion board
2	Approaching academic expectations	LO 2 – Show an understanding of the academic expectations and requirements of higher education modules
3	Time and task management skills	LO 3 – Set themselves a realistic study plan for the semester, through managing time and tasks
4	How to interpret the task	LO 4 – Analyse criteria and essay question
5	Methods of finding sources	LO 5 – Discover relevant academic resources effectively
6	Methods of reading academic sources (including reasoning, critical evaluation and weighing up evidence)	LO 6 – Show awareness of active and critical reading methods when dealing with academic sources
7	Note taking	LO 7 – Use effective strategies to record information and take notes
8	Developing an argument	LO 8 – Show understanding of the information presented within resources, by organising and restructuring ideas to create a coherent argument
9	Incorporating sources and avoiding plagiarism	LO 9 – Incorporate sources wisely, by paraphrasing, summarising and quoting, and show an understanding of what is meant by plagiarism and referencing
10	How to structure an essay	LO 10 – Understand the mechanics of structuring an essay
11	Redrafting and organising ideas	LO 11 – Show an ability to redraft and plan ideas within an essay
12	Editing and proofreading	LO 12 – Use methods of editing and proofreading essays
1–12		LO 13 – Apply the skills developed through this module and use them in other assignments in their various subject contexts

important that the design encompass all the aspects related to the overall course, to facilitate 'concepts of holistic […] thinking' (Ryan & Tilbury, 2013, p. 25). The embedding of learning development provision also involves 'students more actively in the process of learning' (Ryan & Tilbury, 2013, p. 16) and therefore empowers students to become more committed to their learning experience. This, it was felt, would better prepare students for the appropriate assessments required across their other discipline-specific modules.

Learning development has emerged over the past thirty years to become more discipline-focused than generic (Hicks, 1999, as cited in Stefani, 2003; Baillie, 2003), a development that is supported by the argument for integrating the content-skill element into academic studies (Wingate, 2006; Horne & Peake, 2011). However, ensuring that 'writing […] [is] taught explicitly within the subject context, by subject tutors' (Wingate, 2006, p. 464) is not always possible or practical. Therefore the initial collaborative stages that were implemented during the design process of this module played an important role in ensuring that the skills component was a seamless element of the learning, instead of being 'bolt-on provision' (Wingate, 2006, p. 457).

The success of a collaborative approach such as this has been proven and documented in a variety of literature (Horne & Peake, 2011) where 'educational development could and arguably should occur within the disciplinary base' (Stefani, 2003, p. 19). Therefore, module design, identification of student need, assessment methods and discrete aspects of academic study for the module were identified through discussions with lecturers (via surveys, telephone calls and email interaction). This is advocated in Hogg and Doig's study (2012) that sees merit in learning development teams working closely with academic staff. Building strong and productive working collaborations with academic staff at a cross-departmental level from the outset is instrumental in the success of teaching and learning activities and helps 'foster cross-disciplinary learning and interaction', which subsequently enables students to cross boundaries (Ryan & Tilbury, 2013, p. 24). Furthermore, since discrete topic foci for the module were developed directly from discussions surrounding student need, this raised student engagement (Healey et al., 2014) and channelled 'student perspectives to improve teaching' (Ryan & Tilbury, 2013, p. 16).

Assessment Methods and Marking Criteria

The carrying out of discussions and close collaborations as an exploration into the types of assessments students would be expected to submit for these subject-based modules ensured parity across disciplines and transparency in the collaborative process. Consequently, the following assessment methods were set:

- submit a 500-word reflective piece to the discussion board (LOs 1 and 2);
- create a study framework in the form of a weekly work schedule (LOs 1-3);
- a 500-word analysis of an essay question (LOs 2 and 4);

- a short referencing task and a 250-word synthesis from three sources (LOs 2 and 9);
- a reflective essay/series of reflective essays of up to 1,500 words outlining how each student has managed his or her studies over the semester, referring to one or two other modules, and reflecting on time management, research skills, and the writing process (LOs 1-13).

These mirror most of what students would need to submit for their other discipline-specific assessments, which academic staff communicated to the SSC at the outset. This informed the assessment requirements of the skills module in light of student need and discipline expectations, as well as ensuring its full embedding in the wider course curriculum and making it relevant to students' experiences across the course. This aspect of knowledge application is highlighted further by Ryan and Tilbury (2013), who stress the importance of communicating to students how knowledge and learning experiences are transferable and how they can 'integrate and apply different kinds of knowledge' through transparent and explicit learning (p. 24). This module enabled students to cross boundaries in this regard by recognising the need to relocate the 'disciplinary points of focus' (Ryan & Tilbury, 2013, p. 24) to ensure enhanced, flexible learning experiences. The communication to students of information gleaned from this inter-disciplinary collaboration during the course of the module formed a large part of the foundation for weekly topics, in the form of assessment methods and concrete, measurable academic expectations. For example, to help communicate these academic expectations clearly to students, and to enable further transparency, two types of marking criteria were used. Whereas one is based on broader criteria ('threshold', 'good', 'very good' and 'excellent'), the other is far more specific (see Table 2.2).

By offering two criteria types, module expectations were communicated to students in a varied and flexible way and students were able to approach assessment with a higher level of confidence and understanding. This flexible approach to introducing assessment criteria raises student awareness of academic expectations and therefore encourages student participation (Ryan & Tilbury, 2013; Healey et al., 2014). Another means of making the module easily accessible and transparent was by way of a framework overview table of the entire module, which was included as a separate tab on *YPorth* (the e-learning platform used for this distance-learning course). This framework consisted of the weekly topics and their associated assessments (when necessary), the process that students will need to follow when submitting assessments, the percentage weightings for each assessment, and assessments set and due dates. Students could observe the weekly topics and assessments as a whole at any point during the module, which enabled them to understand 'how the whole programme has been put together', one of the key factors that contributes towards how students study effectively (Burns & Sinfield, 2004, p. 163).

Table 2.2. Assessment criterion, per assessment method

Assessment method	Specific assessment criterion, per assessment method
1	Submit a reflective response to specific questions set on the discussion board, responding effectively and sensitively to other students' comments. The comments should be clearly expressed and show that the student has taken time to organise ideas.
2	Show evidence of careful planning and setting realistic targets in relation to an awareness of academic expectations. For example, consider where, when and how you will manage your workload, taking into consideration deadlines and quality assessment methods, as well as foreseeing challenges that you could face which will cause you to deviate from your planned schedule.
3	Show an understanding of the aims of the essay and the requirements of the question; interpret assessment criteria and complete a written exercise which presents your ideas and your initial response to the essay question. The work should be expressed clearly and show evidence of organising and developing ideas.
4	Appropriate and correct use of the Harvard referencing system; awareness of how and when to reference, by summarising, paraphrasing and/or quoting directly, bringing together comparisons between sources. The work should co-ordinate the main points of the three sources clearly and succinctly.
5	Display a firm knowledge of how to reflect, structure, reference, think critically, organise ideas, edit and redraft, when submitting examples of how to apply skills across modules. The work should show detailed understanding in a logical manner, clear expression and evidence of organising and developing ideas.

Content Facilitation

In addition to the collaboration between academic staff and the SSC, the two-year materials development stage also originated from the personal experience of the author as an online distance learner, by way of a 4-week online SEDA course, to gain online experience and to better understand how to facilitate the online learning environment.

During this course, e-learners introduced themselves at the outset by completing a short questionnaire. This self-reflection exercise proved an effective icebreaker, and was later adapted for this skills module, by way of a resource to welcome all students at the beginning. This resource was presented as a condensed module handbook, which included the marking criteria, assessment methods and learning outcomes. Furthermore, students were tasked with posting introductory sentences in addition to the short questionnaire mentioned above, in order to get accustomed to using the online platform. This questionnaire, connected to the Week 1 assessment, includes questions about their interests in, and their first impressions and expectations of, the module, their previous writing experiences, and what they might be anxious about or looking forward to, regarding their upcoming study experience. Kelly (2003) explores events planning in her work, and although module design differs somewhat to organising conferences, the points raised regarding pre-content delivery stand out as relevant considerations when presented with any teaching and learning scenario. For example, Kelly (2003) outlines the importance of identifying needs to help determine the 'purpose and desired outcomes' (p. 41) both of which are key considerations in the planning stages. Ryan and Tilbury's 'learner empowerment' pedagogy is similar in this regard, in the way that it stresses the importance of giving students the opportunity to specify their learning goals at the outset. This encourages content engagement and realisation of their expectations, fostering self-reflection and imparting responsibility on the learner.

This material development process continued with the aid of CADARN (2014–2017), a learning portal that aims to 'stimulate the use of technology in education and the production of educational resources, and then to use these resources to inspire new students into higher education'. E-learners during the SEDA course participated by posting their observations on a set reading task or slide presentation, later being introduced to an academic guest-speaker based abroad, who gave a presentation via audio and PowerPoint slides. From a personal viewpoint, being introduced to a new 'voice' within the course added a new and welcome dimension to the learning environment, which was then applied to the skills module following a successful application by the SSC to gain CADARN support. This involved collaboration between a Media graduate student, IT Services and the SSC. The finished product consisted of short videos of staff from various disciplines across Bangor University sharing their observations of what they expect from an undergraduate written assignment, as well as videos of undergraduate, second and third year students sharing their remarks. Ensuring cross-disciplinary representation in this regard was key to maintaining student engagement. The information gleaned was adapted for a range of learning media used as materials for the skills module, such as videos, a quiz (embedded into Xerte Online Toolkits) and written exercises, highlighting the fact that 'technology can enable new choices for learners' (Gordon, 2014, p. 3). The SSC used these videos as the main resource for the module's Week 2 activity, as a means to raise awareness of academic expectations.

To ensure transparency and accessibility, another flexible approach to module facilitation is aided through clear explanation of basic but vitally important elements of e-learning, especially to new e-learners, which became grounding principles of the skills module. For example, making explicit how contributing towards online discussion boards and responding to others' posts is an essential part of the assessment process and learning experience, as well as being an influential aspect of peer learning, which in itself is central to building a flexible online community. Ryan and Tilbury's (2013) 'social learning' pedagogy is realised in these peer-to-peer interactions, which were deemed to be at the heart of the course by some of the SEDA course participants, giving structure to knowledge acquisition and facilitating the social aspect, namely that students are still psychologically tuned into the course. These learning spaces can help foster a sense of community and enable students to perceive their learning from different perspectives in relation to their peers (Ryan & Tilbury, 2013). Maintaining clear and effective communication at both peer-to-peer and tutor-to-peer levels, especially when students are encouraged to engage with discussion boards, is of vital importance to ensure positive and constructive learning environments.

Student Participation

In addition to the above module requirements, this module also helped students to reflect on and develop methods of dealing with key fields of academic study through their own participation and engagement with course materials and other students on the module that assist them to grow as independent learners. To further enhance these elements, and to maintain a strong social aspect among distance-learning students, students were expected to participate in various modes of learning. These consisted of engaging in conversations facilitated through weekly discussion boards, adding to suggested reading lists and web-links, and collecting a portfolio of cross-disciplinary field notes throughout the course (including the skills module and other subject-specific modules). These collections of documents served as ready material to incorporate into students' final reflective assignment. Striving for dynamic provision for the learner can be difficult, especially within an online setting, and has been proved by Kunøe (2016) to be associated with how knowledge is exchanged over the course of a learning experience. For example, Kunøe (2016) conducted an experiment that revealed how the novelty factor of innovative teaching practices can subside over time. This demonstrates that teaching practices need to evolve to fulfil ever-changing student expectations.

One way of ensuring that teaching methods and learning opportunities are flexible and varied is by offering a range of formative assessment methods with which students will need to engage that directly supports their summative assessments. For example, being accustomed to expressing their own views on common topics on a continual basis via discussion boards and written exercises can enable students to engage more confidently to academic discourse, feel less isolated (Hogg & Doig, 2012) and maintain participation and engagement. To further students' contribution to academic discourse, sharing best practice and techniques within the module in the form of easily accessible, self-built reading lists and resources had the potential to foster a sense of belonging and build constructive peer relationships. Contributing to these reading lists and discussion boards through the medium of Welsh facilitates the creation of a more inclusive learning environment, which 'deconstruct[s] a dominant pedagogical frame' (Ryan & Tilbury, 2013, p. 20) that is English-led education among Welsh speaking communities. Welsh e-learners have the opportunity to think, write, read and approach their studies through their mother tongue. Enabling students to teach each other, and to share best practice and ideas within a cross-cultural and cross-disciplinary learning environment, raises students' awareness of others' backgrounds, cultures, and underlying assumptions and discipline requirements. Consequently, this facilitates a range of different learning dimensions, 'reaching towards an appreciation of the wider world and of diversity' (Ryan & Tilbury, 2013, p. 20).

Further to the above, students were encouraged to view, respond to and participate in weekly exercises via an online resource. These weekly exercises were developed using Xerte Online Toolkits and were delivered as introductory presentations at the beginning of each week to refresh and remind students of their upcoming assessments, as well as to act as the 'workshop' element of the module. Therefore, this was the platform in which students were signposted to other online resources, asked to participate in various written and interactive exercises, shown examples of past student texts and excerpts of academic articles to elicit discussion, as well as reminded of assessments and the need to gather notes for their final assessment. Burns and Sinfield (2004) stress the importance of building timed activities into the programme design, to communicate purposefully and make connections between the purposes of each element of the module.

To ensure balanced delivery, embedded into the module design were weekly feedback forms and an 'I didn't know that…' form. The purpose of both forms was to enable students to gather and collate enough documents for their portfolio of field notes, and to facilitate critical thinking and reflective learning over the duration of the module, which would later become applicable for their final assignment and other assessments across the course. These reflective forms, submitted on a weekly basis, provided instant and continuous accounts of student learning and reflections, which helped to shape the teaching and development of the module, as well as informed students themselves of their own learning, since 'without reflection there is no learning' (Burns & Sinfield, 2004, p. 185). Palloff and Pratt (2007) stress this further, with their 'interaction and feedback' loop, which provides students with a tool to check their level of knowledge attainment. These forms also give students 'the opportunity to express this thinking in frequent, short writing exercises' which promotes a process of 'writing to learn rather than learning to write' (Burns & Sinfield, 2004, p. 136). Students were therefore responsible for directing module content and assessing their current approach to learning by responding to the following questions posed on the feedback form:

- What do you hope to gain from this week's topic focus?
- Do you have a better understanding of X?
- Describe what you have learned this week.
- Did this week's topic focus meet your expectations? If so, please explain how. If not, please help us understand why not.

- In what way have you managed to apply and use the skills introduced this week for your other modules on the course?

Further to the above, the 'I didn't know that...' form posed questions that helped students reflect on what they learned each week and how their observations might have been relevant to the final task and to their other assignments. These questions encouraged the practice of self-reflection (Hanesworth, 2016) and directed students' critical thinking skills towards course material as well as towards their own learning process (Burns & Sinfield, 2004), which encouraged knowledge transfer and application. Ensuring flexible teaching, by fostering a self-monitoring environment to test students' own knowledge and progression, and building it into the module design in the way of sixty-four hours of private study time and weekly activities can facilitate effective social learning. 'Students should know what they are doing and why' (Burns & Sinfield, 2004, p. 70) and formulating written accounts of the process locates students at a better position to take responsibility for their learning, to understand what they have learned, and to consider how they might transfer knowledge across modules.

In addition to these typical weekly activities, the module consisted of various learning experiences. For example, students participated in pair work as 'study partners', advocated by Burns and Sinfield (2004, p. 71), as an exercise to hold each other accountable when designing and reviewing their weekly time planners, complete a quiz and respond to embedded activities, such as a YouTube video and the short videos of academic staff and students. The online quiz was used as a tool to gauge students' understanding of academic expectations at the outset, and once students answer each question they were shown encouraging statements for each submitted answer. This medium enabled students to assess their own current knowledge and to come face-to-face with feedback relating to academic-level studies and requirements, which is central to Ryan and Tilbury's (2013) 'learner empowerment' pedagogy. Furthermore, the facilitation of online drag and drop exercises and sequencing through Xerte Online Toolkits provided students with informal feedback. These formative exercises enabled students to experiment with their writing, reading and thinking skills without 'the fear of being judged' (Burns & Sinfield, 2004, p. 137) and let them find their own academic 'voice' through practice and responding to constructive feedback.

CONCLUSION

The above discussion has addressed some key stages and considerations during the planning, design and delivery process of online content. Modelling an approach on various pedagogical studies, such as Ryan and Tilbury (2013), ensures above all that the teaching and learning experience becomes transparent and applicable. This locates the student at the centre of both provision development and provision delivery. Facilitating constructive social opportunities for students within the realms of the course, where they can interact with each other, reflect on their learning process, ask questions about how applicable content can be across modules, and be immersed in learning in their first language are the four key principles that underpin this discussion. These elements enhance engagement, advocate learning that is transferable, make effective use of learning spaces and enable an inclusive academic dialogue (Ryan & Tilbury, 2013).

The teaching and learning activities associated with this module ensure increased student interaction and empowerment (Ryan & Tilbury, 2013) and less emphasis on content exchange (Hanesworth, 2016), giving students the space to engage with course content at their own pace (Honey et al., 2000; Gordon, 2014). To ensure the effectiveness of this process, it is important to move away from the common misconceptions surrounding 'study skills' as something which can 'fix' students' writing (Harris, 1995; Lea & Street, 1998; Lillis & Scott, 2007; Lillis et al., 2015) to a place where students can reach new realisations and find their own academic 'voice'. Ensuring that the tutor has more of a facilitative role, taking the role of 'the learner' rather than 'the expert' (Harris, 1995; Clair, 2015; Matsuda & Cox, 2004; Palloff & Pratt, 2007) is manifested in the way students interact with each other through the discussion boards and how they reflect and think critically when completing the reflective forms.

Since the provision is shaped by student need, which stemmed from cross-disciplinary discussions around assessment and acquisition, this enabled it to focus on more discrete aspects of study. For example, by avoiding provision that explores academic writing in general, topics could be narrower to target these needs, as was the case with this module, targeting key academic topics such as paraphrasing, structuring paragraphs to build an argument, conveying counter-arguments, analysing texts, working across two languages, exploring academic 'voice', and incorporating signposts and transitions. Therefore, building course content that directly targets assessment and disciplinary acquisition requires an embedded approach to implementing 'study skills', an understanding of student diversity and an awareness of cross-cultural structures when constructing learning environments that are inclusive.

Implementing a heuristic approach enables a person to discover or learn something in a practical way (Clair, 2015). Therefore, encouraging students to respond to exercises, quizzes and videos via an online resource, to participate in discussion boards and to maintain a critical, reflective approach to the processes introduced to them help learners acquire something from that experience (Cowan, 2003). Indeed, e-learners recorded a higher number of positive comments (Honey et al., 2000), which suggests a constructive and effective learning experience. Therefore, the activities provide students with opportunities to think, reflect, write and consider their learning process (Wingate, 2006), which helps make the learning experience transparent (Warren, 2002), transformative and transferable.

REFERENCES

Baillie, C. (2003). Development in the disciplines. In P. Kahn & D. Baume (Eds.), *A guide to staff and educational development* (pp. 143–158). Routledge.

Burns, T., & Sinfield, S. (2004). *Teaching, learning and study skills: A guide for tutors*. Sage.

CADARN: Y Porth Dysgu/The Learning Portal. (2014–2017). Retrieved from https://www.cadarn.ac.uk/about

Clair, R. S. (2015). *Creating courses for adults: Design for learning*. Jossey-Bass.

Cowan, J. (2003). Learning from experience. In P. Kahn & D. Baume (Eds.), *A guide to staff and educational development* (pp. 192–211). Routledge.

Ellington, H., & Race, P. (1993). *Producing teaching materials: A handbook for teachers and trainers* (2nd ed.). Kogan Page.

Gibbs, J., & Tang, C. (2011). *Teaching for quality learning at university*. Open University Press.

Gillespie, P., & Lerner, N. (2004). *The Allyn and Bacon guide to peer tutoring* (2nd ed.). Pearson Longman.

Gordon, N. (2014). *Flexible pedagogies: Technology-enhanced learning*. HEA.

Hanesworth, P. (2016). *Approaches to equality and diversity in higher education teaching: Thinking about the practical implications* [Web log comment]. Retrieved from http://www.teaching-matters-blog.ed.ac.uk/?p=1156

Harris, M. (1995). Talking in the middle: Why writers need writing tutors. *College English, 57*(1), 27–42.

Healey, M., Flint, A., & Harrington, K. (2014). *Engagement through partnership: Students as partners in Learning and teaching in higher education*. Higher Education Academy.

Hogg, S., & Doig, A. (2012). Engaging blended learning students: An evolving approach to engaging students through the VLE. *Dialogue, 2*, 5–10.

Honey, P., et al. (2000). *Attitudes to e-learning: A national survey 2000 undertaken by the Campaign for learning*. Southgate Publishers.

Horne, D., & Peake, K. (2011). Writing hazards. In M. Deane & P. O'Neill (Eds.), *Writing in the disciplines* (pp. 103–119). Palgrave MacMillan.

Kelly, D. (2003). Planning and running events. In P. Kahn & D. Baume (Eds.), *A guide to staff and educational development* (pp. 40–60). Routledge.

Kunøe, G. (2016). Using persuasive marketing methods and mobile phones as active learning devices to enhance students' learning. *Journal of Pedagogic Development, 6*(1), 64–70.

Lea, M. R., & Street, B. V. (1998). Student writing in higher education: An academic literacies approach. *Studies in Higher Education, 23*(2), 157–172.

Lillis, T. (2006). Moving towards an 'academic literacies' pedagogy: Dialogues of participation. In L. Ganobcsik-Williams (Ed.), *Teaching academic writing in UK higher education: Theories, practices and models* (pp. 30–45). Palgrave MacMillan.

Lillis, T., & Scott, M. (2007). Defining academic literacies research. *Journal of Applied Linguistics, 4*(1), 6–31.

Lillis, T., Harrington, K., Lea, M. R., & Mitchell, S. (Eds.). (2015). *Working with academic literacies: Case studies towards transformative practice*. The WAC Clearinghouse.

Macmurray, J. (2012). Learning to be human. *Oxford Review of Education, 38*(6), 661–674.

Mason, R., & Rennie, F. (2008). *E-learning and social networking handbook*. Routledge.

Matsuda, P. K., & Cox, M. (2004). Reading an ESL writer's text. In S. Bruce & B. Rafoth (Eds.), *ESL writers: A guide for writing center tutors* (pp. 39–47). Boynton-Cook.

Palloff, R. M., & Pratt, K. (1999). *Building learning communities in cyberspace: Effective strategies for the online classroom*. Jossey-Bass.

Palloff, R. M., & Pratt, K. (2007). *Building online learning communities: Effective strategies for the virtual classroom* (2nd ed.). Jossey-Bass.

Ryan, A., & Tilbury, D. (2013). *Flexible pedagogies: New pedagogical ideas*. HEA.

Severino, C. (2004). Avoiding appropriation. In S. Bruce & B. Rafoth (Eds.), *ESL writers: A guide for writing center tutors* (pp. 48–59). Boynton-Cook.

Stefani, L. (2003). What is staff and educational development? In P. Kahn & D. Baume (Eds.), *A guide to staff and educational development* (pp. 9–23). Routledge.

Warren, D. (2002). Curriculum design in a context of widening participation in higher education. *Arts and Humanities in Higher Education, 1*(1), 85–99.

Wingate, U. (2006). Doing away with 'study skills'. *Teaching in Higher Education, 11*(4), 457–469.

Wisker, G. (2003). Carrying out a needs analysis: From intuition to rigour. In P. Kahn & D. Baume (Eds.), *A guide to staff and educational development* (pp. 24–39). Routledge.

Young, B. R. (2005). Can you proofread this? In B. Rafoth (Ed.), *A tutor's guide: Helping writers one to one* (pp. 111–126). Boynton-Cook.

CHRIS LITTLE AND MATTHEW STREET

3. GREATER THAN THE SUM OF ITS PARTS

Coalescing Digital and Physical Learning Spaces in Temporary Online Learning Communities

INTRODUCTION

This chapter will explore the coalescence of, and interplay between, physical and online spaces in creating online learning communities (OLC) which are temporary and transitory. Two case studies will be discussed, offering practitioners two different approaches to creating temporary online communities, which can encourage social learning across personal and public boundaries.

Case study 1 centres on the use of a virtual learning environment (VLE) platform, in this case Blackboard, used here for an online debate within a postgraduate certificate (PGCert) module for academic and professional staff as part of a wider Masters programme in teaching and learning in HE. This case study is examined from the perspective of a module leader and learning technologist. The second case study explores the use of the student response system (SRS) *Mentimeter* to empower learners through an act of shared, anonymous reflection, a process that gives students insight into the transitional anxieties and confidences of fellow new starters. This teaching strategy is being utilised by a centrally-based learning developer with new international students, across a range of academic levels, schools and faculties, as part of their pre-induction welcome and orientation activities.

Each case study will provide an indicative session plan or scheme of work for practitioners wishing to utilise this strategy in their own teaching. Discussions of social and interdisciplinary learning and their transformative capabilities (Mezirow, 1997) will be foregrounded throughout the chapter. These case studies demonstrate how in practice each of these boundaries operate across a continuum altered by the context they are placed in. Furthermore, learner empowerment and co-creation, key elements of the flexible pedagogies highlighted by Ryan and Tilbury (2013) are central in each one.

CASE STUDY 1: USING AN ONLINE DEBATE FOR TEMPORARY ONLINE COMMUNITIES

This case study is focused on a traditional conceptualisation of an OLC through the use of discussion forums and blogs as formative assessment, but it presents an innovative take on this established strategy by allowing participants to interact through assumed character roles. Through these roles, participants are empowered to challenge their own preconceptions regarding students' behaviours in online environments, to reflect on their experience as learners in an online space, and to become creative with arguments. The roles undertaken during the activity release participants from the professional personas and power dynamics that may exist outside of these OLCs (Bullingham & Vasconcelos, 2013).

The online debate is an activity in the first of two 30-credit modules forming a PGcert in Teaching and Learning with Technology. It is scheduled midway through the first module of the programme and is preceded by taught sessions discussing online identity and social media. Overall the PGcert focuses on developing participants' ability to reflect on their teaching practices and encourages them to identify the most appropriate educational technology to address specific learning needs. The summative assessment for the module is a reflective portfolio encouraging consideration of practice in relation to the content covered. Participants have the option to choose to reflect on certain topics covered during the module. This means the participants are able to explore in more detail specific areas of the module. However, reflecting on the online debate is mandatory but can be approached in whatever way the participant feels appropriate to them.

Social learning, defined by Ryan and Tilbury (2013) as 'developing cultures and environments for learning that harness the emancipatory power of spaces and interactions outside the formal curriculum, particularly through the use of new technologies' (p. 5), is encouraged throughout the module with discussion and reflection being integral and central to its delivery. For example, typical sessions are structured with short presentations and followed by facilitated discussion, reflection and sharing of teaching practice. This encourages the participants to work in partnership with the module leaders and allows the cultural contexts and influences that surround each participant to be drawn into the learning experience. Sfard (1998) highlights that 'learning activities are never considered separately from the context within which they take place' (p. 6). This maxim is useful for considering the appropriate conditions to encourage active learning, as is the perspective of Brown et al. (1989), who use the metaphor of tools to describe how to engage with knowledge:

> tools [can] only be fully understood through use, and using them entails both changing the user's view of the world and adopting the belief system of the culture in which they are used. (p. 33)

This is facilitated in the module through discussion and active pedagogies that empower the learner and scaffold this developing perspective. The module leaders recognise during this transition that it is important to encourage practitioners to consider educational theory explicitly when applying technology to their practice. Practice-based examples from the participants create an authentic experience for the participant (Brown et al., 1989) and working in partnership creates an inherently flexible and active learning environment.

GREATER THAN THE SUM OF ITS PARTS

The online debate has two main aims. The first is to introduce the participants to a range of different technologies promoting flexibility. The activity makes use of the group's function inside the institutional VLE, Blackboard. This function is used to separate participants into groups of 4 or 5, exposing each group to a subset of tools in the VLE (e.g. discussion boards, blogs and wikis). Here participants are encouraged to collaborate and create their arguments in preparation for the debate. The debate then takes place on a blogging platform (*Blogger*). We discuss with the participants whether they wish for the blog to be accessible on the web or hidden from view. Using these educational technologies gives participants an example of how these tools could be used in practice to create an engaging learning experience and provides them with an experience similar to that of their own students. The second is to encourage critical reflection upon the pedagogical approach taken to the online debate, the good practice demonstrated, and the supporting literature discussed during the face-to-face sessions to prepare the participants for the assessment. These aims help to create an authentic experience for the participants and will be explored in more detail as the case study develops.

The use of role play is also combined with educational technologies, thereby facilitating a blended delivery model. A blended delivery model aims in part to address a gradual shift in the expectations of students in HE as

> Online experiences are raising the bar of student expectations e.g. high quality MOOCs, online courses, digital content, TED talks, etc. Against this background, harder to manage expectations. (Beetham & White, 2013, p. 2)

The online debate is an example of creating a participatory, reflexive and applied pedagogy and uses role-play to facilitate this (Ryan & Tilbury, 2013). The use of role-play in HE is well evidenced (Beckmann & Mahanty 2016; Fong, 2015). Beckmann and Mahanty (2016) suggest that role-play is a well-established tool used by educators to aid student understanding. We might also consider the following definition here:

> [An activity] designed to increase understanding of real life human interaction and dynamics.
> Participants assume a role in someone else's shoes or in someone else's situation
> To do authentic tasks in an authentic context
> Involving substantial in-role human interaction such as collaboration, negotiation, debate
> Interaction between roles is substantially in an online environment. (Wills et al., 2007, p. 2)

Having discussed the approach that underpins the learning taking place within the module, we can focus now on the structure of the online debate. The online debate is set up in four stages. To begin with, the group being taught is separated into subgroups of four or five. The total number of groups are then split into opposing sides and given the task of arguing either for or against a topic. Example topics have included 'Students today are different – they are 'digital natives' who have grown up surrounded by digital technology – the use of technology is second nature to them' or 'The British HE sector needs to adapt to meet the needs of this changing student body or risk falling behind'. Second, each group member selects a role from four or five choices (dependent on group size); for example, a secondary school teacher, parent, student or graduate employer. It should be noted that the same roles are used within each group. Third, each group constructs a series of arguments about the topic, with each member assuming the perspective of his or her allocated role. Each group has access to a series of discussion tools in the VLE which they are encouraged to use. At this point, the subgroups can only see their own interactions, comments and responses. The online debate activity runs concurrently with a scheduled break in the sequence of face-to-face sessions, allowing time for the participants to become familiar with the technology being used, the literature being discussed, and their roles. The fourth stage follows approximately one week after the first three stages where a blog is opened up and the participants are encouraged to debate the topic using the arguments they have constructed in their roles. This blog is left open for a week, but it can be left open for longer, on negotiation between the participants.

In the taught sessions prior to the online debate activity the participants are introduced to a broad literature base, including Salmon's (2004) 'five stage model', to highlight ways in which online discussions can be undertaken and to provide insight into how to create an engaging environment online. Participants are also introduced to the concept of Web 2.0, including different approaches to using social media (Terras, 2012) and certain research studies highlighting how students can sometimes perceive a gap between online activities undertaken informally in social media and activities undertaken in the classroom (Greenhow & Robelia, 2009). The concept of 'identity tourism' (Bullingham & Vasconcelos, 2013) – the notion that when users of social media adopt roles that are different to that of their perceived self, there is a tendency to act in a way aligned to the perceived stereotype of the role being adopted – is also discussed. Alongside this, the advantages and disadvantages of anonymity in online spaces are addressed using Benfield (2002). This literature provides the theory that frames the debate for the participants in class and helps to place the online activity in literary context providing a balance between theory and practice, and an opportunity for discussion and reflection on practice before and during the online debate.

Following the online activity, face-to-face sessions encouraged participants to reflect on the experience through discussion. This brings the content from the temporary OLC into the workshop setting for discussion, reflection and further exploration. The activity therefore is not bound to a wholly online experience, thereby blurring the boundaries between online and physical spaces. Encouraging reflection on what it is like to be involved in this type of activity as a student, what it feels like to be exposed to a variety of tools in the VLE, and to be arguing a topic from a perspective that as professionals they might not agree with, helps builds links directly between their practice and their learning experience. It also has the added benefit of promoting flexibility as an attribute of learners. This makes the learning experience more authentic, while viewing the activity holistically in this way makes the application of theory and practice more transparent for the participant. This is reinforced as the participants are academic and professional staff reflecting on their own practice, upon the impact of being involved in an online debate as a student, and the content being discussed as a practitioner.

Social learning and empowerment run through this learning activity: the participants are actively involved in the learning development process (Ryan & Tilbury, 2013). The activity also recognises that the participants are situated in a culture within an organisation where hierarchies exist outside of the classroom environment and may be brought into the classroom, altering the dynamics between participants. The use of roles removes these underpinning hierarchies. This activity draws on the ideas of Bullingham and Vasconcelos (2013) who use the work of Goffman as a framework to describe online behaviour. This approach is based on the concept of frontstage and backstage to suggest that people's interaction and behaviour is different in an online environment. In the online debate, this difference in behaviour is encouraged through the use of role-play to create engagement and to model 'identity tourism'. Bullingham and Vasconcelos (2013) describe how bloggers and users of online spaces like *Second Life* often choose to represent different versions of themselves online 'behav[ing] and talk[ing] in a stereotypical way with the result that they later feel they know how it is to inhabit this 'other' skin' (Bullingham & Vasconcelos, 2013, p. 103). When participants of the online debate take on roles, we begin to see more stereotypical behaviour acted out online by participants whilst in role.

Benfield (2002) suggests that anonymity can be an advantage in online discussions. In the context of this activity the groups are often small so anonymity would not be possible. The use of roles has a similar effect as anonymity in allowing each participant the flexibility to engage and contribute outside of his or her institutional identity thereby providing differing perspectives to the argument and activity. Beckmann and Mahanty (2016) support this perspective in the context of role-play, highlighting that anonymity was not needed to create engagement. As with all forms of asynchronous communication, one of the advantages to having the debate online and discussion groups is that it allows for reflection before contribution. This is especially important in a role-play situation as it allows time for the individual to think through how they will enact their role; it also allows people to contribute away from any location and at any time that is suitable to them (Beckmann & Mahanty, 2016).

The online debate combined with the face-to-face discussions and reflective assessment aligns the activity closely to the above definition. Combining online discussion, as a student in a specific role, with reflecting on your own teaching and learning practices, and sharing these experiences to inform the participant's own and others' professional development, allows learners to explore the application of the learning and teaching methods being used and how to adapt them to their own contexts. Bringing these strands together helps participants to recognise reflexive and applied pedagogies in action (Ryan & Tilbury, 2013). The participants come from a range of disciplinary contexts and from a range of roles including professional staff, senior lecturers and staff holding senior learning and teaching roles in the university. This mix, alongside the use of roles in the online debate, adds value to the face-to-face discussions around the online debate, providing the space for participants to reflect on their experience.

CASE STUDY 2: *MENTIMETER* AND TEMPORARY ONLINE COMMUNITIES

This second case study will discuss utilising SRS software, *Mentimeter*, in induction sessions for international students to provide an anonymous and temporary OLC focused upon sharing transitional experiences and anxieties prior to commencing their studies in the UK. This use of SRS is enhanced by the locale within which it is implemented, as will be discussed. In these temporary communities, the SRS is used to empower learners through anonymity to share personal reflection, which is a useful way of engaging learners (Heaslip et al., 2014; Poirier & Feldman, 2007). This allows learners to gauge how the rest of the community is feeling, how they are learning, and to participate without fear of public embarrassment. Furthermore, by using learners' devices, this methodology blurs the boundaries between formal and informal learning, and of the personal and public use of communicative technology. Learning activities are offered which allow a flexibility of engagement and involvement, with students able to answer whichever questions they like but still receive much the same learning. We utilise this technology in an education setting as a positive enabler of flexible, student-led interaction.

There is relatively little published academic literature on the use of *Mentimeter*. What little literature there is, however, does generally agree that it can lead to increased engagement through its correct use (Glassman, 2015). Johnston (2016) found that utilising technology such as *Mentimeter* to positively reframe the use of mobile devices in classrooms led to an increase in student-student collaboration and overall engagement. Additionally, it was found that this approach to mobile device usage benefitted students who were learning in a second language, allowing them to translate difficult concepts to their native language during classes. In this instance, the use of technology not only improved engagement and collaboration but actively provided a solution to learning being stopped completely by language issues. The devices are used here as a learning resource as well as a piece of positive disruptive technology (Flavin, 2012) utilised to share knowledge and ideas.

The above benefits were also found in Van Daele, Fijns and Lievens' (2017) work on *Mentimeter*. They found high reported levels of satisfaction, collaboration and engagement when utilising *Mentimeter* to engage students on a personal and cognitive level during classes. Furthermore, staff also reiterated these benefits from a practitioner perspective, despite some small concerns with the logistics of planning out appropriate questions. *Mentimeter* has a wide range of features and uses for practitioners who wish to enact some of the above findings in their own practice (Little, 2016; Mentimeter AB, 2017).

The above benefits have been found in studies examining use of the traditional 'clicker' hand-held device too. These devices are often institutionally owned and handed out and collected in by the class facilitator in each session. Clickers have been found to be linked to increased academic attainment, but it remains incredibly complex to untangle the device from the teaching style of the teacher and other socio-educational factors such as interest, motivation, and many other factors (Morling et al., 2008; Poirer & Feldman, 2007; Tlhoaele et al., 2014; Trees & Jackson, 2007). Often the clicker is indicative of a wider approach to teaching and learning that focuses on active learning and interactive engagement. Valle and Douglas (2014) also noted that clickers allow the possibility of responsive teaching that responds to the clicker answers provided by the class and that this can lead to incredibly valuable unplanned learning activities. Finally, it has also been found that a clicker can provide a safe and private space for individual reflection and private social comparisons without the need to conform (Brady, Seli, & Rosenthal, 2013).

On a local-level, SRS, of any type, offer real opportunities for student-led teaching and learning, as well as flexible socialisation (Gordon, 2014). Utilising *Mentimeter* for this purpose has allowed these sessions to share the benefits of physical and online spaces. Students are able to participate actively without fear of embarrassment but with an acute knowledge that the people next to them, and sharing the wider physical space, are contributing to their learning and sharing experiences with them. Furthermore, these benefits are obtained with very little educational risk. This particular form of 'meaningful learning could involve discomfort' (Kember & McNaught, 2007, p. 21) and, by appreciating the student needs/incomings, learners can feel that their sessions are truly unique and not merely a repeat of a class delivered a dozen or so times previously. Undoubtedly, using SRS should be done with caution and genuine educational intent, not tokenistically, but it can encourage learners to think and provide a flexible means through which they are able to reflect. In short, it encourages some serious learning and it is often through this 'doing' approach that real, deep learning can take place, as opposed to superficial surface learning (Biggs & Tang, 2011). Giving students the opportunity to give a 'wrong' answer without the risk of public embarrassment provides multiple opportunities for learners to adjust their mindsets (Dweck, 2010). Through making learning active and transformative, we can facilitate learners to a more autonomous way of thinking, ultimately giving students more opportunities to develop adaptability, critical awareness and reflexivity (Gordon, 2014; Mezirow 1997, 2003; Ryan & Tilbury, 2013).

Session Plan

This use of *Mentimeter* particularly lends itself to roles with sporadic or limited contact time with cohorts of students. The following session plan was designed and implemented by a centrally-based learning developer for sessions around key academic practices in order to promote a reflective approach to learning to new, non-EU international students. Non-EU students often attend pre-sessional stays in order to ease their transition into their degree programme of study and it is here that this use of *Mentimeter* has been particularly useful. The software was used to enact a flexible form of shared, cross-disciplinary reflective practice amongst new, non-EU international students as part of their pre-sessional induction programmes in the weeks prior to the commencement of their degree courses. This, in-turn, creates a shared learning environment that is both physical and online, offering multiple access points and an inclusive experience for those that participate. Here, what Gordon (2014) refers to as 'm-learning' (p. 6) is utilised to encourage an ontological flexibility in the student, preparing them for future sessions in their formal curriculum that they are about to encounter.

At the start of the session, all students are briefed on the purposes of the *Mentimeter* exercise and assured of its total anonymity by showing the quiz set-up being set to 'anonymous', reassuring them and demonstrating accountability (Valle & Douglas, 2014). Learners who do not wish to participate are given the opportunity to simply sit in and observe. Learners are then given 5 minutes to sign into the *Mentimeter* session indicated to them. Students simply open a web browser on their device (mobile phone, tablet or laptop) and go to www.menti.com, then enter the session code. The quiz is built utilising a teacher-paced setting allowing practitioner control over what questions are released and when – this allows you to discuss each question and result in turn without students continuing to work ahead on other questions. Table 3.1 indicates the questions asked and the format of said questions for the use of fellow practitioners.

The above session has been delivered in four 'welcome' sessions over the 2015/16 and 2016/17 academic years with four separate cohorts of international students entering the University in September and January of each academic year. These cohorts cover almost every undergraduate course and discipline area in the institution, with this session particularly highlighting the value of shared reflection and appreciation of cross-disciplinary working. This method of delivery has been experienced by approximately 351 students over the two academic years and has been positively evaluated by learners via a student evaluative questionnaire (SEQ). When asked to rate how helpful they felt the session had been in developing academic performance, an average score of 4.1 on a 1–5 Likert scale was achieved (1 = not at all helpful, 5 = very helpful).

The most highly rated aspects of this practice were the opportunity to see the anxieties of other students, an early opportunity to discuss the key study skills they felt they needed for studying in UK-based HE, and the signposting to useful resources to ease their transition into HE. Students also reported that the session would encourage them to engage with academic staff more fully. Students involved in this study reported finding it 'comforting to see that most students feel the same way'. The use of an anonymised, interactive, shared reflective lecture session is

Table 3.1. Example Mentimeter *question scheme*

Question	Question format
1. How prepared for your undergraduate degree do you feel?	Likert scale 1–5 (1 = Not at all prepared, 5 = Completely prepared)
2. How do you feel about starting your undergraduate degree?	Word cloud
3. What are you most looking forward to with regards to starting your undergraduate degree at Keele?	Word cloud
4. What are you least looking forward to with regards to starting your undergraduate degree at Keele?	Word cloud
5. Which of the following academic skills do you feel most confident in?	Multiple choice (Respondents can select multiple options)
6. Which of the following areas do you feel the most confident in?	Multiple choice (Respondents can select multiple options)
7. I have a clear idea of what I would like to do after university	Likert scale 1–5 (1 = Strongly disagree, 5 = Strongly agree)
8. I am aware of the academic support that is available to me	Likert scale 1–5 (1 = Strongly disagree, 5 = Strongly agree)
9. How challenging do you expect the transition to university-level study to be?	Likert scale 1–5 (1 = Not at all challenging, 5 = Extremely challenging)
10. How challenging do you expect the transition to living in the United Kingdom to be?	Likert scale 1–5 (1 = Not at all challenging, 5 = Extremely challenging)

a format that fellow practitioners could easily adopt and integrate into their own induction practices.

The approach is participatory, committed to empowering learners as partners in shaping this session, and wholly respectful of what students can add to the session itself (Ryan & Tilbury, 2013). Here, SRS provided an anonymous platform for learners to actively contribute not only to each other's knowledge but to the construction of the session and to the lecturer's knowledge (Valle & Douglas, 2014). Practitioners can use the given responses to tailor the session to their own group at any point (Glassman, 2015). Questions 4 and 5 offer opportunities to signpost and demonstrate recommended learning resources and service, while questions 7–10 directly offer the opportunity to highlight institutional services and support structures that can support transitions to education from an academic and pastoral perspective.

Table 3.2. *Selected responses to 'what did you find most useful about this workshop and why?'*

What did you find most useful about this workshop and why?
Talking to us about things that actually concerned us, it's a better use of time
The word quizzes, it helped me see how everyone else felt and it kept me focussed
Comforting to see that most students feel the same way
Seeing that everyone was in the same boat
The word clouds describing how students felt/are feeling about studying at Keele
The problems, things students are anxious about and good at. I am glad to know we are all on the same page

By creating a temporary online community, within a temporarily-used physical space, we create a mixed-modality contested space where students can publicly reflect. Here, flexibility is found in the interplay between online and physical spaces. As practitioners, we have all been in the situation of asking if students understand the content being delivered only to be met with silence, particularly in larger classes and lecture halls. This use of SRS enables students to have disagreements or to share important values and concepts with the person next to them without having to broker that difficult conversation face-to-face. These interactions are separated from pre-existing cliques or social groupings, allowing students to disagree privately with peers or social groups who may be in close physical proximity to them. Feedback from learners often indicate that the most useful aspect of sessions like this is knowing what the person next to you is thinking in a safe, judgement-free way.

Mentimeter, in this instance, provides a site which enacts and enables educational experiences that cross cultural and disciplinary boundaries. It gathers shared anxieties and opinions by engaging groups of learners from differing programmes in a teaching and learning strategy which is reflexive and promotes 'the ability to reflect on tensions between alternative sets of values and priorities' (Ryan & Tilbury, 2013, p. 24). Furthermore, this approach will also encourage a more open and reflective stance for practitioners. Opening oneself up to honest and anonymous feedback from students mid-session which may drastically alter any pre-planned direction of said session can cause anxiety. However, it will also provide a student's perspective on the content delivered which will ensure that it is more relevant and, consequently, more engaging.

CONCLUSION

The above case studies demonstrate two approaches to enabling students to share their practices across educational and disciplinary boundaries, working towards the fulfilment of several of the 'new pedagogical ideas', notably social learning

(Ryan & Tilbury, 2013). These two case studies, which work with different student groups entirely, offer two approaches to establishing temporary online communities. They share commonalities around building student capabilities, promoting flexible pedagogies to stakeholders, and a form of democratic, co-creation of learning which can only empower learners.

Both case studies provide learners with experiences which encourage 'lightbulb' moments with a view to building learner capabilities, and the inherent flexibility in both teaching methods is a significant part of their successes. The first case study places teaching staff in the position of students. Offering a 'role' to enact provides an authentic experience of what it is like to be set independent study via the VLE which requires asynchronous input from peers in a temporary online community. By doing so, it encourages staff to think about how they might have previously framed their own version of such teaching strategies and thus change their ways of conceptualising such tasks moving forward. The second case study utilises shared, synchronous, reflective practice to demonstrate common anxieties and confidences to a disparate group of students. This practice challenges preconceptions students might have around concepts of orientation and isolation, and of academic confidence and pressure.

Case Study 1 explicitly promotes the use of OLCs as a vehicle for implementing what might be described as flexible pedagogies (Gordon, 2014; Ryan & Tilbury, 2013) for teaching staff to experiment with, use and critically reflect upon. Case Study 2, however, promotes such flexibility to students demonstrating that 'flexibility can and should be considered as an attribute of both learners and educators' (Ryan & Tilbury, 2013, p. 9). By allowing the teaching, and consequent learning points, to be driven entirely by the responses of the temporary online community and the manner in which they navigate these online and physical locales, both case studies model for their learners flexible and reflective practice, and a willingness to utilise a range of paces, places and modes of learning. The teaching practitioners in these examples are demonstrably making efforts to create learning experiences and environments that are inclusive and multi-platform, and which empower students to take control of what, how and from where they might learn (Barnett, 2014).

The case studies presented here have shown, at their heart, a willingness to use OLCs, both synchronously and asynchronously, to involve learners in a flexible and democratic co-creation of learning. The use of *Mentimeter* here exposes students to the mechanics of constructing teaching and learning activities, actively requesting their input, *there and then*, and placing immense value on their pre-existing knowledge and experiences. Similarly, the innovative use of a VLE in Case Study 1 affords teaching staff opportunities to adopt a student role and encourages them to view their learning through a student perspective. This use of a VLE uncovers for teaching staff the challenges facing our learners when negotiating VLE-based work. Such inclusive teaching practices have the potential to utilise pace, place and mode of learning to alter learner-educator dynamics and develop students and staff whose outlook on learning can be truly future-facing – this must be the purpose of truly flexible pedagogies.

The session plans and schemes of work within this chapter provide workable examples which colleagues may like to utilise in their own teaching and learning practices. In discussing the benefits and risks of two such approaches to utilising temporary online communities, we have considered their transformative potential (Mezirow, 1997). Future work is in hand to explore and research the approaches detailed here. This work will seek to examine and evaluate these approaches with a view to disseminating further. This chapter has provided a theoretical exploration of two approaches to utilising temporary online communities to enact flexibility and, indeed, accountability for both students and teaching staff.

REFERENCES

Barnett, R. (2014). *Flexible pedagogies: Preparing for the future.* HEA.
Biggs, J. & Tang, C. (2011). *Teaching for quality learning at university: What the student does* (4th ed.). Society for Research into Higher Education & Open University Press.
Beckmann, E., & Mahanty, S. (2016). The evolution and evaluation of an online role play through design-based research. *Australasian Journal of Educational Technology, 32*(5), 35–47.
Beetham, H., & White, D. (2013). *Students' expectations and experiences of the digital environment.* Jisc.
Benfield, G. (2002). *Designing and managing effective online discussions.* Retrieved from http://cs3.brookes.ac.uk/services/ocsd/2_learntch/briefing_papers/online_discussions.pdf
Brady, M., Seli, H., & Rosenthal, J. (2013). Metacognition and the influence of polling systems: How do clickers compare with low technology systems. *Educational Technology Research and Development, 61*(6), 885–902.
Brown, J. S., Collins, A., & Duguid, P. (1989). Situated cognition and the culture of learning. *Educational Researcher, 18*(1), 32–42.
Bullingham, L., & Vasconcelos, A. C. (2013). The presentation of self in the online world: Goffman and the study of online identities. *Journal of Information Science, 39*(1), 101–112.
Dweck, C. S. (2010). Mind-Sets and equitable education. *Principle Leadership, 10*(5), 26–29.
Flavin, M. (2012). Disruptive technologies in higher education. *Research in Learning Technology, 20*, 102–111.
Fong, M. (2015). Using technology to support discussions on sensitive topics in the study of business ethics. *Journal of Information Technology Education: Research, 14*, 243–256.
Glassman, N. R. (2015). Texting during class: Audience response systems. *Journal of Electronic Resources in Medical Libraries, 12*(1), 59–71.
Gordon, N. (2014). *Flexible pedagogies: Technology-enhanced learning.* HEA.
Greenhow, C., & Robelia, B. (2009). Informal learning and identity formation in online social networks. *Learning, Media and Technology, 34*(2), 119–140.
Heaslip, G., Donovan, P., & Cullen, J. G. (2014). Student response systems and learner engagement in large classes. *Active Learning in Higher Education, 15*(1), 11–24.
Johnston, K. A. (2016). The use, impact, and unintended consequences of mobile web-enabled devices in university classrooms. *Issues in Informing Science and Information Technology, 13*, 25–46.
Kember, D., & McNaught, C. (2007). *Enhancing university teaching: Lessons from research into award-winning teachers.* Routledge.
Little, C. (2016). Mentimeter smartphone student response system: A class above clickers. *Compass: Journal of Learning and Teaching, 9*(13). Retrieved from https://journals.gre.ac.uk/index.php/compass/article/view/328
Mentimeter AB. (2017). *Mentimeter – Features.* Retrieved from https://www.mentimeter.com/features

Mezirow, J. (1997). Transformative learning: Theory to practice. *New Directions for Adult and Continuing Education, 74*, 5–12.

Mezirow, J. (2003). Transformative learning as discourse. *Journal of Transformative Education, 1*(1), 58–63.

Morling, B., McAuliffe, M., Cohne, L., & Di Lorenzo, T. M. (2008). Efficacy of personal response systems ("Clickers") in large, introductory psychology classes. *Teaching of Psychology, 35*(1), 45–50.

Poirer, C. R., & Feldmann, R. S. (2007). Promoting active learning using individual response technology in large introductory psychology classes. *Teaching of Psychology, 34*(3), 194–196.

Ryan, A., & Tilbury, D. (2013). *Flexible pedagogies: New pedagogical ideas.* HEA.

Salmon, G. (2004). *E-moderating: The key to teaching and learning online.* Routledge-Falmer.

Sfard, A. (1998). On two metaphors for learning and the dangers of choosing just one. *Educational Researcher, 27*(2), 4–13.

Terras, M. M. (2012). The impact of social media on the dissemination of research: Results of an experiment. *Journal of Digital Humanities, 1*(3). Retrieved from http://journalofdigitalhumanities.org/1-3/the-impact-of-social-media-on-the-dissemination-of-research-by-melissa-terras/

Tlhoaele, M., Hofman, A., Naidoo, A., & Winnips, K. (2014). Using clickers to facilitate interactive engagement activities in a lecture room for improved performance by students. *Innovations in Education and Teaching International, 51*(5), 497–509.

Trees, A. R., & Jackson, M. H. (2007). The learning environment in clicker classrooms: Student processes of learning and involvement in large university-level courses using student-response systems. *Learning, Media & Technology, 32*(1), 21–40.

Valle, M., & Douglass, C. (2014). Clicking for health: Use of a student response system in a large interdisciplinary health class. *Academy of Educational Leadership Journal, 18*(3), 87–92.

Van Daele, T., Frijns, C., & Lievens, J. (2017). How do students and lecturers experience the interactive use of handheld technology in large enrolment courses? *British Journal of Educational Technology, 48*(6), 1318–1329.

Wills, S., Rosser, E., Devonshire, E., Leight, E., Russell, C., & Shepherd, J. (2007). *Encouraging role based online learning environments.* Retrieved from https://ro.uow.edu.au/cgi/viewcontent.cgi?article=1114&context=asdpapers

NICOLA POOLE AND SOPHIE LESLIE

4. ENHANCING THE STUDENT EXPERIENCE

Examples of Joint Student-Staff Partnerships to Create and Embed Online Peer Networks within Programmes of Study

INTRODUCTION

The Learning & Teaching Development Unit (LTDU) is a central department within Cardiff Metropolitan University that supports the development of learning and teaching across the institution. The unit consists of three main strands: Quality Enhancement, Academic Development and Learning Technology. The aims of the unit are to develop and promote innovative approaches to learning, teaching and assessment alongside the development of a high quality student experience.

The Quality Enhancement team work specifically on improving the student experience and work closely with all schools – of Management, Art & Design, Health Sciences, Education and Sport – within the institution, as well as other centralised professional services that impact upon the student experience. The areas of work include retention, student satisfaction, induction, transition and student partnerships. The team utilise a range of datasets to help support programme teams to provide the best quality student experience through enhancement activities and have funded a number of projects in order to do so. Previously the team have led team intensive projects to help support individual programmes in response to a review of key performance indicators, programme specific induction projects and learning and teaching calls for thematic projects, all supported by students as partners.

Dunne and Zandstra (2009) outlined the different ways students can be integrated into educational change through their work on a 'Students as Change Agents' framework. They use a scatter plot graph to explain the varying degrees of engagement with students, the Y axis ranging from *Emphasis on the student voice* to *Emphasis on student action,* the X axis ranging from *Emphasis on the university as driver* to *Emphases on the student as driver.* Dunne and Zandstra also outline four key roles for students as partners in educational change: *students as evaluators of their HE experience, students as participants in decision-making processes, students as partners, co-creators and experts*, and finally *students as agents for change*, with each role taking a further step up the participation ladder towards true partnership. These four key roles identify a range of opportunities for students to engage as partners in the enhancement of different aspects of HE provision.

The use of online communities is a strand of the team's work which draws on the 'students as partners' ethos as to how students can become co-creators of materials, resources and programme content alongside academic members of staff. This partnership approach can help to improve student engagement, retention and the overall student experience as well as support the idea of 'learner empowerment' by changing the dynamics of the student/staff relationship. By providing students with a sense of ownership over their learning, participation in online communities might help to instil a sense of confidence and improve engagement with their programme, academic staff and the institution as a whole, and in turn improve retention. As these case studies demonstrate, the role of student interns in creating the online learning communities has helped to facilitate the implementation of a number of these roles within educational change. Historically, emphasis was placed on capturing the student voice with the university as the driver, but now with greater levels of integration it is moving towards student action and using the student as the driver for change. This has opened up a number of different avenues where students as partners can be utilised to improve learning and teaching provision, as well as enhancing the student experience; such an approach might also be employed effectively in the development of professional service activities. Ryan and Tilbury's (2013) idea of learner empowerment outlines this 'positioning students as peers with valuable contributions to make to curriculum design and teaching approaches, as well as the broader culture, practice and experience of learning in HE' (p. 16). This approach was also adopted within the Students' Union (SU) in terms of their 'Student Representation' structure, allowing for a more student-centred approach that provides feedback to and from the students in order to enact change within the institution. This chapter will examine two case studies based in the Cardiff School of Health Sciences and one from Cardiff School of Art & Design.

QUALITY ENHANCEMENT PROCESS – INSTITUTIONAL PHASES

Within the institution, the team support programmes and academic staff in improving their student experience by a 'Quality Enhancement Process'. The process begins with data collection. Students engage in this process not only by participating in a variety of collection methods, but also in the promotion of surveys and feedback opportunities by highlighting how their engagement can affect change. Once the data is collated, it is analysed and presented for discussion to the programme teams and Schools within the institution. It is also reviewed by the Learning & Teaching Development Unit (LTDU) and aligned with existing activities; out of this analysis, possible areas of new activity that might improve the student experience are highlighted. The process then has two pathways in which the enhancement of the student experience can take place.

The first pathway is a School-based approach that involves focus groups with both staff and students in order to gather more detailed feedback on the data and a student perspective from the current cohort (one of the flaws in the NSS is that the students are no longer at the institution to be able to investigate further). This allows careful consideration of the data and, in particular, the use of open comments and qualitative data, in order to identify trends or particular cohort issues. The Schools then work with LTDU to develop School-based action plans, which are monitored by each School's Deputy Dean of Learning & Teaching and shared with students within the school. Updates on the action plans are submitted to the institutional Learning & Teaching Board and discussed with LTDU throughout the academic year.

The second pathway begins with LTDU identifying individual programme teams that would benefit from additional support to make enhancements to their programmes. LTDU carry out focus groups with students using an appreciative inquiry approach. This provides an opportunity for students to present their own ideas and solutions as well as to identify good practice. This also empowers the students and raises their confidence in their own programmes and how they are impacting upon their own and future students' experience. Following the focus groups, an action plan is put together with the programme team and identifies additional support from LTDU. This can include staff development, bringing in guest speakers and experts, hiring student interns or sometimes all three.

APPRECIATIVE INQUIRY

The role of the focus groups with staff and students is to provide more detail around current issues and to identify solutions. Appreciative inquiry has existed since the 1980s and is a method that can assist transformation and change in a positive direction (Cooperrider, 1986), particularly within the current climate and ongoing changes within the HE sector. As stated by Cockell and McArthur-Blair (2012).

> [i]t creates energy and generates positive change as people discover and build upon their positive core and life giving forces to co-create their futures. (p. 2)

The idea of the participants identifying the solutions provides a sense of ownership for them, empowering the students as learners, and therefore a sense of belonging with the programme. However, the appreciative inquiry model is about asking the right questions within the focus group, encouraging engagement with the participants, and preventing the group from constantly raising concerns that feel out of their control. In our work with students as partners this model has become key to engaging students in a process that they feel is positive, impactful and student-led, making a genuine collaborative process. The model also invites more insightful comments from the participants in terms of not only what they would want but also how they can achieve it. As stated by Cooperrider, Whitney, and Stavros (2003),

> AI seeks out the best of 'what is' to help ignite the collective imagination of 'what might be'. (p. 103)

Cooperrider, Whitney, and Stavros (2003) also outline the following areas as a way of achieving this: (1) Discovery – What gives life?; (2) Dream – What might be?; (3) Design – How can it be?; and (4) Destiny – What will be? Students are asked about the state of their programme in the discovery phase, then asked, in a perfect world, how they would see the programme being shaped for the dream phase. They are then asked during the design phase how this may be achieved. The final stage – destiny – is where realistic targets can be set. There is no point in setting unachievable targets as this would only lead to expectations not being met and a possible lowering in satisfaction with their experience. Meaningful collaboration with students is therefore embraced to provide a positive outcome for all. This approach has been very successful at Cardiff Metropolitan University and will be demonstrated in the following case studies.

CASE STUDIES

Speech & Language Therapy – Online Journal Club and Placement Support

LTDU initially approached the Speech and Language Therapy (SLT) programme to help improve the student experience following discussions around NSS scores, particularly in response to placements. The programme is a four-year degree and involves three placements, therefore the students are off campus and not in contact with their peers for long periods of time. The placement element of the degree can also cause anxiety for some students who may be unsure of what to expect. In order to address this, LTDU worked with the programme to develop an online community as a way for students to keep in contact with each other and share experiences and advice. Following appreciative inquiry based focus groups with students on the programme, two main strands of work were identified: a society called SALTSoc and an online community for the students.

LTDU worked with the programme in a number of areas to improve the student experience including the hiring and supporting of student interns, staff development training for the programme team, and most importantly supporting the interaction between staff and the student interns. Four student interns were hired with support from LTDU to run an SLT Society called SALTSoc, which is funded by the SU. The society runs events aimed at developing a professional identity for the students on the programme; in doing so, it develops an online learning community. The purpose of this community was to develop an online space for students to interact and share experiences of their placements, as well as to ask each other questions. This was enhanced by the inclusion of useful resources, job postings and journal articles relevant to the programme.

In order to meet the requirements of the two work strands, a close working relationship was required by the programme team and student interns to ensure the content on the website was relevant and up to date, and that it met the confidentiality requirements that all students on the programme must adhere to when on placement.

The online community, and SALTSoc, are completely student-led, allowing students to speak more freely or ask questions they may be less likely to ask in front of a member of their teaching team. However, due to the nature of the programme, which includes placements within clinical settings, all of the students involved in the online community are provided with extensive guidance in relation to confidentiality and ethics, thus promoting professional values, in particular when sharing experiences of different placements they have attended. LTDU acted as an intermediary between the programme team and student interns initially and helped to establish expectations for both staff and students. This relationship structure has since been embedded within the programme team as an ongoing partnership approach between staff and students.

Following the success of the online community, one student intern requested the development of an online journal club. The idea of an online journal clubs stems from clinical practice within the discipline where practitioners are required to keep up to date with research in order to further promote the development of professional values. The Royal College of Speech & Language Therapists recognise student involvement in journal clubs and can be included in their portfolio as a continuous professional development activity. This required additional duties for the intern in locating journals, reading materials, sharing them with students within the journal club, and posting questions for students to respond to. The intern worked alongside a member of academic staff in order to relate the articles to the programme content and to formulise questions that would help to develop the students' critical and analytical skills. The club works on a six-week cycle and is optional for students to participate in. Students who are participating in the cycle are required to answer a certain number of questions in order to receive a summary of the responses at the end of the cycle. The journal club also provided students with the opportunity to challenge learning relationships, engage in peer learning, and work collaboratively with academic staff.

The flexibility of the journal club was one of its defining features, not only for the opt-in or out nature of the cycles, but also due to its online nature. This allowed students who are out on placements or with commitments outside of their programme to participate in an activity when it suited them, interact with other students on their programme, and maintain a sense of community while developing skills essential to their development within the field of Speech and Language Therapy. The online tool promoted inclusivity by allowing all students to contribute meaningfully, thereby highlighting the value of technologies in heightening the accessibility of the student learning experience. It is in this way that such technologies can foster the development of social learning scenarios.

As the journal club and online community have developed, the programme team have maintained a close working relationship with the student interns and have helped to embed the journal club in particular within their programme content and induction activities. This has helped to maintain student engagement with the community and provide a degree of importance in involvement with the journal club. The programme team and student interns have become completely self-sufficient and the journal club runs within the programme without LTDU support. The idea of an online journal club has been discussed and trialled in other discipline areas within the School of Health Sciences as a way of developing skills, professional identity, and a sense of community within a programme. Since LTDU began working with the programme, there has been a steady increase in the programme's NSS scores for student satisfaction and personal development.

The student intern who developed the idea of the online journal club was awarded Regional Student Employee of the Year for Wales by the National Association of Student Employment Services, further developing their employability by providing evidence for future job applications.

Health & Social Care – Programme Information & Professional Identity

LTDU began working with the Health & Social Care (H&SC) programme team in response to low student satisfaction scores and high student withdrawal rates. Following focus groups with the students, LTDU identified issues around employability and professional identity amongst their students, due to the large number of topics covered and the lack of formal accreditation or vocational identity upon graduation. The focus groups suggested an enhancement of the current Personal and Professional Development module to support the students and provide clearer programme information.

LTDU assisted the programme team to hire two student interns who were to help redevelop the existing compulsory Personal and Professional Development module. The student interns identified that the module did not necessarily reflect the content being provided in other modules and lacked structure. The idea was to create an online community where the students could be provided with supporting materials for the module, as well as an area where they could communicate with other students on the programme. This programme also had a placement element to it as well as a requirement for volunteering throughout; therefore the online community also provided a place for students to share experiences when not on campus with their peers, a key benefit of the peer learning networks and social learning.

The online community was mapped to the main topics covered throughout the degree. This exercise also allowed for the provision of additional materials for students; for example, case studies developed within a fictional town called Oaktown. The student interns worked closely with the programme teams to develop individual case studies for each of the nine thematic areas covered throughout the programme and to provide realistic scenarios for the students to experience with an opportunity for critical and analytical skill development. This is a prime example of co-creation as outlined by Bovill et al. (2011, as cited in Ryan & Tilbury, 2013) who identifies students as just one of several stakeholders working in a variety of collaborative relationships. As the student interns continued to develop materials, the online community started to take shape. Four areas were created for each theme:

Careers, Volunteering, In the Field and Case Studies, each containing videos and quotes from alumni relating to their own experiences. The case studies and materials were then embedded within the programme content via the Personal and Professional Development module and learning activities were centred on the case studies. The case studies and additional materials are updated annually to keep materials up to date and relevant.

The online community also incorporated a specific area dedicated to programme information. Within this area the student interns provided videos of each module leader discussing their module and the potential routes for progression into specific careers. This helped to provide students with a better understanding of the module content and programme journey as well as allowing them to make more informed study choices.

LTDU worked closely with the student interns to help develop their own skills and supported them in developing a close working relationship with the programme team, a different dynamic of co-creation this time between a professional unit and the students. The student interns attended a number of conferences with LTDU and developed their presentation and communication skills as part of promoting the work they had been undertaking, such as the 'Future Directions Conference' at Glyndwr University in 2012. As the student interns came to their final year of study, the programme team further embedded the materials within their teaching content and took on responsibility for updating the materials. This has included moving the materials from a SharePoint site to Moodle in order to embed them more appropriately within programme content.

Since working with the programme and student interns on developing their sense of community and professional identity, the programme has seen improved student satisfaction scores via the NSS, and improved personal development scores.

Architectural Design & Technology – Online Resources and Tutorials

LTDU worked with the Architectural Design & Technology (ADT) team in response to low student satisfaction scores via the NSS. LTDU led focus groups with the students which identified a need for additional resources to help support the technical requirements of the programme content. Suggestions were made for an online space to share resources and develop skills. Due to the nature of the programme, students are required to use specialist software included CAD and Revit in order to design buildings and architectural plans. This software can be quite complex, and although the programme content provided an introduction to the software, more detailed support for students within timetabled sessions could not be provided. Therefore the idea was to develop an online community where students could share useful software tutorials or tips they have either developed themselves or found online. This would create a bank of resources for students that would be easily accessible and relevant to their studies. Thus a new learning space would be created that extended beyond the existing parameters of the peer learning networks seen previously in the institution, one based on a model that was responsive to student demand for specific content and learning.

Two student interns were hired to collate useful resources and develop an online resource of software tutorials and guidance materials. LTDU worked closely with the interns and programme team to develop ideas that related to programme content and prioritised areas or skills required by the students. The student interns decided to make a small number of their own tutorials to kick start the online community and to show students how easy it can be. LTDU provided the student interns with training and support in making their own tutorials and developing the content for the online community. The student interns then wrote guidance for the students on how to develop their own resources and share them via the online community, a prime example of learner empowerment.

Working with the student interns required the development of clear working objectives and guidance in terms of what is expected of both the interns and the academic members of staff involved. Again, clear boundaries were set early on about how the programme team would not only be supporting the development of the interns and the community, but also how they would later embed these materials in their own teaching.

Within the online community, a number of additional materials, including programme and staff information, as well as useful resources for students to use, were also made available. One of the principal purposes of the online community was to empower students by encouraging them to produce their own tutorials and to post them on the website. This became an embedded activity within the teaching for first year students where they were required to produce their own video tutorial of how to complete a short skill within a piece of software and upload it to the community to share with all students. This has helped to develop a sense of community amongst the students, as well as to adopt a more open and sharing practice throughout their studies and learning from each other.

The student interns who were working on the online community have further developed their own skills and have been instrumental in engaging other students in the online community. Since working with the programme, the programme has received increased student satisfaction scores and increased personal development scores via the NSS.

CONCLUSION

Benefits

Between 2011 and 2015, LTDU undertook a number of projects to improve the student experience. The unit worked closely with a number of programme teams, each one looking at a different aspect of the student experience bespoke to their programme. The majority of these projects have included the hiring and supporting of student interns in order to better inform the process, develop student-friendly materials, and to engage the wider student cohort in new activities or communities.

These projects have produced a large number of benefits to both the student cohort and the programme team, including increased engagement, retention and an improved student experience, and these positives can be directly linked to the application of certain flexible pedagogies, notably learner empowerment. This has been highlighted via student satisfaction within the NSS as one measure of impact, as well as additional student feedback mechanisms and student withdrawal data held internally. All programmes that have worked with LTDU via this quality enhancement process have received an increase in NSS overall satisfaction. Many have received 100% student satisfaction and seen increases in personal development scores.

The projects also produced a number of benefits for LTDU and the Quality Enhancement Team, including increased and improved links with other centralised professional departments across the university, such as our IT department, the SU, Marketing and Student Recruitment, and Library and Information Services. The projects have also enabled the team to develop the 'students as partners' ethos, promoting co-creation and social learning. This has increased student engagement with the Quality Enhancement process and understanding of learning and teaching methods used within the institution. Feedback from the student interns has often reported an increased knowledge of how the institution works and the demands placed on academic staff, therefore providing a better understanding of the staff and student experience.

Challenges

The success of these projects is largely based on the continuous feedback being provided to the students within the programmes by members of academic staff. The role of the student intern was key to the success of the projects and in developing a closer relationship with the programme teams, which developed better communication channels between the two. This allowed for more embedded learner empowerment and particularly the idea of successful co-creation. This improvement in communication also allowed students to provide their own feedback and developed a much more open environment for sharing, not only issues or concerns, but also in celebrating successes and identifying solutions. Developing these communication channels and supportive environments was sometimes new to the programme teams and often required the intervention of LTDU in order to establish these connections and manage expectations, and to outline the pedagogical ideas of learner empowerment and co-creation. Often student interns felt unsure of how working with the programme teams could potentially impact upon their academic studies and how the programme teams would respond to direct student feedback on programme design and content. Following initial discussions and setting of ground rules within projects, the partnerships between programme teams and students flourished, and open communicative environments were established. The development of clear objectives and expectations for both staff and students involved in enhancement work is key to the success of the projects.

One of the main challenges faced with evaluating the outcomes of these projects was how success can be measured. The initial data used in discussions with programme teams is from the NSS and is both qualitative and quantitative. Therefore, the NSS has been used to identify if the enhancements have had a positive impact upon the student experience. However, focus groups and informal feedback from students have provided some of the more profound aspects of their impact and we will continue to use these to evaluate our quality enhancement approaches. Evaluations were also collected via Programme Committees and Student Staff Liaison Committees.

Initially these projects were designed to run for a single academic year. However, this was often not enough time to hire interns, establish the project and evaluate the outcomes using the next cycle of NSS data. Therefore it was extended to an eighteen-month process, which sometimes proved difficult in terms of funding and maintaining motivation and student involvement through the summer. However, this allowed for longer term improvements and more robust evaluation of outcomes.

Future Developments

As stated in the QAA Quality Code, there is an expectation for

> [t]he participation of students in quality enhancement and quality assurance processes, resulting in the improvement of their education experience. (Chapter B5)

The use of appreciative inquiry and student engagement outlined in the previous case studies has also helped to engage students in further conversations around quality assurance and has led to enhancements in student engagement. Students are now engaged with the validation and periodic review process in a number of ways, including by acting as panellists at the review event and by taking part in focus groups as part of the review process in preparation for their self-evaluation document. This ensures that students are engaged in all aspects of learning, teaching and the student experience, from validation of programmes, right through to graduation, and to 'equip people with an understanding of the constraining hierarchies and transmissive or 'top-down' educational models that guide their HE experience' (Ryan & Tilbury, 2013, p. 16). This has also enabled further collaboration between LTDU and the Academic Standards and Quality Unit within the institution and closer working between the two.

The case studies provided were carried out over a number of years and involved a number of support departments within the institution. One of the many benefits for running these projects was the development of a close working relationship with the institution's SU. The SU provided additional support for them, as well as later providing a service for hiring students as interns and managing the advertising, interviewing, hiring and payment of the interns. The closer links with the SU have been sustained in the years since and have provided LTDU with vital opportunities in gathering student feedback, providing feedback to students, and also in developing a supportive and effective student experience for our students.

Through working with programme teams and departments across the university, a number of case studies have been developed as good practice that can be shared across the institution. This has provided staff with tools and resources they can use in their own teaching by seeing how other programmes may benefit from using students as partners in the enhancement process. In many cases, this has involved the building of online communities. This has allowed for flexibility of support that many students now require due to the varied commitments that exist external to their student life. For example, some of the students had little IT knowledge in the past, with digital literacy being raised as a concern during the focus groups when the use of online communities was suggested. This is an area that is being investigated further by the institution, as to how students can be supported to increase their ability and confidence to engage with the new platforms that are being recruited to support learning communities.

In conclusion, the quality enhancement process and involvement of students as partners within it has been key to the success of the enhancement projects. Cardiff Metropolitan University has a strong sense of community and student involvement and engagement is at the heart of it. Setting expectations, communication between staff and students, and providing students with more freedom to design their own learning and support were vital elements in all of the case studies mentioned here. Indeed, by embracing the concept of 'learner empowerment', the power dynamic that exists between the student and staff within the institution was challenged, with the student learning experience being enriched as a result. This process has continued to be used within the university and the work with students as partners has expanded across all Schools to ensure the best possible student experience in building learning communities.

REFERENCES

Cockell, J., & McArthur-Blair, J. (2012). *Appreciative inquiry in higher education: A transformative force*. Jossey-Bass.

Cooperrider, D. L. (1986). *Appreciative Inquiry: Toward a methodology for understanding and enhancing organizational innovation* (Unpublished PhD thesis). Case Western Reserve University, Cleveland.

Cooperrider, D. L., Whitney, D. K., & Stavros, J. M. (2003). *Appreciative inquiry handbook: The first in a series of AI workbooks for leaders of change*. Berrett-Koehler Publishers.
Dunne, E. J., & Zandstra, R. (2009). *Students as agents of change* [Presentation]. University of Exeter.
Quality Assurance Agency for Higher Education (QAA). (2012). *UK quality code for higher education*. Retrieved from http://www.qaa.ac.uk/assuring-standards-and-quality/the-quality-code
Ryan, A., & Tilbury, D. (2013). *Flexible pedagogies: New pedagogical ideas*. HEA.

MOIRA MCLOUGHLIN AND WENDY SINCLAIR

5. A CLASSROOM WITHOUT WALLS

Academic and Student Nurses Co-Curating Twitter in Partnership

INTRODUCTION

> Today in our cities, most learning takes place outside of the classroom. The sheer quantity of information conveyed by press-mags-film-tv-radio far exceeds the quantity of information conveyed by school instruction & text. This challenge has destroyed the monopoly of the book as a teaching aid & cracked the very walls of the classroom. (McLuhan, 1957, p. 1)

The aim of this chapter is to present and explore qualitative findings from an innovative and contemporary 'classroom without walls' project which made use of social media as part of a pedagogical approach for nursing undergraduates at the University of Salford. Using Ryan and Tilbury's (2013) 'new pedagogical ideas' as a framework for an examination of this project, we assess the extent to which the students involved developed greater confidence when using social media, particularly in contexts related to the development of their professional identity, through what we call 'curation', the responsibility of creating social media content and steering the direction of any interactions. We argue that there is still a great deal of debate, perhaps even confusion, about the role of technology in higher education (HE) settings; this chapter demonstrates one way in which it might be integrated successfully into the student learning experience.

Few things have disrupted the *status quo* more than the internet, and, in particular, social media, which is considered to be an important communication and learning tool for academics in the twenty-first century (Sinclair, McLoughlin & Warne, 2015; Miah, 2013; Schmitt et al., 2012). More recently, Prensky's (2001, 2012) papers on 'digital natives' and the later 'digital immigrants to digital wisdom' suggest that student thinking patterns are changing radically and that many are already fully engaged with digital technologies on arrival to HE. This is much more the case as greater technological advances occur. He maintains that the locus of knowledge in the twenty-first century has moved from the teacher to the internet, where information on any subject is readily available in a couple of clicks, meaning that the role of the teacher is becoming increasingly facilitative. We argue that in order to equip millennials with the confidence needed to use technology-enhanced learning effectively, academics working in the area of nurse education need to empower these students in such a way as to give them a greater sense of control of their learning whilst, at the same time, allowing them to draw upon their experiences of the world. For example, in recent years, technological shifts have had a significant impact on healthcare and the Department of Health (DH) (2014) argues that for many healthcare professionals, including social workers, doctors and nurses, 'the arrival of the digital age has often been experienced not as a force for good but rather as an intrusive additional burden in an already pressured existence' (p. 8). Yet they also make it clear that human interactions should always provide the foundation of good quality care, but that these interactions could be 'better informed, more efficient and better organised if supported by data and technology services' (p. 10).

Ryan and Tilbury (2013) highlighted that it has become increasingly important to consider ways of

> Building the capability of learners to anticipate and engage with the future and to navigate through complexity, uncertainty and change. (p. 4)

Although it is clearly not a homogenous group of 18–30 year olds who access nurse education locally, or, indeed, across the UK, the majority of the student community appears to be already engaged with social media and digital technologies on arrival to HE. It is therefore not unreasonable to expect academics to be as engaged with this technology. It is worth noting that OFCOM (2016) data reports that in 2016, eight in ten (81%) UK adults aged 16+ of those surveyed (N=3737) reported that they had broadband access at home, with 87% stating that they used the internet regularly either at home or in other locations. Both of these measures appear to have remained unchanged since 2015. However, in previous years, differences by age group were considerable. For example, 97% of 16–24s reported that they use the internet; in comparison, only 42% of those aged 75+ did the same. Two-thirds of UK adults (66% of these survey respondents) accessed the internet through a mobile phone, an increase of five per cent on the same statistic collected in 2015. 89% of 16–24 year olds surveyed were doing this, compared to 19% of those aged 65+.

When considering the adoption of Twitter as an alternative form of communication, it was assumed that by working in partnership with students we could engage them with learning in familiar spaces – for example, via their mobile phones or iPad – but, more importantly, perhaps encourage them to start using social media platforms with the notion of becoming a professional role model in the future, as advised by Moorley and Watson (2015). Access to Twitter is possible on a range of devices, including smartphones and tablets, which many students possess when they enter HE. Interactions on Twitter can enhance the learning taking place in curriculum-based teaching. Broadly speaking, despite the difficulties of measuring its impact on learning precisely, Twitter achieves this enhancement by encouraging active participation in online discussions, sometimes with professionals working in the field. Its benefits are revealed particularly clearly by this feedback from a student curator:

> I was able to participate in some really wonderful discussions, and saw tweets from accounts that I didn't follow personally (although I did end up following some of them as a result) and it was amazing to be able to put ideas and discussion topics out there, and see people engaging with things I was saying.[1]

Kettle (2013) states that the main aim of HE learning should be the development of learners' independence and autonomy, and this should involve students engaging actively with academics, to develop in themselves a repertoire of learning strategies and practices that enhance positive learning dispositions for the future. Ryan and Tilbury (2013) challenge educators and students to question the 'how', 'what', and 'why' of their HE experiences. It is our contention that we are attempting to do this in partnership with students and that it is an imperative for academics to engage with the use of social media in teaching and learning as it is changing the boundaries of classroom education, as highlighted here by another student nurse curator:

> As well as support from peers there is also invaluable support from lecturers and professionals from the world of Twitter.[2]

This highlights the impact of social media in allowing students to hold meaningful discussions with academics in and beyond the classroom to enhance their learning. The Nursing & Midwifery Council (NMC) (2010, 2016) believes that appropriate use of information forms a key part of professional practice. This is reflected in the educational standards developed for pre-registration nursing programmes, where students are expected to demonstrate responsible use of social media. Indeed, Skiba (2011) advocates the need for more transparent social media policies in schools of nursing, so all are clear about how these platforms can be used for the development of students as responsible members of the professional community, of which they will be a part on completion of the programme. In addition, the use of social media should allow students, as learners, to explore the opportunities it affords, the experts with whom they can connect, and the organisations they might follow. However, for nurses in the UK, the NMC offer only guidance on social media use rather than policy; yet, it is their opinion that this guidance can be applied to many other forms of online communications (NMC 2016). This guidance advises on responsible social media use. It is very clear about protecting individual professionalism and the reputation of the user by ensuring that use is always in line with the NMC (2015) code of conduct in both the theory and practice elements of nurse education programmes of study. It was therefore important to ensure that the students are aware of the significance of these factors in the process of becoming future nurses. As Qualman (2014) tweeted:

> We don't have a choice on whether we do social media; the choice is how well we do it.

OVERVIEW

In January 2014, a school Twitter account (@nursingSUni) and accompanying WordPress blogsite (salforduniversitynursing.wordpress.com) was set up by a small team of academics with the express purpose of engaging students with this form of social media from the outset of university life. It would also serve as a useful way of enhancing existing communication channels. All student nurses enrolled at the University were invited to volunteer to curate the account, either individually or to co-curate it in partnership with other students or academics. For the past three years, twice a year, in March and September, all new (and returning) students have an introductory session in the first week on using social media professionally. They are invited to open a Twitter account of their own or if they use Twitter already to follow @nursingSUni. Student nurses were then invited to volunteer to curate the account following callouts or occasionally direct invitations via the virtual learning environment announcements page. Some students who volunteered were already confident about using Twitter and felt ready to speak to a much larger audience. Other students were just beginning to use Twitter and wanted to develop their digital and social media skills with support and guidance from academic staff. By empowering students to do this, they are able to tailor their Twitter learning experience to meet their own personal learning needs. Doing this requires them to undertake a self-assessment of their skills in this area. Such an approach has been highlighted as a crucial factor in personal development planning (Karimjee & Craig, 2010).

Kettle (2013) suggests that one of the key drivers for enhancing the student experience is by engaging students as partners in learning. Enhancing the quality and flexibility of pedagogical approaches may achieve this objective. For example, Ryan and Tilbury (2013) suggest that the promotion of social learning as an active component of flexible pedagogies helps students to identify informal learning and social interaction as key factors in learning development. The extension of learning spaces from classrooms into virtual environments in particular, such as the Twittersphere, encourages interaction, collaboration, and the sharing of knowledge (Zhao et al., 2012). From such spaces, belonging and trust about being in this community of practice can emerge (Lin, 2008). Furthermore, improving the impact of pedagogical practice by harnessing the benefits of technological change may lead to the development of more flexible dimensions to teaching and learning (Kettle, 2013).

The overarching aim of this project was to encourage both engagement and digital professionalism, initially with undergraduate nursing students. Individual students or pairs were able to volunteer to take control of the Twitter account from 7am on a Monday morning for one week. Guidelines were developed to support curators; they included pointers such as:

- setting up an account if you do not already have one;
- logging on, tweeting and responding to tweets at least once every day;

- always seeking advice if unsure of any external requests;
- always considering how the NMC (2015) Code should be applied in this virtual setting (see Appendix 1).

A small team of academics assisted student curators, as and when required. These good practice guidelines were developed in-house and amended over time to withstand the dynamic fluidity of social media use. The guidelines devised were closely linked to the NMC Code (2015) and NMC (2016) guidelines (see Appendix 1).

From an academic perspective, the School's Twitter account has been a huge success with followers increasing on an almost daily basis. With over 8,850 followers in February 2018, some of the student curators have reported that curating the account for such a large and growing audience has not only developed their digital skills, but also their professional competence, communication, and their confidence to start conversations with those who they previously assumed were unreachable. We are also beginning to see a change in the way students use social media for learning and personal development, with real consideration for their professional image and digital footprint. We believe locally this is largely due to the student and academic partnership element of this model, along with the participative and discursive nature of the account, as opposed to some accounts which have the aim of simply providing one-way broadcasting. As one student reflected in the blog post:

> I've also had the opportunity to speak to some lovely people that I have things in common with whom I wouldn't have otherwise met [...] one of the highlights was speaking to a person who has overcome depression [...] Tweeting will build your confidence, your connections and increase your debating and critical thinking skills.[3]

Ryan and Tilbury (2013) noted the more recent proliferation of new technologies in HE which have triggered ideas related to connecting differently and flexibly with students for the purpose of enhancing teaching and learning. As 'tweeting academics', we are connected to and are part of a large and steadily increasing online community of nurses and healthcare professionals using Twitter to connect and learn. For example, the voluntary organisation @WeNurses has several community accounts for healthcare professionals, such as @WeAHPs, (occupational therapists), @WeGPNs (general practice nurses), and @WeCYPnurses (children and young people nurses). The @WeNurses account alone has over 71,700 followers, evidence that points to the potential for student nurses to access a huge professional and educational resource beyond the classroom. Reviewing the themes that emerged from the reflective blogs undertaken by student curators for this project, it became increasingly evident that using social media in this form can enhance learning and encourage students to extend their learning 'beyond the classroom walls' in a way that is both accessible and underpinned by flexible pedagogies.

This qualitative evidence suggests that being involved in and curating the @nursingSUni Twitter account can provide students with a transformative learning environment. Mezirow (1997) describes this environment as one in which learners have equal opportunity to assume various roles, can reflect on assumptions by working with facilitators who often encourage critical thinking, are empathetic listeners, and who are willing to search for common ground or are just able to hear a synthesis of different points of view. Students tweeting on behalf of the School can do this and become a participant in a community of practice. Lave and Wenger (1991) suggest that communities of practice are

> much more than the technical knowledge or skill associated with undertaking some task. Members are involved in a set of relationships over time. (p. 98)

Eraut (2007), in contrast, suggested that informal learning often happens in social scenarios. However, what we felt was emerging here was a sense of community for a lot of these students both within and without the university setting, realising the initial aims of encouraging engagement and digital professionalism in undergraduate nursing students.

DISCUSSION

Learner Empowerment

Learner empowerment lies at the heart of the six 'new pedagogical ideas' proposed by Ryan and Tilbury (2013). They describe the pedagogy of learner empowerment as

> involving students in learning development and processes of co-creation that challenge learning relationships and the power frames that underpin them. (Ryan & Tilbury, 2013, p. 5)

We argue that by offering student nurses the opportunity to curate the @nursingSUni Twitter account, it has given students a platform for their voice to be heard by a much wider and more varied audience than one just consisting only of their peers and one academic in a classroom setting. For example, once students have completed a week of curation we ask them to write a blog using the link in the Twitter profile. We ask that it is no more than 500 words and is generated using a reflective approach to their learning based on their experience of undertaking this activity. However, in completing this task, students have employed a variety of creative and innovative ways of expressing their learning, including video logs (vlogs), writing poems, and taking photographs. These expressions of creativity, we argue, reflect the positive impact on the student curators of being empowered in their learning in this arena. Such empowerment is also reflective of an unspoken challenge to the perceived power balance in a HE setting, which has in turn positively affected the relationship between involved students and academics. Conversations are more personal and go beyond the subject matter covered in the classroom. For example, a third-year student undertaking a management and leadership module developed a Twitter relationship with a professor of nursing at another university who invited the student to shadow her for a week and attend meetings to observe leadership characteristics in senior-level interactions. This example highlights that the @NursingSUni account has offered students a platform on which the boundaries that usually prevent someone with no perceived legitimacy from engaging in 'professional' conversations with either an academic or practitioner from a clinical background might be broken down.

Future-Facing Education

The second pedagogical idea put forward by Ryan and Tilbury (2013) is that academics in HE consider:

> refocusing learning towards engagement and change processes that help people to consider prospects and hopes for the future across the globe. (p. 5)

There have been a number of examples where social media has been used to effect positive change through the use of a transformational approach, such as the #hellomynameis campaign launched on Twitter by Kate Granger, who wanted healthcare professionals always to introduce themselves to patients and users of the National Health Service (Granger, 2012). This campaign was exceptionally well received and by encouraging our students to use Twitter we have exposed them to important campaigns related to healthcare, such as this one, and others related to caring for people with dementia (@TommyNtour). Awareness of these account has expanded the students' capacity to see and consider the views and perspectives of people that they may not have previously heard or otherwise considered. Along similar lines, many students have discussed their future careers with qualified nurses, professors, and professional body members and have actively used the information gathered for personal development. For example, students have publicly requested to attend relevant conferences for little or no cost through the use of Twitter. When they have been successful, they have shared their learning by live tweeting from the event, encouraging others to do the same, and, more importantly, acted as professional role models to other students both locally across the UK and often globally.

Decolonising Education

Ryan and Tilbury (2013) suggest that academics should be

> deconstructing dominant pedagogical frames that promote only Western world views, to create experiences that extend inter-cultural understanding in the HE system and the ability to think and work using globally sensitive frames and methods. (p. 5)

Through the development of the Twitter account, we have connected with schools of nursing not only locally in the UK but across the globe, including Europe, Australia, the USA and Saudi Arabia. This, in turn, has enabled students not only to make global connections, but also to learn about cultures beyond their own boundaries.

For example, one student nurse was able to contact a school nurse in the USA to learn more about care provision before applying for an international placement. As the Code (NMC, 2015) makes clear, nurses of the future should be able

> to use a range of verbal and nonverbal communication methods, and to consider cultural sensitivities to better understand and respond to people's personal and health needs. (p. 7)

The @nursingSUni account therefore offers students an opportunity to learn about the culture and perspectives of the very people they will be caring for at the end of their programme. Students have also been able to share their experiences of being on international placements to a wider audience, encouraging discussion about healthcare provision and education in other countries, a benefit identified more recently by a Masters of Nursing student (mental health field) (Harvey, 2016).

A final point concerns guest curators. Whilst we have not had guest curators from across the globe yet, we do receive requests to curate the account from student nurses at other universities in the UK. We have enabled this, as we believe it creates a more cohesive community in which students are able to learn about diversity in nurse education. We believe that this is also helpful for students who are beginning to build their own professional networks, for it will ultimately enhance the development of their future careers.

Transformative Capabilities

Transformative capabilities refer to

> creating an educational focus beyond an emphasis solely on knowledge and understanding, towards agency and competence, using pedagogies guided by engaged, 'whole-person' and transformative approaches to learning. (Ryan & Tilbury, 2013, p. 5)

For student nurses entering a course of study that eventually leads to professional registration, facilitators of learning in HEIs should be encouraging students to use the medium of social media in an appropriate way when developing their knowledge and understanding of issues for practice (Sinclair et al., 2015). The ultimate outcome of any undergraduate nurse education programme is for each student to emerge as a qualified practitioner who is 'fit for practice' (NMC, 2010, p. 147). As this intervention makes clear, social media has the potential to facilitate future-facing education by privileging learner empowerment and by developing agency engendering transformative capabilities in learners. This project highlights the potential for social media to break down the walls of the classroom naturally by empowering learners, and, at the same time, creating agency and competence in graduates.

Healey, Flint, and Harrington (2014) argue that

engaging students and staff effectively as partners in learning and teaching is arguably one of the most important issues facing higher education in the 21st century. (p. 7)

Partnership is essentially a process for engaging students rather than an outcome in itself, and, as Bryson (2014) has pointed out, 'the future of student engagement lies in partnerships' (p. 240). Creating meaningful partnerships often represents a significant challenge to universities; but this project has revealed how effective partnerships might be developed through the simple use of social media. This Twitter account idea started as a small seed but is growing into a mighty oak that is now central to student learning.

The potential of this approach for developing transformative capabilities lies in the inherent responsibility of curating the School's Twitter account. Students tweeting on behalf of the School need to consider the content of their tweets carefully and how each one will be received by a large and growing Twitter following. Furthermore, by curating the account, students also have to think broadly about issues and be prepared to continue discussions through an ability to listen and – when appropriate – to challenge in a professional manner alternative perspective. The power of these discussions often prompts students to think about aspects of an issue that they had perhaps not yet been exposed to, as evidenced through some of the reflective blogs:

> The thing I most enjoyed about my week on Twitter was taking part in the Twitterchats. There are so many thoughts, theories and opinions out there, and it felt like I learnt a lot. After I had finished one of the @WeNurses chats I sat back and read through the evening's discussion. There were some really interesting points of view and reasons for different approaches to care. I had never thought Twitter could be a tool for learning. It is not just a Social Media outlet it is a place where people learn from each other, share ideas, develop and most importantly connect with like-minded people.[4]

Crossing Boundaries

Ryan and Tilbury (2013) propose that educators should

> generate interdisciplinary, inter-professional and cross-sectoral learning, to maximise collaboration and shared perspective, while tackling bias and differences of perspective. (p. 5)

There are numerous accounts that students can access to learn about other professions once they begin to use Twitter, such as @WeHealthVisitor (predominantly for those working in the field of health visiting) and @WeDocs (connecting, driving and supporting the doctor community). There are also greater opportunities to interact with people, who before the advent of Twitter were previously considered to be unreachable, such as the Chief Executive Officer (CEO) of the Nursing and Midwifery Council, @JackieSmith_nmc, who uses Twitter to engage with healthcare professionals and has proved to be approachable and amenable to conversing with students about Nursing and Midwifery Council business. Creation of this Twitter account has also provided students with greater opportunity to learn from student nurses at other universities, including those at the University of Plymouth, who are assessed as first year student nurses on how they use Twitter as part of digital professionalism (Jones et al., 2016). We have had students from both Plymouth and Salford collaborate in live Twitter discussions, blogging and curating via @WeNurses. We have actively sought professions outside of nursing to interact with curators of the account to enable development of inter-professional working. For example, we have had guest academic curators from Podiatry and Midwifery. We have encouraged students from other universities to curate the account to build networks and learn from each other. The success of these activities is consistent with the findings of Beetham and White's (2013) study on student expectations and experiences of the digital environment. One key recommendation that emerges out of their study is that technology should be carefully integrated into the learning experience in such a way as to promote academic success. For example, as evidenced by this quote from a student blog after curation (November 2016):

> I was able to have some interesting conversations with people from around the country [...] I was able to gain some great insight on what both students and mentors expect from the relationship – students want assistance and guidance in both skills and knowledge about the placements, mentors would like the students to have done at least some background reading about the placement.[5]

Social Learning

The final pedagogical idea presented is social learning (Ryan & Tilbury, 2013). This is arguably the most relevant of the 'new pedagogical ideas' to this project for it is very closely linked to using a dedicated Twitter account to enhance learning. As this example demonstrates, the Twitter platform promotes the co-creation of content between academics and students. As such, it enables social learning to take place and allows both a culture and an environment for learning built on the 'power of spaces and interactions taking place outside the formal curriculum to develop', as proposed by Ryan and Tilbury (2013, p. 5). This is clearly illustrated by a student from another university who had volunteered to curate the account to connect socially with other nursing students:

> It's October 2015 and I am connecting with other healthcare professionals (including students), hearing service-user voice and acquiring knowledge about services, policies and research informing evidence-based practice. I am still learning ways to benefit from social media in a professional sense, but do we ever stop learning? Our neighbours came to talk to us about using social media (#SoMe) professionally and fortunately for me I was presented with an opportunity to curate the Salford University's Nursing School Twitter account.[6]

The very nature of nurse education programmes means that student nurses are taught in the university for 50% of their time and in clinical placement for 50% of the time (UKCC, 1986; NMC, 2010). Sinclair, McLoughlin and Warne (2015) explain that the authenticity of the responses in professional Twitter chats, such as those facilitated by @WeNurses, gives students an opportunity to reflect with others and apply theory to their own clinical practice. When curating the School Twitter account, students are actively encouraged to participate in open professional discussions and offer reflections about their clinical practice experience. Not only do students reflect on their own practice, they use the opportunity to ask professionals about their practice, enhancing their understanding of the roles of others, and in return engage with tweeting professionals, including doctors, social workers and other members of the multi-disciplinary teams they work with. Student viewpoints are also challenged, with exchanges that go some way to encouraging critical thinking and debate. When student nurses are on placement in clinical practice, they can be away from the University for long periods of time when they may feel distant from their support networks. This is when students may experience a level of vulnerability and where the potential for withdrawing from the programme is real (Royal College of Nursing, 2008). This time can be isolating; it actually encourages students to separate practice learning from academic learning. Eraut (2011) states that when developing a student's ability to make effective use of what has been learned off the job, work-based learning is important. He also maintains that it can help with knowledge development as it is situated in the context in which it is acquired; yet it also requires additional learning for its application, which often takes place through later reflection and facilitation of this learning. By engaging via Twitter, many students are able to maintain contact with both staff and students, not only for support, but also to discuss and consolidate their learning, further closing the theory-practice gap.

The NMC (2015) social media guidelines state nurses put their registration at risk if they act 'in any way that is unprofessional or unlawful' (p. 5). Indeed, Jones-Berry (2016) has reported that eight nurses have been removed from the register because of inappropriate postings on Facebook and other social media in the past. Anecdotally, students have reported, from the experience of curating the account, that they have subsequently edited the biography pages in their personal accounts in order to present a more professional identity. This can also be evidenced through blogging and focus group findings undertaken following the completion of each curator's turn. Therefore, as this example demonstrates, utilising social media and working in partnership with students can lead to greater engagement in learning that occurs in familiar spaces; more importantly, it generates greater awareness of professional responsibility when using such platforms. For example:

> Curating the university Twitter account has been a great experience, and I feel that tweeting has boosted my confidence. For me it's all about learning and sharing information, expanding knowledge, and experience in order to understand and promote best practice. Furthermore, I feel that it is important to

acknowledge and thank the nursing lecturers who have introduced and created the university Twitter account who strongly believe in the value of social media in nurse education.[7]

CONCLUSION

Using the framework of Ryan and Tilbury's (2013) 'new pedagogical ideas', this chapter has explored the development of a creative and innovative project entitled the 'classroom without walls', a dedicated Twitter account for undergraduate student nurses. We recognise that many leading organisations and governing bodies, such as the NMC, already use social media to engage with both practitioners and the public and by doing so it can be assumed that they are setting a standard that as a school of nursing, within a university, is important to follow. Since the account began there have been approximately fifty-five student curators, with many curating as first year students and then returning in the second or third year for another opportunity. There have also been a number of guest curators, both students and academics, who volunteered as a way of developing their Twitter skills. One of the questions posed locally following this initiative was: is there something unique about student nurses that means they are more willing to experiment in this way with social media? This is a difficult question to answer, but we suggest that curation of this account has developed greater confidence amongst the students in using social media in a constructive and professional way. For healthcare professional students, both before starting a course of study and throughout the programme, it can be the first place to see a breaking news item on health, or highlight new resources, procedures or toolkits. Nursing students can become involved in Twitter chats and begin to discuss new ideas for service improvement and care delivery, hear about case studies, or read a recently published research article that may have relevance for the care that they are delivering. It may also provide insights into more theoretical pieces of work they are undertaking. As Ryan and Tilbury (2013) suggest, and as this case study highlights, 'pedagogies geared towards flexibility in the learner and flexibility in the very nature of those pedagogies' (p. 31), as ideas, might only be brought closer together by educators who are willing to challenge the learning dynamic. By presenting opportunities to connect with colleagues around the world, and by offering a breadth of learning from a global landscape of tweeters, social media – and, more specifically, Twitter, offers educators a powerful means of achieving the goals set out by Ryan and Tilbury.

NOTES

[1] See salforduniversitynursing.wordpress.com
[2] See salforduniversitynursing.wordpress.com
[3] See salforduniversitynursing.wordpress.com
[4] See salforduniversitynursing.wordpress.com

⁵ See salforduniversitynursing.wordpress.com
⁶ See salforduniversitynursing.wordpress.com
⁷ See salforduniversitynursing.wordpress.com

REFERENCES

@nursingSUni . (2017). Retrieved from https://twitter.com/nursingSUni
@WeNurses. (2017). Retrieved from https://twitter.com/WeNurses
Beetham, H., & White, D. (2013). *Students' experiences and expectations of the digital environment.* Retrieved from http://repository.jisc.ac.uk/5572/1/JR0006_STUDENTS_EXPECTATIONS_EXEC_SUMMARY_v2.pdf
Bryson, C. (Ed.). (2014). *Understanding and developing student engagement.* Routledge.
Department of Health. (2014). *Personalised health and care 2020: Using data and technology to transform outcomes for patients and citizens. A framework for action.* HM Government.
Eraut, M. (2007). Learning from other people in the workplace. *Oxford Review of Education, 33*(4), 403–422.
Eraut, M. (2011) Informal learning in the workplace: Evidence on the real value of Work-Based Learning (WBL). *Development and Learning in Organizations, 25*(5), 8–12.
Granger, K. (2012). *The other side.* Author .
Harvey, E. (2016, March 22). *From Salford to Sweden – Undertaking an Erasmus international placement and reaping the benefits for my future career.* Retrieved from https://salforduniversitynursing.wordpress.com/2016/03/22/from-salford-to-sweden-undertaking-an-erasmus-international-placement-and-reaping-the-benefits-for-my-future-career-by-emma-harvey-sept-13-ma-nursing-emmaharveyhk/
Healey, M., Flint, A., & Harrington, K. (2016). Students as partners: Reflections on a conceptual model. *Teaching & Learning Inquiry: The ISSOTL Journal, 4*(2), 1–13.
Jones, R., Kelsey, J., Nelmes, P., Chinn, N., Chinn, T., & Proctor-Childs, T. (2016). Introducing Twitter as an assessed component of the undergraduate nursing curriculum: Case study. *Journal of Advanced Nursing, 72*(7), 1638–1653.
Jones-Berry, S. (2016). Revealed: The price nurses pay for ill-judged postings on social media. *Nursing Standard, 30*(24), 7.
Karimjee, R., & Craig, G. (2010, July). *How can personal development planning assist progression from access courses into a career in nursing: mapping best practice?* Retrieved from http://www.bbk.ac.uk/linkinglondon/development-projects/Ref34FinalReportCity.pdf
Kettle, J. (2013) *Flexible pedagogies: Employer engagement and work-based learning.* HEA.
Lave, J., & Wenger, E. (1991). *Situated learning: Legitimate peripheral participation.* Cambridge University Press.
Lin, H. (2008). Determinants of successful virtual communities: Contributions from system characteristics and social factors. *Information and Management, 45*, 522–527.
Miah, A. (2013, July 26). Top 5 social media platforms for research development [Blog post]. Retrieved from http://blogs.lse.ac.uk/impactofsocialsciences/2013/07/26/a-to-z-of-social-media-for-academia/11/12/2017
McLuhan, M. (1957). Classroom without walls. *Explorations, 7.* Retrieved from http://tcpd.org/Thornburg/Handouts/McLuhan.pdf
Mezirow, J. (1997). Transformative learning: Theory to practice. *New Directions for Adult and Continuing Education, 74*, 5–12.
Moorley, C., & Watson, R. (2015). NMC code advice on digital communications. *Nursing Times, 111*(14), 22–23.
Nursing and Midwifery Council. (2010). *Standards for pre-registration nursing education 2010.* Retrieved from https://www.nmc.org.uk/globalassets/sitedocuments/standards/nmc-standards-for-pre-registration-nursing-education.pdf
Nursing and Midwifery Council. (2015). *The Code: Professional standards of practice and behaviour for nurses and midwives.* Retrieved from https://www.nmc.org.uk/standards/code/

Nursing and Midwifery Council. (2016). *Social media guidance*. Retrieved from https://www.nmc.org.uk/standards/guidance/social-media-guidance/

Ofcom. (2016). *Internet use and attitudes: 2016 metrics bulletin*. Retrieved from https://www.ofcom.org.uk/__data/assets/pdf_file/0023/63950/Internet-use-and-attitudes-2016.pdf

Prensky, M. (2001). Digital natives, digital immigrants. *On the Horizon, 9*(5), 1–6.

Prensky, M. (2012). *Digital natives to digital wisdom: Hopeful essays for 21st century learning*. Corwin.

Qualman, E. (2014, November 13). *We don't have a choice on whether we do social media, the choice is how well we do it*. Retrieved from https://Twitter.com/equalman/status/533090727081689088

Royal College of Nursing. (2008). *Nursing our future*. Royal College of Nursing.

Ryan, A., & Tilbury, D. (2013). *Flexible pedagogies: New pedagogical ideas*. HEA.

Schmitt, T., Sims-Giddens, S., & Booth, R. (2012). Social media use in nursing education. *The Online Journal of Issues in Nursing, 17*(3), Manuscript 2.

Sinclair, W., McLoughlin, M., & Warne, T. (2015). To Twitter to woo: Harnessing the power of Social Media (SoMe) in nurse education to enhance the student's experience. *Nurse Education in Practice, 15*(6), 507–511.

Skiba, D. J. (2011). Nursing education 2:0 the need for social media policies for schools of nursing. *Nursing Education Perspectives, 32*(2), 126–127.

United Kingdom Central Council for Nursing Midwifery & Health Visiting. (1986). *Project 2000: A new preparation for practice*. UKCC.

Zhao, L., Lu, Y., Wang, B., Chau, P. Y. K., & Zhang, L. (2012). Cultivating the sense of belonging and motivating user participation in virtual communities: A social capital perspective. *International Journal of Information Management, 32*, 574–588.

SHEILA L. AMICI-DARGAN, AMBER M. MOORCROFT AND
STEPHEN M. RUTHERFORD

6. SHADOW MODULES AND STUDENT-LED ONLINE LEARNING COMMUNITIES

Supporting Learning, Engagement, and Student Empowerment within, and across, Institutions in Higher Education

THE ROLE OF SELF-REGULATED COLLABORATIVE LEARNING IN HIGHER EDUCATION

One of the fundamentals of HE is the development of independent self-regulated learners (Biggs & Tang, 2011; Daily & Landis, 2014; QAA, 2014). Central to this aim are approaches which develop active and deep learning strategies. However, the logistical constraints of some disciplines, such as the Biosciences, with typically large class sizes (often 300+ students) may tend to drive educational practitioners more towards the use of didactic methods for teaching. A limitation of didactic teaching methods is that they are generally less effective for promoting deep learning than active learning methodologies (Prince, 2004; Biggs & Tang 2011), such as inquiry-based, case-based or problem-based learning. Large-scale didactic teaching particularly limits several of the core values of the 'new pedagogical ideas' of Ryan and Tilbury (2013), in particular learner empowerment, social learning and the transformative capability of learning, to move beyond basic surface-learning considerations of knowledge and understanding. One way of addressing this disparity is the adoption of peer-led or collaborative learning.

Student-led learning initiatives (e.g. peer/near-peer teaching and/or collaborative peer-learning), through their discursive and collaborative nature, have the potential to encourage social learning, moving learners beyond knowledge and understanding (Ryan & Tilbury, 2013) towards deeper learning and the cultivation of effective 'communities of practice'. Collaborative learning as a pedagogic approach is deeply embedded within sociocultural models of learning, for example, Mercer's concept of the 'Intermental Development Zone' (IDZ) (Mercer, 1996; Mercer & Littleton, 2007). The IDZ is a reimagining of Vygotsky's 'Zone of Proximal Development' (ZPD), where an expert designs activities to lessen the knowledge gap between them and a novice (Vygotsky, 1978). However, the IDZ is a space that is mutually negotiated, either between a novice and expert, or between two novices. The IDZ is narrowed by 'exploratory talk' between parties (Mercer, 1996, p. 104), during which each side benefits by constantly revising their own perceptions. This mutual development of understanding empowers learners to take ownership of their learning, and develop social networks and learning partnerships (Ryan & Tilbury, 2013). This interaction is particularly potent between two novices who might have limited understanding of a subject. Exploratory talk will identify knowledge gaps, utilising the relative expertise of each party (greater in different individuals for different aspects of the issue being discussed). It also promotes metacognition and critical thinking by encouraging learners to question their own assumptions, challenge each other's perceptions, and come to an agreed and shared understanding (Littleton & Mercer, 2013).

Student-led collaborative learning initiatives, through their enhancement of social learning, have the potential to foster deep learning within large student cohorts, and to empower learners to become active agents in their own learning, rather than passive consumers of knowledge. This facilitation of agency in learners has great transformative potential, leading students beyond the limiting scope of focusing only on knowledge and understanding (Ryan & Tilbury, 2013), and offers a broader opportunity to deepen their ability to apply that knowledge to solving problems and being creative. However, there are many challenges to doing this effectively. In particular, it is important to scaffold interactions so that effective peer-led learning can take place *outside* of the classroom. The aim of this chapter is to reflect upon and share our own experiences of establishing effective, student-led collaborative communities of practice.

COMMUNITIES OF PRACTICE IN HIGHER EDUCATION LEARNING

A 'community of practice' (CoP) is a discipline-specific group who interact with each other over a period of time on a shared interest or concern (Lave & Wenger, 1991). Lave and Wenger's model of 'Legitimate Peripheral Participation' involves learners becoming progressively more engaged with their CoP through interactions with more knowledgeable individuals. In HE we can actively cultivate this process of social learning by providing opportunities for our students to interact with each other (peers), with individuals in higher year groups (near-peers) and/or with academic staff (community experts). Successful CoPs (see Webber, 2016, for a practical guide) require a minimum of two core components: a shared domain of interest, and good interaction between members of the community to develop a repertoire of shared resources (e.g. sharing experiences, solving problems together, sharing useful tools or learning materials). As students become more engaged in a CoP of learners, they desire to gain the skills and expertise of the individuals they respect – a powerful driver for learning. The following components must be considered when establishing an effective CoP: Meaning (experience), Practice (doing), Community (belonging) and Identity (becoming) (Wenger, 1998).

POTENTIAL IMPACT OF COLLABORATIVE LEARNING IN HIGHER EDUCATION

Collaborative learning requires individuals to work together on a task and challenge each other's assumptions and ideas to negotiate shared understanding (Mercer &

Littleton, 2007). Care must be taken not to confuse collaborative learning with co-operative learning (Dillenbourg, 1999), where a task is generally split up into sub-tasks on which individuals work independently before collating findings with the group (Johnson, 1999). Co-operative learning can be effective for developing transferable skills, such as taking responsibility for a task and meeting the social expectations of a group (Brufee, 1999), but collaborative learning is a more powerful educational tool because it requires 'effortful interactions' between students (Järvelä et al., 2007, p. 77), developing metacognitive strategies, which promote deeper understanding. However, collaborative learning requires 'scaffolding' (structures or activities that encourage interaction, guide discussions, and manage the collaborative process) to be fully effective (Bruner, 1978, p. 254).

The impact of well-scaffolded collaborative learning is well-established (Scott et al., 2014a); however, once the learner is outside of the structured classroom environment, this scaffolding disappears. The challenge, therefore, is how to effectively scaffold extra-curricular collaborative learning activities so that interactions are fruitful, and the social learning is effective. Recent developments in collaborative Web 2.0 technologies can help address this particular problem. Collaborative technologies complement physical collaborative learning interactions to make collaborative learning even more powerful (Rutherford et al., 2015; Scott et al., 2014a). There are, however, many challenges and questions to be addressed to enable us to establish effective and sustainable online collaborative learning communities. For example: what are the best online tools to use? (e.g. wikis, blogs, curation tools, social media). Should we be trying to create bespoke blended learning packages or providing students with 'e-tool kits'? Who should be invited to participate in these learning communities, and how do we get the balance right between academic and student input? How do we ensure inclusivity and maximise engagement? Our research focuses on exploring such issues and aims to identify major barriers and motivations for engaging in collaborative learning initiatives.

'SHADOW MODULES' – A FLEXIBLE PEDAGOGY FOR STUDENT ENGAGEMENT

In our experience, we have found that the didactic delivery of material to large student cohorts limits opportunities for students to take an active role in their own learning. To empower students to overcome these limitations, we developed an approach to facilitate peer interaction and collaboration, and the formation of learning communities. This approach, termed 'Shadow Modules' (Scott et al., 2014b), aims to support the development of student-led, semi-formal learning communities, which parallel taught modules, providing spaces for students to re-visit material in the taught syllabus, reinforce understanding, and develop/curate materials to support their learning. The key aspect of Shadow Modules is that they are student-focused and (more importantly) student-led, thus empowering students to be active agents in their own learning, rather than passive consumers (Ryan & Tilbury, 2013).

The shadow module process is summarised in Figure 6.1. A volunteer shadow module leader is chosen from the student cohort (or a previous cohort), to undertake organising, facilitating, and (in some cases) peer-teaching the shadow module sessions. These sessions are typically either a collaborative group working on a single issue, a peer-taught class (either didactic or active learning), or a peer-led virtual community via social media. The most effective shadow modules are a combination of all three of these approaches, using facilitated active learning, whereby the participants identify existing resources (web sites, videos, journal articles and reviews) or develop new materials (text descriptions, mind maps, flow charts, question sets) which can be shared through collaborative platforms or social media. Student-authored learning resources can be reviewed critically by academics to give feedback to the current cohort and/or incorporated into core teaching to make it more engaging for future student cohorts. However, we have found that the student body as a collective is highly effective at reviewing and critiquing the validity and accuracy of resources, without the need for academic involvement, again empowering the participants to be critical and moderate their own learning.

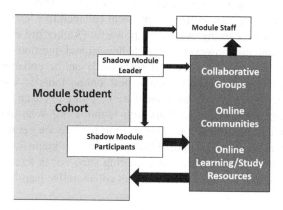

Figure 6.1. The shadow module[1]

The key factor for a shadow module, which makes it different from an *ad hoc* study group, is that Web 2.0 technologies are used to share outputs. Platforms such as Google Drive, wikis, Prezi, Facebook and the University's Virtual Learning Environment (VLE) are used to share these resources to peers. These platforms also act as a long-term resource bank, for future years, meaning that shadow modules build in depth and impact, year-on-year. The shadow module therefore benefits different groups of stakeholders (summarised in Figure 6.2): the highly-engaged shadow module participants (who gain significant benefit from the active learning underpinning the construction/curation of the resources); less-engaged participants (who gain some benefit from active learning, and have access to other people's work on the resources); and 'lurkers' (students who did not participate but who view and

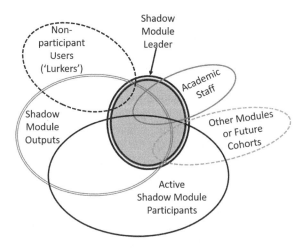

Figure 6.2. Interactions between shadow module constituencies[2]

use the resources or answers to questions in social media). In addition, there are also some students on the module who will not engage with the shadow module or its materials. Evidence shows that high levels of participation with a shadow module is associated with improved module outcomes for participants (Scott et al., 2014a). Despite this benefit, the numbers of active participants are small (typically 10–20% of the module cohort, Scott et al., 2014b). However, numbers of lurkers who actively use the resources are substantially higher, and access records show extensive use of resources by many students, especially prior to examinations.

Student-led shadow modules exemplify the potential impact of social learning (Ryan & Tilbury, 2013). Effective cultures of student-led collaborative learning can be cultivated by creating opportunities for learners to interact in physical spaces and virtual environments outside of the formal curriculum. Student-led collaborative learning sessions encourage learners to recognise the benefits of social learning by exploring and showcasing the expertise of individual members of the group, so that they can work together effectively to co-create a shared understanding. This learner empowerment is core to the shadow module's potential to provide mutual support, both to highly-engaged and peripheral members of the community. The shadow module format empowers participants to take control of their own learning, and that of their peers/near-peers, counterbalancing and thereby challenging the traditional top-down structure of most HE learning approaches (Ryan & Tilbury, 2013). Informal small group sessions make students feel more comfortable to share their ideas and give them the confidence to discuss them directly with academics which can significantly empower the student voice. This reversal of roles moves students beyond the 'student voice' merely commenting on their learning experience and instead makes them active partners in the HE experience by placing all participants in the role of 'teacher' (Ryan & Tilbury, 2013).

DEVELOPING SHADOW MODULES AS ONLINE COMMUNITIES

Experience of observing shadow modules over several years suggests that a key factor to the success of a shadow module is the development of an online community. Despite the fact that the majority of undergraduate students are active users of social media and other online platforms, they do not appear to use these tools effectively for supporting their own learning and professional development (Rutherford & Standley, 2016). Furthermore, there is no consistency as to where individuals sit on the 'visitors or residents' continuum (White, 2011) for various online collaborative technologies. Both of these factors mean that students need supporting in digital literacies required for effective online collaboration. Over the past few years we have expanded the shadow module paradigm to include online learning communities using various free online platforms: Blackboard CourseSites, Facebook, Learnium and Yammer. In keeping with the shadow module ethos of student-led learning we were keen to use online platforms that permit students to set up their own groups as 'administrators' and invite academics into the community as desired. We felt it was important that the online platforms should be easy to use, with the ability to support all multimedia formats (e.g. documents, videos), and due to our large student cohorts it was also important to select a platform onto which a large number of participants could be enrolled easily. As an online extension to the shadow module, the shadow module leader managed and moderated activity in the online community. With modules that have large student cohorts, we have found it helpful to recruit an additional 3–5 student volunteers, to act as a steering group to assist the shadow module leader in promoting continuous activity in the online community.

Similar to our previous findings with the traditional shadow modules, only a small percentage of students from the core taught module (approximately 30%) actively participated in voluntary online interactions. Limited engagement could potentially disempower learners, so this prompted us to explore potential barriers to student participation and to evaluate the suitability of the online platforms we were using to support and develop shadow modules. The intention of this research was to generate data to inform strategies for increasing student participation and tailoring online communities to meet actual (rather than perceived) wants and needs of our students.

Qualitative data from semi-structured interviews and focus groups were generated to evidence the experiences and views of different types of students: highly engaged participants, less-engaged participants, 'lurkers', and non-engaged students. Table 6.1 summarises some of our key findings, based on data (surveys, reflective logs, interviews and focus groups) collected from individuals who participated in online learning communities, to highlight the main benefits and limitations of using each platform.

Table 6.1. Evaluation of the benefits and limitations of online platforms for creating online learning communities based on our own experiences

	Blackboard CourseSites	Facebook	Learnium	Yammer
Benefits for supporting shadow modules	Designed as an educational tool	Designed for social interaction	Designed for academic interaction	Designed for academic interaction
	Separates academic work from social life	Many students already have an account and know how to use it	Separates academic work from social life	Separates academic work from social life
	Familiar to our students (= open source version of Balckboard VLE)	Simple layout	Collaborative documents (Microsoft)	Collaborative documents (Microsoft)
	High flexibility allows creation of topic folders and layout design (within reason)	Easy to use	Phone App	Phone App
		Phone App	Chat groups	Chat groups
		Visually appealing (can set cover photo for group)	Notifications	Notifications
	Has many Web 2.0 technologies (e.g. wikis, web logs, discussion boards)	Scrolling feed (live content updates)	Scrolling feed (live content updates)	Scrolling feed (live content updates)
		Students can 'add' other members	Can browse for other communities of interest	Can browse for other communities of interest
	Quick set up guide enables the use design templates to tailor the site to the needs of your community (e.g. Lab format, Social Learning)	Good for informal discussions	'Boards' to group resources	Post pictures from your phone
			Single Sign On – can login using university email and password.	Easy to upload resources to email from Yammer
		Can share videos, interests and trending topics	Can embed code into folders on VLE to log in from taught module	Easy to search for resources
			The developers are keen to work with academics and students to improve the platform, and they always act rapidly on feedback	Supported by the university and easy to access from student and staff intranet
				Intuitive to use without training

(cont.)

Table 6.1. Evaluation of the benefits and limitations of online platforms for creating online learning communities based on our own experiences (cont.)

	Blackboard CourseSites	Facebook	Learnium	Yammer
Limitations for supporting shadow modules	Students need to create an account (only enthusiastic students engage)	Risk of going unnoticed amongst other social groups	Need to pay a licence fee if you want to enrol users with different email domains (e.g. for cross institutional online interactions)	Students find daily notifications from 'all groups' annoying
	No automatic notifications	Long news thread (need to scroll to relocate resources and posts)	Mobile Phone App currently has less functionality than their website (but is improving)	Cannot edit collaborative documents from phone
	No collaborative documents	Non-inclusive (not all students want to use it, many describe it as a 'distraction' and others don't want academics in their social space)	Students did not find it intuitive (especially with the use of collaborative documents), so some training was required	
	Students found it difficult to use and struggled to easily locate content	Considered "too social" by students		
	Hard to make it visually engaging	Limited specialised functionality (restricted to 'groups' or 'pages')		
	Each discussion thread must be opened to view content, so students found it rather time consuming			

Clearly, both shadow modules and student-led online communities require getting the level of academic input right – too much and it is seen as 'extra work' by the students, but too little and students do not see the benefit over social networking. Online communities must be launched at the beginning of the academic year, and students need to be reminded they exist and encouraged to use them. However, they must not be pushed too hard by academic staff, since this also puts students off. The benefits of interacting online and developing an online professional persona must be made explicit, and a culture of promoting collaborative learning in a safe and non-judgemental environment needs to be actively nurtured. Examples of what the students can do in the online community should also be provided so they have some guidance as to how they can interact online to support their own learning and professional development. Pre-populated platforms/communities are more attractive to students than starting with a blank page. Students like to see what their near-peers used the online communities for, and, ideally, have an opportunity to interact with them. Online learning communities, in our experience, work better if you can cover broad topic areas within them, and if you can get students interacting online as soon as they start university.

POTENTIAL FOR DEVELOPING LEARNING COMMUNITIES ACROSS MODULAR AND INSTITUTIONAL BOUNDARIES

Another way we used online platforms was to develop CoPs within, and between, HEIs, following models of transformative capabilities and crossing boundaries (Ryan & Tilbury, 2013). For example, we have started to establish online communities for students studying specific scientific disciplines, which they can use to develop 'student-led societies'. This approach enables students to interact with learners in different year groups (without releasing specific contact details to them). We are also using online platforms to support the establishment of cross-institutional CoPs, to encourage 'life-wide' learning by incorporating different spaces and settings, giving our students a wider perspective of their chosen discipline and exposing them to external opportunities. These interactions are beneficial in breaking down artificial barriers between student groups created by cohort boundaries. The educational focus here goes beyond knowledge and understanding towards empowering students to develop agency and competence, and aims to encourage a transformative learning mindset, that learning is a 'life-long' mission, not just about passing the next upcoming exam. By nurturing the growth of online communities and facilitating discussion within them, we are aiming to expose students to opportunities beyond their current educational focus (e.g. undergraduates can talk to postgraduates and get advice on how to prepare accordingly for a PhD). If used well these communities can help students develop as a 'whole person' by increasing awareness of the transferable skills and competencies required for their desired profession.

REFLECTION – PERSPECTIVES AND IMPACT ON STAFF, STUDENT MODULE LEADERS AND PARTICIPANTS

The three major *active* stakeholders in the shadow module process are the participants, student shadow module leaders, and academic staff leading the module that the shadow module parallels. Our evidence suggests that these individual constituencies each have differing experiences of the shadow module, in terms of gains, expenditure, and perceptions. The following reflections are based on analyses of participant interactions in group sessions and online platforms, through focus groups of participants and non-participants, and interviews with shadow module leaders and academic staff. The key benefits of shadow module engagement for active participants, shadow module leaders, academic staff, and a fourth constituency, 'lurkers', are summarised in Figure 6.3, mapped against four of Ryan and Tilbury's (2013) six dimensions for flexible pedagogies.

Participants

Participation in shadow modules was primarily driven by students' motivation to achieve. Many participants expressed a need to attend to remedy gaps in understanding certain topics, but most were motivated to be involved for fear of missing out on vital teaching points or extra information needed to succeed. Shadow modules gave participants an outlet for problem solving amongst peers, with students declaring overwhelming support for social learning. Although many participants of these shadow modules evidenced enthusiasm for peer learning, many were in addition frustrated by the lack of academic involvement, and craved guidance and/or support through their studies, which varied from pastoral needs to problem solving issues. Conversely, however, participants also stated that, with an academic present, they would be afraid to offend or appear 'stupid' to an individual who might potentially be involved in evaluating their academic progress

Attendance levels were low in most shadow module sessions, generally due either to students being unaware of the sessions, or due to conflicting priorities. In particular, individuals highlighted that when shadow module sessions were active, coursework deadlines seemed continually to conflict with them, unfortunately leading to shadow module participation becoming a lower priority for students, as it was considered an 'optional extra'. Carefully planning the timing of shadow module content should, therefore, be implemented to maximise student engagement and impact. General motivations for, and barriers to, engaging in shadow modules are shown in Figure 6.4.

When using online platforms, student participants raised questions to their peers that extended beyond simple gaps in knowledge and understanding, using the online tools as a professional social platform for more general queries about their course. Using online platforms specifically developed for academic purposes enabled students to keep their social and professional lives separate, a barrier that is often crossed with some networking platforms. Student perceptions concerning

SHADOW MODULES AND STUDENT-LED ONLINE LEARNING COMMUNITIES

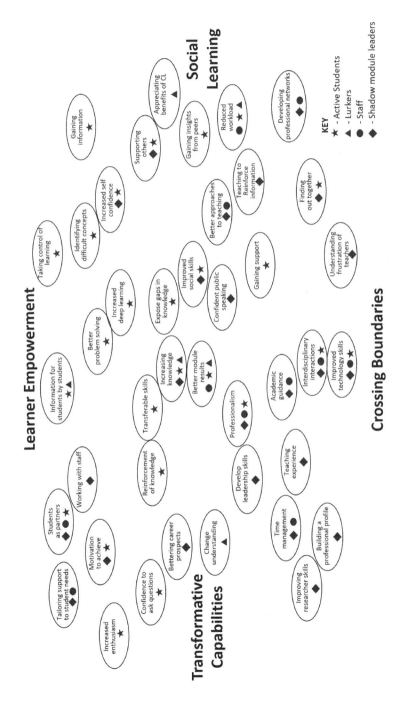

Figure 6.3. Potential benefits of shadow modules on key stakeholders[3]

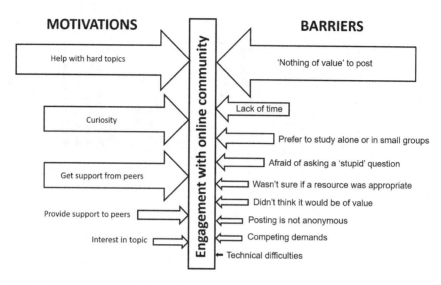

Figure 6.4. Summary of the key motivations and barriers to student engagement in online communities specifically for supporting shadow modules[4]

anonymity when asking online questions to peers were conflicting. Most individuals recognised the need to state their name in online discussions to establish an element of social professionalism and take ownership of their work. However, many students, despite recognising the need for professionalism, expressed that a major barrier to participation was the inability to maintain anonymity, primarily for the fear of asking 'stupid questions' and consequently being judged negatively by their peers.

Student Shadow Module Leaders

The key to the success of this shadow module approach is largely dependent on the student shadow module leader, who liaises closely with the academic(s) leading the taught module. As can be seen in Figure 6.2, the shadow module leader is central to all of the interactions on the module. The shadow module leader may either be a member of the module itself, a near-peer (e.g. a student from the previous year's cohort of the module), or a far-peer (e.g. a post-graduate student). Either is effective, although each has advantages and disadvantages (summarised in Table 6.2). For student shadow module leaders, demonstrating an ability to teach large cohorts of students on their CV was a major benefit, with many individuals stating that leading a shadow module provided enhanced evidence of leadership and management, as well as more adept social skills for employers.

Engaging students as shadow module leaders provided a safe environment for student participants to be open and honest about their knowledge base. Indeed, shadow module leaders typically vocalised that this would not be the case if academic

Table 6.2. Comparison of the benefits and limitations of true-, near-, and far-peer teaching

	True-Peer	Near-Peer	Far-Peer
Definition	Student from the same academic year (usually the same module)	Student from a more-senior academic year (typically a student from the previous year's cohort of the module)	A more-senior student, such as a post-graduate
Benefits to the shadow module	Experiencing the same module activity as the other participants	Typically more confident to lead the student group	Wider knowledge base and a broader overview of how the subject sits within the discipline
	Known to the participants, so may have a closer relationship	Has a wider understanding of the module, having completed it previously	Might have teaching or demonstrating experience
	Has a vested interest in the success of the Shadow Module	Can see more linkages with other subjects	Typically more confident
	Is at the same educational stage as the other participants, so can see the potential needs	Is at a later educational development stage, so may have more transferrable skills	Is at a later educational development stage, so may have more transferrable skills
	Will pitch the activities at the appropriate level	Typically more-confident at liaising with academic staff	Quite used to liaising with academic staff
	Typically is passionate about the subject. Feels empowered and transformed	Has taken the module before, so knows the areas of challenge	May have taken the module before, so knows the areas of challenge
	Is undertaking the module with the other participants, so is directly experiencing the same difficulties/confusions	May already have overcome particular areas of confusion or difficulty	Able to view module from a more-distant perspective

(*cont.*)

Table 6.2. Comparison of the benefits and limitations of true-, near-, and far-peer teaching (cont.)

	True-Peer	Near-Peer	Far-Peer
		May be more enthusiastic or have an emotional connection to the module	May be more confident than an Undergraduate student
		Typically is passionate about the subject	More confident interacting with academic staff
Limitations for the shadow	Seen as less-knowledgeable and/or less-reliable	Has no personal investment in the shadow module outcomes	Has no personal investment in the shadow module outcomes
Module	Has less of an overview than a near- or far-peer	Timetable might not be compatible	May not be as close-to the subject as a current or recent module participant
	May be less confident to lead peers and/or interact with academic staff	Unknown to the other participants	May be seen as too-distant, or a surrogate for an academic, therefore not a 'peer'
	Might deliver incorrect or misinformed information	Might deliver incorrect or misinformed information	Might deliver incorrect or misinformed information
		May be seen as a 'source of inside information' for completing coursework assignments or exams	Due to greater knowledge base, may find it difficult to judge appropriate level

staff were present. Instead, a student-led environment fuelled discussions, and permitted honesty when answering questions, whilst also maintaining a professional expectation to ensure boundaries were not overstepped.

Shadow module leaders were not experts in the subject areas for which they delivered sessions, and their own potentially limited knowledge base was a recurrent concern. However, shadow module leaders all felt that not being recognised as experts made them more approachable to participants. Indeed, rather than this being a barrier, shadow module leaders reported mutual benefits of 'finding out together' with participants. Furthermore, directing students towards peers for problem solving drove deep learning; therefore it was beneficial that shadow module leaders acted as facilitators in student discussions rather than as teachers or the source of answers.

Low levels of student participation was the main challenge vocalised by shadow module leaders. They occasionally became exasperated by dwindling numbers, but conversely felt strongly that they had a duty to deliver the best session possible for those students who did continually attend. Being confident, enthusiastic and friendly during sessions was universally felt to be essential to enhancing student learning and tackling unexpected logistical issues. Shadow module leaders typically felt that their own enthusiasm would have a direct and proportionate impact on participants being much more likely to engage and immerse themselves in learning.

Positive benefits recognised by shadow module leaders were considerable, with frequent references to feelings of excitement and euphoria after collaborative sessions. The impact on the shadow module leader's personal growth and development appears significant. Shadow module leaders also reported considerable gains in their own confidence, agency, and feelings of empowerment, as a result of their role in the educational process. The shadow module therefore provides a means of empowerment, and can be a transformative experience, for those involved, both participants and leaders.

Academic Staff

For staff whose modules were paralleled by shadow modules, there were considerable benefits from working in partnership with students. In several cases, the shadow module itself had a significant impact on the academic module, either through the production of learning resources, or the identification of areas of difficulty within the curriculum. Moreover, in those cases where there was effective two-way communication between the module and shadow module leaders, the results were often transformative. In some cases, considerable portions of the curriculum were revised to better support student learning, based on shadow module leader observations. Such revisions might be the manner in which material was presented, the chronological order of curriculum delivery, or to highlight areas that students found particularly challenging. The partnership endemic in this interaction empowers learners and encourages them to cross the boundaries between learner and teacher (Ryan & Tilbury, 2013). In particular, the participants, shadow module leaders, and staff all began to feel that they had truly developed an integrated CoP around the curriculum of the module where each member of the community, regardless of their role or status, could learn from the others.

Concerns voiced by academic staff related primarily to the extent of their expected involvement (and resultant workload impact), and the accuracy/validity of student-authored answers and resources. The degree of input from academic staff varied between individuals. However, the best outcomes were when academic staff had active engagement with the shadow module leader, but minimal involvement with the shadow module itself. The most effective input from academic staff was to remind or encourage students to participate in the shadow module, and to provide logistical support (provision of learning materials such as rooms, interactive whiteboards, pens, printing facilities, and write-access rights for the VLE). More potent was advising the shadow module leader over areas that might be addressed in shadow module sessions, or offering subject-specific guidance and information. However, it was generally found that with shadow module leaders who were proactive and highly motivated, the input required from the academic was minimal. Conversely, in those instances where the academic had more significant and visible input (e.g. attending group sessions or being prominent in online discussions), the shadow module itself typically failed and was abandoned, with students voicing that they perceived it as simply another teaching session, rather than a student-led, peer-learning activity. Therefore, experience suggests that less academic involvement resulted in more productive peer learning, even though students themselves vocalised that they desired more active involvement from academic staff.

THOUGHTS FOR THE FUTURE: ENGAGING STUDENTS AS PARTNERS AND BROADENING COMMUNITIES OF PRACTICE IN LEARNING

Shadow modules and online learning communities have provided the means by which several aspects of Ryan and Tilbury's 'new pedagogical ideas' can be fulfilled. The most clearly evidenced of these approaches is the opportunity for our students to become active agents and to be empowered to take control of their own learning (and that of their peers/near-peers) and feed back into the development of the core curriculum. These educational initiatives have purposefully challenged the power relationships that exist between academics and students, within student cohorts, and between peers and near-peers. Accordingly, it has been easier to work with students as partners/co-creators to improve the content and mode of delivery of core teaching sessions, and tailor teaching to current learning needs and preferences. Working closely with students through these initiatives has made academics more aware of the different needs and ambitions of learners.

Student-led collaborative learning sessions require learners to explore the expertise of individual members of the group, so that they can work together effectively to co-create shared understanding. As stated above, shadow modules typically attract a small percentage of the module cohort, which enables extra-curricular small group teaching to occur, and such groups have different dynamics to large cohorts taught in formal core teaching sessions. Small group sessions make students feel more comfortable to share their ideas, and empowers confidence to discuss ideas in a more informal setting, which again empowers the student voice. Feedback from shadow module leaders can have significant impact on the ongoing development of module delivery. Overall, the shadow modules exemplify the many benefits of working in partnership with our students, as active contributors to their own learning communities, rather than passive consumers of teaching.

ACKNOWLEDGEMENTS

The authors would like to acknowledge the contributions of Jon Scott, Galina Limorenko, Abby Huckridge, Victoria Jeffs, Kane Malone, Alice Birch, Harry Davies, Sumit Mistry, Drs. Andrew Doherty, Stephen Fitzjohn, Joanna Howarth, and Prof. Bernard Moxham; also the various shadow module leaders and participants over recent years. This work was facilitated by the generous support from a Physiological Society David Jordan Teaching Award (to SLA-D), Higher Education Academy Teaching Development Grant GEN1030 (to SMR), and HEA Wales Learning & Teaching Innovation Grant (to SMR).

NOTES

[1] Engagement with shadow module activities is voluntary but actively encouraged, and so shadow module participants are members of the module's student cohort. The shadow module leader(s) organises and often produces outputs that encourage learning activities for shadow module participants, and forms a link between the module's student body and academic staff. The participants in turn also produce online outputs or discussions, which can be used by/impact on their peers, and also on the academic staff in developing module content.

[2] The shadow module leader (double black line, grey shading) forms a nexus point between shadow module participants (black line), the online discussions and outputs of the shadow module (double grey line), non-participant users ('lurkers'; dotted black line), students on other modules or future cohorts (dotted grey line), and module academic staff (grey line).

[3] The potential positive impacts of engaging with shadow module activities are highlighted, mapped against four of the six dimensions highlighted by Ryan and Tilbury (2013). Several benefits are shared by several different constituents, and these are represented by: star (active participants), diamond (shadow module leaders), triangle ('lurkers') and circle (academic staff). Impacts are identified from interviews and focus groups with stakeholders, and from monitoring online activities and comments.

[4] Size of each arrow is a direct representation of the proportion of students expressing that opinion in surveys.

REFERENCES

Biggs, J., & Tang, C. (2011). *Teaching for quality learning at university* (4th ed.). Open University Press.

Brufee, K. A. (1999). *Collaborative learning: Higher education, interdependence and the authority of knowledge* (2nd ed.). Johns Hopkins University Press.

Bruner, J. (1978). The role of dialogue in language acquisition. In A. Sinclair, R. Jarvella, & W. Levelt (Eds.), *The child's conception of language* (pp. 241–268). Springer.

Daily, J. A., & Landis, B. J. (2014). The journey to becoming an adult learner: From dependent to self-directed learning. *Journal of the American College of Cardiology, 64*, 2066–2068.

Dillenbourg, P. (1999). What do you mean by 'collaborative learning'? In P. Dillenbourg (Ed.), *Collaborative learning: Cognitive and computational approaches* (pp. 1–19). Elsevier.

Järvelä, S., Näykki, P., Laru, J., & Luokkanen, T. (2007). Structuring and regulating collaborative learning in higher education with wireless networks and mobile tools. *Educational Technology and Society, 10*, 71–79.

Johnson, D. W. (1999). *Learning together and alone: Cooperative, competitive, and individualistic learning* (5th ed.). Allyn and Bacon.

Lave, J., & Wenger, E. (1991). *Situated learning: Legitimate peripheral participation.* Cambridge University Press.

Littleton, K., & Mercer, N. (2013). *Interthinking: Putting talk to work.* Routledge.

Mercer, N. (1996). *Words and Minds: How we use language to think together.* Routledge.

Mercer, N., & Littleton, K. (2007). *Dialogue and the development of children's thinking: A sociocultural approach.* Routledge.

Prince, M. (2004). Does active learning work? A review of the research. *Journal of Engineering Education, 93*, 223–231.

QAA. (2014). *UK quality code for higher education part A: Setting and maintaining academic standards.* Retrieved from http://www.qaa.ac.uk/en/Publications/Documents/qualifications-frameworks.pdf

Rutherford, S. M., Mistry, S., & Scott, J. L. (2015). Assessing the potential of Web 2.0 technologies for supporting collaborative learning in higher education, in formal and informal learning environments. In R. Gillies (Ed.), *Collaborative learning: Developments in research and practice* (pp. 265–294). Nova Science Publishers.

Rutherford, S. M., & Standley, H. J. (2016). Social space or pedagogic powerhouse: Do digital natives appreciate the potential of Web 2.0 technologies for learning? In M. M. Pinheiro & D. Simões (Eds.), *Handbook of research on engaging digital natives in higher education settings* (pp. 72–97). IGI Global.

Ryan, A., & Tilbury, D. (2013). *Flexible pedagogies: New pedagogical ideas.* HEA.

Scott, J. L., Mistry, S. L., Moxham, B. J., & Rutherford, S. M. (2014a). Using Web 2.0 technology to support and enhance collaborative activity outside of the taught curriculum in higher education. In S. Rutherford (Ed.), *Collaborative learning: Theory, strategies and educational benefits* (pp. 149–174). Nova Science Publishers.

Scott, J. L., Moxham, B. J., & Rutherford, S. M. (2014b). Building an open academic environment – New approaches to empowering students in their learning of anatomy. *Journal of Anatomy, 224*, 286–289.

Vygotsky, L. S. (1978). *Mind in society: The development of higher psychological processes.* Harvard University Press.

Webber, E. (2016). *Building successful communities of practice: Discover how connecting people makes better organisations.* Tacit.

Wenger, E. (1998). *Communities of practice: Learning, meaning and identity.* Cambridge University Press.

White, D. S., & Le Cornu, A. (2011). *Visitors and residents: A new typology for online engagement.* Retrieved from http://firstmonday.org/ojs/index.php/fm/article/view/3171/3049

SUE BOND-TAYLOR AND CERYL TELERI DAVIES

7. YOUTH JUSTICE LIVE!

Flexible Pedagogies in an Online/Offline Community of Practice

INTRODUCTION

This chapter explores the experiences of staff and students within Lincoln University's *Youth Justice Live!* project, an educational development project testing new, collaborative approaches to curriculum design and delivery involving staff, students and local youth justice professionals. The aim of the *Youth Justice Live!* project was to create a sustainable level 2 undergraduate Youth Justice module, developed collaboratively by staff and students from levels 1 to 3, and also to foster a lasting relationship with the Youth Offending Service (YOS) in Lincolnshire. Here we reflect upon the pedagogic potential in establishing a community of practice (CoP) supported by digital technologies, in order to challenge traditional HE power hierarchies and prioritise relational approaches to learning grounded in a slow scholarship. It argues that such a CoP offers a unique setting in which flexible pedagogies can be fostered and explores the role of digital technologies in facilitating and sustaining such a CoP.

In considering the role of flexible pedagogies within the future of HE, Ryan and Tilbury (2013) highlight the ways in which flexibility might support new modes of thinking, debate and action, and thus help us to rethink the purpose and nature of the university. They advocate an understanding of flexible pedagogies which goes beyond the ubiquitous debates around flexibility in the *delivery* of HE programmes. The increasing integration of technology which facilitates 'flipped classroom' techniques, distance learning and the rise of the MOOC clearly promotes greater flexibility and broader choices for learners in the 'pace, place and mode' of their learning (Gordon, 2014, p. 3), but emphasis on student choice and satisfaction in relation to programme delivery does not necessarily promote flexibility in the learner. Indeed, it may do just the opposite as students demand that university courses adjust to their expectations and cater for their schedules.

Ryan and Tilbury therefore advocate a focus on pedagogical ideas and approaches which promote flexibility as an *attribute* in both learners and educators. They understand flexibility as 'the ability of people to think, act, live and work differently in complex, uncertain and changeable scenarios' (Ryan & Tilbury, 2013, p. 4) and thus for HE to produce graduates capable of anticipating, preparing for, and responding to change in society. Without flexible pedagogies, they argue, HE merely promotes skills for engaging with existing social practices, the world as it is now, but does not equip graduates with the skills to improve social practices or to adjust to dynamic global working environments. The notion of flexible pedagogies is therefore developed as a means to reposition HEIs as 'beacons for social change' (Ryan & Tilbury, 2013, p. 31).

The development of this new module in Youth Justice, in partnership with Lincolnshire YOS, was intended to prompt students to consider the possibilities of future careers in youth justice, and to highlight for them the realities of what such work might entail. Given the perpetual shifts in government policies and the practice context of delivering youth justice services, the greatest continuity in this service is the prevalence of flux, fostered by an expectation that services respond flexibly to shifts in political, policy and funding priorities. Flexibility and adaptation are therefore key to career development in this sector.

Within this chapter the *Youth Justice Live!* project provides a case study for illustrating and evaluating the possibilities for promoting flexibility within interactions between educators, learners and the wider community, facilitated by digital technologies. Two different but interrelated contexts for these pedagogical developments will be explored. Firstly, there is the educational development project in itself, in which a team consisting of one Senior Lecturer, one PhD student, nine undergraduate students (from all years) and youth justice professionals engaged in a collaborative curriculum design initiative. Students and staff visited youth justice settings, interviewed youth offending staff, created digital learning resources and blogged and tweeted about the process. This provides an illustration of how university departments can broaden the opportunities for developing flexible pedagogies outside the required curriculum and activities of the programme of study by involving students in the wider work of the University.

Secondly, there is the resulting Youth Justice module itself, designed to generate new educational experiences for undergraduate students, in which we can thus explore the emergence of flexible pedagogies within the context of this module. The collaborative design project has resulted in further collaboration in the delivery of the module, with YOS staff supporting or providing teaching sessions, but also attending lectures and visiting guest speaker events as a means to enhance their own learning. Students on the module therefore not only engage with youth offending staff in the classroom, but they are encouraged to participate in this wider *Youth Justice Live!* community, through volunteering, research, organising guest speaker sessions, and engagement with social media. The partnership approach to curriculum planning also continues in the inclusion of students in the annual review process. Students act as 'module custodians' to ensure that the module is attended to and that relationships with YOS are maintained across the eight months of the year when the module does not run. What has emerged therefore is a continuum of practice within the *Youth Justice Live!* CoP, from the collaborative design of module, the delivery of the teaching sessions, social media interactions, and the engagement of the current students in planning for future cohorts.

The focus of this chapter will therefore address the key questions of whether a CoP, supported by digital technologies, can be an effective vehicle for the delivery of flexible pedagogies. The findings discussed here identify two key points: firstly, the benefits of adopting a CoP approach when designing curriculum content and delivery mechanisms which promote flexibility as an attribute; and secondly, the uses and limitations of digital technologies in sustaining a 'live' CoP for this purpose.

YOUTH JUSTICE LIVE! AS A COMMUNITY OF PRACTICE

The importance of Communities of Practice (CoP) has been highlighted within social and situated learning (Lave & Wenger, 1991). This concept equates to a community that shares practice (Hoadley, 2012) revolving around knowledge situation and reflective practice (Ng & Pemberton, 2013). As explained by Wenger, McDermott, and Snyder (2002):

> Communities of Practice are groups of people who share a concern, a set of problems, or a passion about a topic, and who deepen their knowledge and expertise in this area by interacting on an ongoing basis. (p. 4)

There has been a growing interest in the use of CoPs within a HE setting (Lea, 2005), as a community of staff to ensure teaching quality (Jakovljevic et al., 2013), for knowledge transfer with community organisations (Hart et al., 2012), and as a means to deliver learning experiences grounded in shared meaning making (Lea, 2005). Therefore, a CoP is a useful tool for situating community learning within social and professional practices to (re)produce learning materials in a 'live' manner.

As such, the CoP was the chosen mechanism for establishing a collaborative space inclusive of teaching staff, students, YOS Managers and practitioners to develop a 'live' youth justice undergraduate module, with the aim of fostering learning strategies which promoted flexibility. This was a heterogeneous CoP with members from across organisational boundaries and resources both financial and 'in kind' from both organisations, as the goals of both institutions intersect with the aims and objectives of this CoP. As a team, the staff and students had a range of youth justice experiences, but it was clear that the expertise did not lie with the Senior Lecturer CoP leader, since a career in academia does not provide the hands-on experience of the practices of youth justice. By contrast the PhD student had had a previous career in youth justice management and a number of the undergraduate students had worked directly with young people in mentoring and support roles within multi-agency youth justice contexts. The role of the CoP leader (the Senior Lecturer in this case) was therefore to identify the key issues, establish links across the institutional boundaries, shape a clear communication strategy and avoid hierarchy. However, this role went further by fostering a culture of 'knowing' and enthusiasm by bringing both expertise and passion into the group. Initially, the agenda for the work streams of the CoP was established by the CoP lead, but this evolved as the CoP developed its identity based on a model of mutual power between members. To enhance the development and communication of the CoP, social media and technology played a critical role (e.g. blogs, Blackboard learning site, and Google docs), which worked to support the community and the practice. Furthermore, the use of technology and social media sites enhanced the affordance of multimedia formats to disseminate information within the CoP and publicise knowledge to future community members.

Therefore, a key function of this CoP was to jointly develop learning resources and collectively problem solve issues pertinent to developing and launching a new undergraduate academic module, and thus to co-produce knowledge within the identity of the CoP. Therefore, rather than an instructivist approach to knowledge creation, all members were identified as 'knowing' and possessing their own agency, further perpetuating the power of this CoP. Not only did this encourage a 'two-way' process for sharing knowledge, skills and information, it also reinforced the development of a supportive and secure community environment in which 'the greatest threats to creativity (fear of criticism, ridicule and retrenchment) have been removed' (Jakovljevic, 2013, p. 1111). Students were given the power to function as 'Change Agents' (Kay, Dunne & Hutchinson, 2010), to enable new discussions on how they wish to learn and take ownership of their learning experiences to shift the pedagogic landscape. This shift acknowledged undergraduate students as capable researchers and key members of the CoP.

A key motivation for this CoP was to 'slow down' the process of designing a new teaching model to foster collaborative working, shape ideas and produce innovative teaching materials to bring youth justice 'alive'. This 'slowing down' signified an appeal for reflective scholarship in the context of the neo-liberal university, to encourage rich (re-)engagement with this topic in a manner that eliminated unequal power relations. Therefore, this appeal for 'slowness' extended beyond timeframes to address socially constructed institutional power structures (Mountz et al., 2015). This ethos blends further with the 'ethics of care' (Bozalek et al., 2014; Keeling, 2014) as it informs our understanding of students as 'active agents'. The notion of 'care' promotes the concept of *interdependence* with positive relationships modelled on the idea of care framed in an empowering manner. For this group, slow scholarship and ethics of care were about equal collaboration focusing on a mutual mentoring ethos. That is, the CoP benefitted from the creation of a space to discuss ideas and learn from each other, to take care of each other and to change the focus of the conversation when creating teaching materials to ask, '*what matters?*'.

FLEXIBLE PEDAGOGIES

Ryan and Tilbury (2013) identify six 'new pedagogical ideas' for a flexible HE sector: learner empowerment, future-facing education, decolonising education, transformative capabilities, crossing boundaries and social learning. They position the first of these, learner empowerment, as pivotal to the other five, reflecting the centrality of the radical reordering of power and responsibility within the HE experience. For students to acquire the necessary attributes of flexibility, they must be given the opportunities for participation, self-reflection, decision-making, action, application and response. Critical pedagogies which challenge the authority of the educator as 'expert' and develop more collaborative approaches to the co-creation of education are therefore advocated as promoting flexibility within both learner and educator.

Learner empowerment has been central to the ethos of education at the University of Lincoln, through the 'Student as Producer' agenda established there (Neary & Winn, 2009) and the more recent 'Pedagogies of Partnership' project (Crawford et al., 2015). Students are involved in constructing their own learning, within a wider focus on 'critical engagement, challenging assumptions and collaborative discovery' (University of Lincoln, 2012). There is considerable scope therefore for a project such as this to generate flexible pedagogies, through an emphasis on teaching and learning in which 'students create and develop new knowledge in collaboration with their lecturers' (University of Lincoln, 2012). The activity of renegotiating the traditional relationship between 'expert' and 'student' and developing systems of co-creation and collaboration has been key to the *Youth Justice Live!* project. The CoP included a wider range of voices within the community, by working in partnership with the local YOS offline, and promoting the *Youth Justice Live!* community online. Establishing a CoP in which students play a role, and encouraging their contributions to the ongoing development of the module and maintenance of the community in social media, can empower students to become active learners and to help shape the learning experiences of others.

Future-facing education is described as that which enables people to think critically and creatively about alternative visions of the future and to initiate action in pursuit of those visions (Ryan & Tilbury, 2013). In youth justice, the ability to anticipate change, identify alternatives, and to actively work towards achieving these within a political climate and a legislative context are key sector management skills. The youth justice practitioner as 'street level bureaucrat' (Lipsky, 1977) has had considerable influence in mitigating potentially authoritarian policies and generating more progressive alternatives, for example, in diverting young people from custody. The offline aspects of the *Youth Justice Live!* CoP thus exposes undergraduate students to the professional contexts of youth justice practice in Lincolnshire whilst the online community promotes engagement with interdisciplinary, global youth justice debates, for example, around child psychology and the age of criminal responsibility, comparative analysis of youth justice in different parts of the UK and beyond, and the role of social policy in youth crime prevention work. Such global and comparative perspectives therefore also reflect ideas about decolonising education through 'deconstructing dominant pedagogical frames which promote singular worldviews to extend the inter-cultural understanding and experiences of students' (Ryan & Tilbury, 2013, p. 20). Building a CoP which engages students actively with their learning within a wider online community of experience offers a unique opportunity to do this, and to challenge their preconceptions and assumptions about what 'youth' and 'justice' might look like in diverse contexts.

Transformative capabilities are described by Ryan and Tilbury (2013) as 'the capacity to learn, innovate and bring about appropriate change, connecting with ideas of 'competence', such as an appreciation of the contexts in which skills are used, as well as the values and choices around their use in real situations' (p. 22). As part of the CoP developed within the *Youth Justice Live!* project, students are encouraged to reflect on their own experiences, their impact upon youth justice and youth crime prevention practices, and their capacity to make use of their new-found knowledge and skills. Building links with local YOS professionals in the offline CoP has opened opportunities to recruit students for voluntary positions, to engage them in participatory activities (e.g. local consultation on young people's experiences of policing), and to undertake research for the YOS. In addition, engaging with youth organisations within social media opens a wider set of participative opportunities to students, from signing e-petitions on youth issues, to reflecting upon their party political allegiances, and even to finding summer placements and internships.

Crossing boundaries is also promoted when exposing students to the real-world contexts of youth justice within the *Youth Justice Live!* CoP. 'Boundary work', in which individuals spend time thinking and acting at the boundaries between their own knowledge and identities and those of others, is an essential feature of CoPs, as this is where learning is most likely to occur (Hart et al., 2012). For example, criminological theories are frequently presented to students as polarised and opposing options, comparing Classicist ideas about criminal responsibility (the young person has capacity for rational decision-making and thus is held responsible for his/her choices) and Positivist notions of determinism (the young person is subject to a range of internal and external factors which impact his/her actions and therefore they should be provided with support or treatment as appropriate). Understanding the real life application of theoretical principles thus inevitably requires the merging and overlapping of a number of different perspectives (the young person is neither wholly rational nor determined and each individual has a different biography and needs), and therefore students are encouraged to reflect upon the boundaries of 'youth justice' through interaction with the CoP both on and offline. Crossing boundaries between different disciplinary understanding, political positions or professional identities enables a fully contextualised understanding of the youth justice sector. Therefore, the aim of adopting a flexible curriculum design, developed jointly with key youth justice professionals, was to strive to prepare students for the reality of working within this form of dynamic, multi-faceted role.

Finally, the notion of social learning seeks to expand the contexts of HE to produce informal learning opportunities through social interaction 'in addition to (or in tandem with) the interactions triggered within the formal curriculum' (Ryan & Tilbury, 2013, p. 26). This notion is central to the *Youth Justice Live!* project in a number of ways, through both offline and online interactions with others. Offline, at a local level, students had opportunities to network and engage with YOS staff outside of the formal curriculum through, for example, an afternoon of workshop sessions provided by YOS partner organisations. In addition to this, social media played an important role in the CoP. Established by the project team as a way of showcasing their activities and signposting people to the project website, the *Youth Justice Live!* Twitter account soon became a space for social interaction with organisations, academics and professionals with an interest in youth justice and youth crime prevention work. For students, interactions with this community play a vital role in their learning as they immerse themselves in a world outside the classroom, and blur the boundaries between 'study' and 'leisure' activities. Whilst Lave and Wenger (1991) may have distinguished between formal and informal learning situations, it has been recognised that the HE context blurs the line between these two and that a CoP can facilitate such learning (Lea, 2005).

REFLECTIONS ON THE PROJECT

Within the Collaborative Curriculum Design Project

Within the ethos of developing the collective identity of the CoP, the members of the curriculum development team were eager to contribute to a new learning environment for future students and thus were aware of the transformative capabilities which they possessed. Yet the CoP had to offer everyone something in addition to purely altruistic motives in order to avoid one of the pitfalls of a CoP approach, in that '[i]f it is not clear how members benefit directly from participation, the community will not thrive, because the members will not invest themselves in it' (Wenger, McDermott, & Snyder, 2002, p. 17). The process of setting goals or milestones and developing knowledge assets was key to the process of establishing the CoP, with collective reflection upon what information to collect, how to collect it, for whom and for what purpose, representing a decolonisation of knowledge production.

Through the production of key project outputs, both tangible and intangible, staff and student CoP members developed professional confidence through the performance of new skills, for example, interviewing key YOS professionals to create video resources, collating and curating online materials to the Blackboard VLE site, generating a digital reading list, building a social network profile via Twitter (with staff and students tweeting from the account), and using Wordpress for blogging about the project (with staff and students receiving training alongside each other). As the repository of module information and learning tools developed, so therefore did the knowledge and transferrable skills of the CoP as a whole. Yet students may have the most to gain from such an approach as they benefit from learner empowerment opportunities and can demonstrate their autonomy through crossing boundaries and taking on roles usually reserved for staff members, for example, presenting the project at both internal and external conference events on partnership in teaching and learning, and accompanying staff to a secure children's unit for the purpose of module development and fostering new links with key youth justice staff. Even the process of selecting the project name encouraged everyone in the team to feel part of a community of equals, since *Youth Justice Live!* was indeed a creative student suggestion. Working within the team thus facilitated a future-facing orientation in that it gave students an opportunity to gain experience that can be used after university, as part of a safe and mentoring environment, alongside the opportunity to build professional relationships with the YOS. Student feedback commented on the informal team meetings and positive and open relationships created between students and staff, which may be argued to amount to a social learning experience. Both staff and students furthermore shared a responsibility to ensure that a rapport was built between the University and YOS, to enable future collaboration and sustainability of the project.

The limitations of such an approach can be seen when exploring perceptions of the type and level of participation achieved within the project, which varied within the team. When asked to reflect upon the levels of learner participation achieved within the CoP, students characterised this as either 'partnership' or 'delegated power' (Rudd et al., 2006). The former indicates a more limited conception of learner empowerment, with less power and responsibility attributed to learners. However, whether the power imbalances between scholars/practitioners and students can be fully eliminated is questionable. Despite the encouragement of a mutual community space, undoubtedly the existence of professional roles and responsibilities maintains that particular members have a greater degree of power and responsibility, whilst others remain on the periphery. Nonetheless, students in the project team were given the opportunity to undertake roles focused on research, creating resources, and taking the lead on blogging and social media interactions. Therefore, specific aspects were delegated to the learners to encourage them to actively shape their learning experiences and outcomes, and those of other students. Students remained satisfied with the level of participation whether it was described as partnership or delegated power, indicating the importance within a CoP of flexibility with respect to the level of responsibility, contribution and participation which individual CoP members feel comfortable with.

Within the Resulting Module

The launch of the module in January 2016 provided new opportunities to promote flexible pedagogies supported by the wider CoP and facilitated by digital technologies. Flexibility was built into the module delivery in a number of ways. Firstly, the timetable of events required flexibility to enable us to include guest speakers from the YOS to support the sessions, and to accommodate their preferences for method of contribution (a formal lecture or a more hands on workshop for example). We also left one week free for a student directed session, and worked with our community of contacts to facilitate the guest speaker of their choice. Secondly, the content of each session was flexible in that it responded to the latest news and developments in youth justice discussed within our community on Twitter. Twitter was central to keeping abreast of the news in this way and directing students to sources of information. Thirdly, a fairly broad assessment task was set (to produce a briefing paper) but students were then asked to help us decide what a briefing paper should look like. Students searched online for other briefing papers, shared them in Facebook and discussed the features that we should include in the briefing papers for this assessment. Students therefore contributed to the marking criteria during the course of the module rather than receiving them from the outset.

The reflections of students at the end of the module were largely favourable, and students particularly valued the opportunities to hear from practitioners. Students benefitted from gaining knowledge on the range of specialised work opportunities available within the youth justice system as a whole. The overall student attainment was positive with an average module assessment mark of 53% and a maximum mark of 75%. The students themselves rated the impact of the module learning on their knowledge of offending behaviour and their understanding of the youth justice system (25% good/very good rating at start of the module to 93%), practice (30% good/very good rating at start of the module to 93%), multi-agency practice (40% good/very good rating at start of the module to 85%), and theory (10% good/very good rating at start of the module to 85%). Those most engaged students also continued to contribute to the CoP after completing the module; for example, one student supported the police in setting up a young person's advisory panel, by analysing survey data and undertaking focus groups with young people engaged with the YOS. She was then able to share her new 'expertise' with the next cohort of *Youth Justice Live!* students.

However, three areas of student satisfaction were lower, and consideration of these responses has enabled us to reflect upon the challenges of promoting flexibility in the curriculum. Firstly, feedback on the assessment indicated student preference for greater clarity and less flexibility in the assessment instructions or marking criteria, with 30% of students responding that the support for assessment was poor or very poor. One key suggestion was to incorporate further revision/assessment preparation as part of the teaching sessions. Whilst they may be open to flexibility in classroom activities, students demand a more rigid approach to assessment, with any ambiguities interpreted conclusively by staff from the outset. Secondly, some students were less satisfied with the organisation of the module (20% of students responded that this was poor), and this suggests that flexible rather than static teaching arrangements may be interpreted by some students as less effective organisation. Thirdly, feedback on the quality of teaching was difficult to interpret, since the students had clearly appreciated the professional contributions to the module, and indeed their perceptions of their own learning gain were positive, yet 20% responded that teaching on the module was poor. For the teaching team, this posed the question of what counts as 'teaching'? Does this include only formal delivery of material by the lecturer? Does it include external speakers? Does it include material delivered in a digital environment, and are alternative, active and independent learning strategies perceived as 'teaching'? Significantly, this illustrates the need for further consideration of whether flexible pedagogies pose problems for staff faced with traditional module evaluation and student satisfaction surveys, which focus on 'teaching' over 'learning' and may indeed be institutionally 'risky' in the current climate increasingly dominated by the Teaching Excellence Framework.

CONCLUSIONS

The design of the *Youth Justice Live!* project was fostered by the theoretical and ethical beliefs of the staff leading the project whose experience in undertaking research with young people has prompted a commitment to break down structures of power and inequality (Bond-Taylor, 2012; Davies, 2019), encourage co-production and to develop an ethic of care through a relational approach to knowledge production. This is achieved through the creation of a CoP in which collaborative approaches to curriculum design offer students unique opportunities to develop as active and equal participants within a community of learning and action, with clear benefits in preparing them for future employment in the field:

> In the 'community of practice' approach, the learning process is not seen as delivery or production, but as induction. It is the journey learners take on their way to becoming active participants and practitioners in a particular trade, profession, discipline or discourse. The emphasis is on building relationships – not only between teachers and students, but between students and other students, at the same and differing levels of study. (Streeting & Wise, 2009, p. 3)

The construction of a CoP therefore can be seen to provide a strong framework for developing the flexible pedagogies advocated by Ryan and Tilbury (2013) as essential to the future of HE, and the use of digital technologies was key to facilitating this, and to expanding the CoP, connecting both online and offline interactions. Learner empowerment is evident in the student involvement in developing the module, and their active engagement within the online/offline community, both in 'real' spaces for interaction and within social media contexts. Social learning is therefore embedded in the use of alternative learning spaces, including social networking, digital learning resources and visits to youth justice settings. These help to blur the boundaries around the edges of course content and encourage students to develop an interest in youth justice outside the classroom, reflecting upon their own transformative capabilities. Delivering the module in partnership with youth justice professionals enables students and educators to cross boundaries between theoretical debates and real-life practice within the contexts of multi-agency service provision. The real time 'live' nature of the module also facilitates future facing and decolonising education as we identify uncertainty and respond to it through participation in public debates, campaigns and consultations, drawing upon global discourses around 'youth' and 'justice' in order to challenge dominant political narratives.

For the future, the intention is to build sustained value as part of the CoP work to foster this type of learning model, and to ensure the sustainability of this CoP beyond the initial creation of the youth justice module. The vision is to establish a group of student peer mentors as part of the module team to foster a culture of creating student and practitioner-led learning materials, updating and developing the learning materials and keeping the module fresh and 'live'. This will necessitate a review and evolution of the functions of this CoP to establish a 'long lived' CoP and keep 'alive' our collective learning, ensuring the sustainable development of flexible pedagogies within *Youth Justice Live!*

ACKNOWLEDGEMENTS

We would like to thank all of the undergraduate students from the Youth Justice Live! project for their contributions to this research. In particular, we would like to acknowledge Kirsty Groom, Abi Ogle, Katie Walker and Candice McKane for their contributions to earlier versions of this chapter presented at the RAISE Conference 2015 and 2016.

REFERENCES

Bond-Taylor, S. (2012). Lessons in listening: Where youth participation meets student as producer. *Enhancing Learning in the Social Sciences, 4*(3), 1–14. http://journals.heacademy.ac.uk/doi/abs/10.11120/elss.2012.04030004

Bozalek, V. G., McMillan, W., Marshall, D. E., November, M., Daniels, A., & Sylvester, T. (2014). Analysing the professional development of teaching and learning from a political ethics of care perspective. *Teaching in Higher Education, 19*(5), 447–458.

Crawford, K., Horsley, R., Hagyard, A., & Derricott, D. (2015). *Pedagogies of partnership: What works.* HEA.

Davies, C. T. (2019) This is Abuse? Young women's perspective of what's 'OK' and 'Not OK' in their intimate relationships. *Journal of Family Violence, 34*, 479–491.

Gordon, N. (2014). *Flexible pedagogies: Technology-enhanced learning.* HEA.

Hart, A., Davies, C., Aumann, K., Wenger, E., Aranda, K., Heaver, B., & Wolff, D. (2013). Mobilising knowledge in community–university partnerships: What does a community of practice approach contribute? *Contemporary Social Science, 8*(3), 278–291.

Hoadley, C. (2012). What is a community of practice and how can we support it? In D. H. Jonassen & S. M. Land (Eds.) *Theoretical foundations of learning environments* (2nd ed., pp. 287–300). Routledge.

Jakovljevic, M., Buckley, S., & Bushney, M. (2013, June 19–21). *Forming communities of practice in higher education: A theoretical perspective.* Paper presented at Management, Knowledge and Learning International Conference, Zadar, Croatia. Retrieved from http://www.toknowpress.net/ISBN/978-961-6914-02-4/papers/ML13-368.pdf

Kay, J., Dunne, E., & Hutchinson, J. (2010). *Rethinking the values of higher education – Students as change agents?* Retrieved from https://dera.ioe.ac.uk/1193/

Keeling, R. P. (2014). An ethic of care in higher education: Well-being and learning. *Journal of College and Character, 15*(3), 141–148.

Lave, J., & Wenger, E. (1991). *Situated learning: Legitimate peripheral participation.* Cambridge University Press.

Lea, M. (2005). 'Communities of practice' in higher education: Useful heuristic or educational model? In D. Barton and K. Tusting (Eds.), *Beyond communities of practice: Language power and social context* (pp. 180–197). Cambridge University Press.

Lipsky, M. (1980). *Street-level bureaucracy: Dilemmas of the individual in public services.* Russell Sage Foundation.

Mountz, A., Bonds. A., Mansfield, B., Joyd, J., Hyndman, J., Walton-Roberts, M., Basu, R., Whitson, R., Hawkins, R., Hamilton, T., & Curran, W. (2015). For Slow Scholarship: A feminist politics of resistance through collective action in the neoliberal university. *ACME: An International E-Journal for Critical Geographies.* Retrieved from http://www.academia.edu/12192676/For_Slow_Scholarship_A_Feminist_Politics_of_Resistance_through_Collective_Action_in_the_Neoliberal_University

Neary, M., & Winn, J. (2009). The student as producer: Reinventing the student experience in higher education. In L. Bell, H. Stevenson, & M. Neary (Eds.), *The future of higher education: Policy, pedagogy and the student experience* (pp. 126–138). Continuum.

Ng, L., & Pemberton, J. (2013). Research-based communities of practice in UK higher education. *Studies in Higher Education, 38*(10), 1522–1539.

Rudd, T., Colligan, F., & Naik, R. (2006). *Learner voice: A handbook from Futurelab.* Retrieved from http://archive.futurelab.org.uk/resources/documents/handbooks/learner_voice.pdf

Ryan, A., & Tilbury, D. (2013). *Flexible pedagogies: New pedagogical ideas.* HEA.

Streeting, W., & Wise, G. (2009). *Rethinking the values of higher education – Consumption, partnership, community?* QAA.

University of Lincoln. (2012). *Student engagement strategy 2012–2016.* Retrieved from http://www.lincoln.ac.uk/home/media/universityoflincoln/globalmedia/documents/SES.pdf

Wenger, E., McDermott, R. A., & Snyder, W. (2002). *Cultivating communities of practice: A guide to managing knowledge.* Harvard Business School Press.

SHARON SMITH AND RUTH HEWSTON

8. OPENING THE DOOR TO THE VIRTUAL SCHOOL

Enhancing Student Engagement through Online Learning Communities

INTRODUCTION

The intention of this chapter is to explore a pedagogical approach for teaching and learning using a Virtual Learning Environment (VLE), enabling students to become more involved in the learning process by co-constructing their own learning journey. In the case study presented here, the emphasis on tutor-led activities is challenged by empowering students to take greater control over their learning. In adopting a flexible approach to learning through the use of a VLE, and building on the work of McLinden, McCall, Hinton, and Weston (2006), the use of problem-based learning (PBL) with a group of foundation degree students has been explored. A flexible approach refers to a variety of opportunities to learn in differing settings, at a variable pace, and through different modes of delivery. The intended learning outcomes were clearly defined; however, students were able to demonstrate their knowledge and understanding against them in a number of different forms, thereby demonstrating flexibility of outcome as well. The concept of PBL requires teaching strategies to focus on the learning through student-focused activities in which learners are required to solve particular problems (Callan, Reed, & Smith, 2012). The approach of McLinden et al. (2006) to PBL is based on Burch's (2001) conception of it as 'a teaching 'strategy' that shifts the classroom focus from teaching to learning,' noting that the

> central premise of PBL holds that most students will better learn information and skills if they need them; need arises as students try to solve specific, open ended problems. (p. 194)

This has enabled a flexible pedagogical approach and empowered the learners to take responsibility for their own learning by embedding a 'Heutagogy' (Hase & Kenyon, 2000) approach which allows the students to be more reflective. This results in more effective interaction in the learning process. A case study of the process of developing and adapting the VLE is presented within this chapter, highlighting the barriers of an online approach for both staff and students. Many staff and students may consider themselves to be 'digital natives' (Prensky, 2001) and the case study highlights how perceived barriers to employing such an approach have been addressed and how the notion of online communities has been developed. *Opening the Door to The Virtual*

School embarks on a journey of technological exploration for both the students and virtual staff.

Historical Perspectives on HE in FE

The Dearing Report (1997) identified that links between higher education (HE) and other parts of the education and training system, particularly further education (FE), are of great importance. In response to agendas opening up opportunities for disadvantaged and under-represented populations in HE, the increased demand for HE places, and the shifting policy and funding context of higher education institutions (HEI) and further education institutions (FEI) settings, increased numbers of HE students have chosen to study for their qualifications within college-based settings. In 1997 there were an estimated 200,000 HE students studying in FE settings. King, Saraswat and Widdowson (2013) also argued that some 10% of all undergraduate HE is delivered within FE college settings. Likewise, Parry's (2012) data suggests that of the 2.2 million HE students in England, 177,000 (one in twelve) are taught within a college setting. Consequently, a large number of students experience their HE studies in partnership with FE colleges.

This repositioning of HE presents a range of challenges for FE settings, staff and students. Gray, Swain, and Rodway-Dyer (2014) argued that the culture and environment within colleges are often seen as being very personalised and responsive to the needs of the local community. However, they also balance this agenda with the need to adhere to academic standards and provide equivalent learning opportunities to those experienced within an HEI. The then UK Department for Business, Innovation and Skills further articulated this position:

> Colleges have displayed particular strengths in reaching out to non-traditional higher education learners including mature and part-time students. They also have a distinctive mission particularly in delivering locally-relevant, vocational higher-level skills such as HNCs, HNDs, Foundation Degrees and Apprenticeships. (DBIS, 2011, p. 46)

Meeting these challenges and managing quality provision raises questions about the practices in place to embed quality learning experiences for students and to facilitate transition between FE and HE contexts, particularly for foundation degree (FdA) graduates who may progress their studies at Level 6 (top-up). Students progressing their studies at top-up (Level 6) have usually completed a foundation degree or two years (Levels 4–5) of a three-year bachelor's degree. This may be within a university environment, within an FE college, or in an alternative setting. It also raises the question of whether good practice in FE, particularly that which focuses on personalisation and responsiveness to diverse learners could, and should, be further embedded within HEIs.

Working in Partnership – HE in FE

Foundation degree qualifications were introduced by the Department for Education and Skills (DfES) in the UK in 2000 in response to national initiatives addressing widening participation and lifelong learning agendas. At this time, the University of Worcester developed the FdA Learning Support (FDLS) to provide a work-based learning and academic programme in supporting learning. The national initiatives encouraged participation of learners who may have previously not considered or entered HE (DfEE, 2000; QAA, 2010). The QAA Characteristic Statement for Foundation Degrees (2015) highlights foundation degree awards integrating academic study alongside work-based learning. They extend opportunities for vocational education within the HE sector and

> equip learners with the skills and knowledge relevant to employment, so satisfying the needs of employees and employers. (QAA, 2010, p. 2)

The course is taught within the University and in partnership with a number of regional FEIs.

In line with the QAA Characteristic Statement for Foundation Degrees (2015) the FDLS provides a stand-alone qualification, but also provides opportunities for further lifelong study on a number of programmes at the University and at alternative institutions, predominantly HEIs. The FDLS is a work-based learning programme and baseline HE qualification for students wishing to enhance their existing practice, skills and knowledge in supporting learning. The overall aims of the programme are to provide students with the necessary skills to support learners in a wide range of educational environments. The programme is also designed to support the development of students' transferable skills that will enable them to enter into professional dialogue with colleagues and confidently tackle issues in their working environment.

Scott (2010) highlighted that the delivery of HE within FE raises a number of issues, tensions and challenges. Davies (2007) also identified a range of tensions, asserting that despite the provision of HE learning within FE being excellent, FEIs often lack a higher education culture, specifically their different teaching demands, the higher teaching hours that are typical in FEIs, and the lack of support for research and scholarly activity within the FE sector. Scott (2010) also argues that from a pedagogical perspective differences in teaching between FE and HE may be difficult to conceptualise. Differences in provision of NQF Levels 4 and 5 may be perceived as small and colleges may benefit from the opportunities for staff to engage in a broader range of teaching. However, students, particularly at Level 5, need to be given opportunities to extend their skills, knowledge and experience (Scott, 2010). Harwood and Harwood (2004) also highlighted that FE staff may be keen to promote more self-directed and independent learning for HE students, but this aspiration is stymied by the constraints of the FE system.

FurtherHigher,[1] a two-year project looking at HE provision in dual-sector institutions providing both further and higher education study, found that once in HE, students reported that they predominantly experienced pedagogic practices seen more as 'traditional' alongside practical skills development and work placements. Particularly in relation to transition between sectors, evidence suggested that having entered HEIs there were differences in learning compared to their previous experience. The student voice in particular indicated that study within HE required a greater degree of independence and self-direction (Bathmaker, 2016). In response to this, this project identified areas of practice which would support the development of independent study skills, prepare students for transition between FdA and BA qualifications, and support the sharing of practice between teaching staff within FEI and HEI settings.

UTILISING A VLE TO FACILITATE PBL

Problem-Based Learning and the 'Virtual School'

In response to students' evaluations and reflection on previous module delivery for the FDLS, the course team recognised that the teaching and assessment pattern for the course needed addressing. The team suggested adopting a structure for the module that would allow for a new approach utilising a VLE to facilitate PBL in order to motivate learners and encourage the development of a deeper understanding of professional practice. Its rationale was to contribute to professional development by encouraging student engagement in an analysis of their own professional practice, that of others, and the inter-relationships between them. Having explored the work of McLinden et al. (2006) and reflecting on the importance of flexible learning as well as the notion of developing problem-based scenarios, evaluation of the teaching strategies employed within the course highlighted some need to provide a more flexible, online approach, which embedded opportunities for students to co-construct their learning at a place, pace and context that meets their needs.

Ryan and Tilbury (2013) recognise that empowering the student challenges the authority of the tutor and makes room for an 'enhanced contribution from the learner'. In doing so, the critical discourse is advanced and tutors are enabled in 'taking cues from the diversity of learner cohorts and profiles in the new HE landscape' (p. 15).

One method of engaging the learners effectively can be identified in the concept of PBL, which requires teaching strategies to focus on the learning through student-focused activities, in which students are required to solve particular problems (Callen, Reed, & Smith, 2010). Not only does this challenge the students' perceptions of learning, but it enables a more adaptive approach to teaching and designing learning strategies, embedding a 'Heutagogy' (Hase & Kenyon, 2000) approach which allows the students to become more reflective. Many students find the shift from tutor-led lectures to more student-led learning difficult to adapt to as they are required to engage with an interpersonal dialogue. In some cases students do not make the link between 'real life' situations and the scenarios they encounter during PBL This is particularly evident in the way students engage with the virtual head teacher and Special Educational Needs Coordinator (SENCo) as part of the problem-based scenario.

Problem-based learning has proven to be an effective teaching strategy which develops students' autonomy through a problem-based scenario (Callen, Reed & Smith, 2010). An online tool was created which enabled the students to engage with a 'virtual school' website and interact with the school's staff through online discussions facilitated by emails to the school. Online 'virtual staff' then responded to the questions. Module tutors enabled this aspect of the module and in doing so created other scenarios to allow the students to reflect on practice. Scenarios would include information given to the student that would create a problem, such as the addition of another pupil's requirements and learning needs.

This 'virtual school' shifted the emphasis of learning from tutor to student, empowering students to make sense of their own learning (Campbell & Norton, 2007). Students were required to use their existing knowledge and skills, respond to challenges and issues, interact with fellow students and virtual staff, and problem-solve real world issues that arise. This pedagogical approach creates learner empowerment which actively involves learners in their own development as 'co-creators' of their own learning. The implementation of the 'virtual school' challenges existing learner relationships, student-student and tutor-student, and the power frames that underpin them (Ryan & Tilbury, 2013). This approach also facilitates Ryan and Tilbury's (2013) concept of transformative capabilities, where learning moves beyond the emphasis on knowledge acquisition and understanding, towards competence and agency. This transformative philosophy is often at the centre of foundation degree programmes and awards.

It was recognised that through exploring the potential of e-learning we can focus on the use of VLEs as a tool to enhance learning rather than a resource repository for modules. In the early development of the module delivery, the content was linear and based on PowerPoint presentations, but its continued development has produced a more interactive learning environment with resources available to promote students' thinking. The use of web-based tools and VLEs did initially challenge some tutors and learners, but ultimately their use promoted a more independent and flexible approach to learning for both students and staff. A case study approach was adopted to explore the efficacy of e-learning and the use of the VLE to further develop the student learning experience. Through reflective research, using course evaluations and empirical evidence, the impact of the VLE on student's engagement and the development of their own autonomy in their learning was examined. The course team were mindful that the interface between students and tutors can become marginalised and a clear pedagogical reasoning should be employed for e-learning to be effective. The project aimed to implement a pedagogical approach that might support the development of students' reflective, self-directed and independent learning. The expectation was that through PBL and the VLE, students could engage in the co-creation of their learning. As a consequence of the research, the 'virtual school' was further developed into an active resource, which, in turn, fostered a sense of ownership for the students.

Working in Partnership

In reviewing the impact of student engagement in using technology-enhanced learning (TEL), Davies, Mullan, and Feldman (2017) highlight a survey of over 7,000 HE students which concludes that TEL impacts positively on student learning. In addition, it confirmed that students value a flexible learning approach that allows them to have continuous access to course notes, online tools and virtual learning environments. In recognising this, Davies, Mullan and Feldman state that there is a requirement by institutions to ensure that the IT skills are in place to support learning and staff capabilities. This key element of developing staff capabilities was highlighted early on in the process of creating the 'virtual school' and in developing a new approach to the delivery of the module that included the creation of an interactive environment. It became evident early on in the module's development that the technical limitations of staff knowledge needed to be addressed. It was therefore important to establish effective partnerships with the IT services to develop the VLE. Ryan and Tilbury (2013) consider this in recognising that new technology can be 'exciting and daunting, adding new dimensions to thinking about core educational purposes in HE' (p. 7).

In exploring new pedagogical approaches in HE, tutors are required to approach teaching and learning with an open mind and to recognise their own limitations. The shifting educational landscape, Ryan and Tilbury (2013) note, considers that not only is the tutor required to embrace these new approaches, but that other stakeholders, as well as financial constraints must be considered. Indeed, they concede that in creating social learning, there is a wider aspect of educational cultures to be considered. It is not only the pedagogical approach that needs to be embraced, but also the IT infrastructure on which it might sit. They highlight that

> [a]lthough the flexible learning arena has not always taken up this radical pedagogical potential this is where IT can act as a significant positive enabler for innovation. (Ryan & Tilbury, 2013, p. 26)

The drive in developing positive collaborative working relationships with colleagues in IT has resulted in module delivery becoming more intuitive in recent years and certainly we have seen a more dynamic approach in designing module content. The development of the 'virtual school' required a cross-institutional partnership approach as the FDLS was delivered across a number of FEIs. The partners were able to make use of content prepared for them which allowed for a consistent approach in delivering the module. However, cross-institutional requirements created some barriers in deciding which VLEs should be used. Developing partnerships that enabled institutional policy and the consistency of students' experiences to be maintained required some negotiation. Ryan and Tilbury (2013) acknowledge that flexible pedagogies require institutional-level commitment, including joined-up and systematic approaches to enhancement. Moore (2012) also suggested that, without this, tension in flexibility and organisational structures may occur. The development of the 'virtual school' required flexibility on the part of the FEIs involved. However, as Barber, Donnelly and Rizvi (2013) argued, the HEIs also needed to adopt change to support organisational models and cultural practices, including sharing of pedagogical practices across the partnership and strategies that worked for both corporate and educational intentions throughout it (Ryan & Tilbury, 2013). Reflecting on our institutional policy, teaching and learning requires a prescribed format for the use of the VLE; however, this can affect flexible pedagogical approaches. Processes of quality assurance and parity of student experience can influence creative and flexible delivery to fulfil institutional requirements. Firkpatrick (2011) suggests '[t]he wisdom of the crowds is not always peer reviewed or quality assured' (p. 20).

In order for flexible pedagogical approaches to be utilised, an approach to learning needs to be maintained that allows for the voice of each student in the cohort to be heard. Across partner delivery, the 'virtual school' remains the same; however, the student dialogue and discourse varies due to the diversity of individual students across the partnership. Although there are benchmark entry requirements to the degree in relation to qualifications and professional experience, across the partnership there are variations in the students' learning journeys. This flexible approach enables students' voices to be heard in the context of their learning and the co-construction of their understanding. Moore (2006) suggested that digital technologies have increased flexibilities. However, Moore also argued that substantial changes in attitudes, policies and operations need to be addressed. Inflexible institutional structures and policies result in squeezes and constraints on pedagogical flexibilities; these may include differing VLE platforms used across the partnership and varied partner expectations on VLE learning. This required adaptations and partnership working to ensure parity of student experience in line with institutional expectations; for example, in face-to-face student teaching and online facilitation. However, Barnett (2014) argues that flexibility is not an absolute good and too much flexibility may lead to a lack of internal integrity and a fragmented student experience, potentially leading to lower standards and quality measures. This argument leads to a consideration of systems flexibility, which has been defined as

> not an end in itself but more properly becomes a means to assist in helping students to take on personal forms of flexibility so that they may be better equipped to face and, indeed, contribute to a fluid and unstable world. (Barnett, 2014, p. 27)

In the context of the 'virtual school', the flexibility of the PBL model allows students to engage with its content at a personal level, in order for them to resolve the scenarios they face. In Davies, Mullan, and Feldman's (2017) review of rebooting learning for the digital age, we can look at the work from University of Greenwich, which uses the notion of virtual environments to engage students. In doing so, it considers the way in which there is more effective engagement within the learning process, thereby enabling a more flexible pedagogical approach for staff and students. The assumption that e-learning is an add-on needs addressing and a recommendation from Davies, Mullan, and Feldman (2017) is to suggest that HEIs have technology built into the curriculum design.

Elements of the cross-partner development of the 'virtual school' also encouraged aspects of social learning for the tutors involved with the module development. Ryan and Tilbury (2013) argued that an important feature of social learning was the organisational concern about improving the learning experience of students. Social learning can be seen through an

> [i]nstitutional lens in which teaching and learning practices are under review, prompting new pedagogical student experiences that are profoundly student-centred. (Ryan & Tilbury, 2013, p. 26)

This social learning enables practice and expertise to be shared and developed throughout the partnership. Garrison (2009) argued that technologies used in distance learning have tended to focus on access and economies of scale, focusing more on two-way communication. However, emphasis has now shifted to focus more on collaborative and constructivist approaches to engage students in the learning process. This supports the development of communities of practice and enquiry. Social learning goes beyond setting up learning tools (i.e. online discussion boards), but to be effective it needs to focus on setting up communities for critical discourse and engagement.

Teaching Strategy

This module requires active participation by the student in the learning process by using a VLE and engaging in a PBL Scenario. The use of the VLE provides an interactive platform for the module content. McLinden et al. (2006) argue Burch's (2001) notion of PBL as a teaching 'strategy' that shifts the classroom focus from 'teaching to learning' (p. 194). The module's teaching strategies moved away from traditional methods, highlighted by Knowles (1990) as 'Andragogy' (p. 7), which he defines as a linear, self-directed learning process. An alternative approach to developing more independent learners is that of 'Heutagogy', which Hase and Kenyon (2000) describe as a more active approach which 'takes account of intuition and concepts such as 'double loop learning', and acknowledges the process of reflection' (p. 20).

This approach identifies the need for flexible learning and student-led negotiated learning, recognising that it does not require the tutor just to deliver content but also to think more about the process of learning.

The 'virtual school' requires active engagement in PBL through both group and written tasks. The group task enables the learners to co-construct knowledge based on theory and work experiences. Within the scenario provided by the 'virtual school', the students engage by creating a presentation which will be used to assist the 'school' in facilitating the transition of a new pupil into the setting. The students have access to two virtual people, the head teacher and SENCo. The roles are played by the tutor(s). The students can email the virtual staff to ascertain some of the needs of the new pupil. However, during this process a number of problems are introduced. Owen and Norton (2006, as cited in Campbell & Norton, 2007) consider that this 'active learning' encourages students to engage with the process and make better sense of learning, rather than simply accumulate knowledge. Indeed, the students assimilate knowledge of relevance to the problem scenario rather than just acquiring factual information about an additional need. The acquisition of purely factual knowledge may often result in a medical model of a pupil's requirements, rather than allowing learners to unpack the social perspective on the pupil's needs and approach to inclusion, a central premise to the aim and learning outcomes for the module.

The approach of McLinden et al. (2006) is based on Burch's (2001, p. 194) notion of PBL as an approach to teaching that shifts the focus from the process of teaching to the experience of learning, which, in turn, concurs with Brown and Duguid's (2002), which states that learning occurs in response to need. It was noted by one student in their final assessment for the 'virtual school' that the process of PBL was quite a difficult concept to comprehend because it required more of an autonomous approach which was not as reliant on the tutors. Mezriow et al. (2000) argue that reflective discourse produces an analytical approach for the learner requiring them to question their beliefs and values. These reflective and co-constructive elements of PBL enable learners to challenge, consider, refine and extend their existing knowledge and skillset. Some students are able to make links between their workplace experience and the scenarios they face in the module. This shared experience provides students with opportunities to construct new knowledge and understanding of practice. Meyer and Land (2005) define this learning as 'threshold concept' and highlight this as 'a new way of understanding emerges, a transformed view of subject matter or landscape, or even a new world view' (p. 373).

This generates experiences that allow for transformative learning to be embedded within the programme. Mezirow et al. (2000) also highlight that the learner requires the tutor to be supportive to 'facilitate the student's willingness to move forward with transformative learning' (p. 23). This factor emphasises the challenge for students and tutors who may see a VLE as repositories for resources rather than active 'learning environments' which require student engagement in a learning process rather than just a tool for 'picking up notes' (Bell & Rothery, 2006). In their studies, students agreed to an accepted level of professionalism in their approach and aimed at completing the tasks without expressing any intentional bias. They became concerned with the language they used in their feedback and as a result relied on positive interaction to guide their comments. This co-construction of learning with fellow students enabled peer feedback to be utilised as a means of active engagement in the PBL process rather than feedback for the purpose of evaluation and assessment.

Assessment Strategy

Brown and Knight (1994) suggest assessment is at the heart of learning and module design. Campbell and Norton (2007) highlight the need to align learning and assessment, ensuring that the learning outcomes are addressed effectively within the assessment task and that the assessment is relevant to the learning process. The students are required to produce a group presentation, which is peer assessed, as well as a reflective account of the learning journey completed whilst experiencing the 'virtual school'. Many of the students find writing a reflective journal difficult. This was highlighted within the work of Callan et al. (2012) as that of an expectation of the practitioner to become more reflective and to explore values and concepts rather than just accepting them at face value. This process is identified by Cowan (1998, as cited in Littlejohn & Pegler, 2007) as one of reflecting 'on action and in action'. The students are required to engage in keeping a reflective diary to record the process they encounter throughout the module. It requires 'snapshots' of their experiences as they are doing it and reflection on how they feel about the process they encounter through PBL. This enables students through the module to become deeper thinkers and tutors firmly believe their role in this learning is to engage the students in 'discourse thinking' (Husband, 2013).

As part of the PBL approach students are required to peer assess each other's presentation. This is done as a group and students use the VLE to upload feedback to the other groups on the module. Students are guided through a taught session on how they feed back to learners at school and how they manage the feedback they receive for summative assessments. Through the activity of peer assessment, the students recognise that the process is not exclusively about developing the presentation; it also highlights the importance of engaging in thought and deeper-level learning. In using such an approach to assessment, the emphasis is shifted from tutor to learner and in many cases more meaningful feedback is provided. The process of peer assessment was challenging for the students and many of them became more aware of the use of the language in their feedback. It was noted by one student that they found peer assessment was a useful tool, as it gave a new perspective to their work, aiding their development as an autonomous learner. This development of peer assessment engaged a more proactive approach to the task and stimulated the students to not only look beyond the finished product but to consider the processes they were engaging with.

Curtis and Pettigrew (2009) argue that assessment should be about placing the learners at the centre of the assessment process, and in so doing, the development of a richer and more meaningful student learning experience can be fostered. PBL allows a shift in the power balance between tutor and student, with the student being able to co-create their learning experience. The implications for this in relation to assessment are important to note. Ryan and Tilbury (2013) argue that co-created models of learning challenge the perceived authority of the tutor. In exploring student perceptions during module development, several students found this shift in dynamic challenging. A student commented that they did not initially feel that the tutor was supporting them since they were thought not to be providing the answers to issues raised. However, as the module progressed, the student realised that the PBL scenarios were as unpredictable as 'real life'. Students' perceptions shifted to recognise that knowing the answer may be less important that the reflection and analysis used in the process of finding the answer. Student evaluations of the module also showed that students valued the opportunities to engage in PBL, particularly in group-orientated activities and tasks. One student commented that in participating in the 'virtual school' they had learnt to worry less about others completing tasks and to trust and support them, a transformation in his/her learning.

CONCLUSION

In conclusion, making effective use of a VLE provides a more flexible approach to learning, and in using PBL as a tool to enhance student engagement, a 'discourse' in students' thinking is created which requires support and an approach that provides scaffolded learning. PBL is essentially part of the FDLS students' everyday work commitments. However, the students expect their learning to be more structured and prescribed; this could be as a result of the pedagogical approaches they have experienced themselves in school. The use of the VLE and PBL within the 'virtual school' has been identified by the team as 'life outside conventional modules', with students co-creating curricula, developing skills and attitudes that can be implemented across their learning experience. Essential to the academic development of the students is a need to engage them in a more transformational approach to their learning. Consequently, HE teaching practices are required to evolve in the face of changing educational landscapes in order to meet student expectations. Furthermore, the changing nature of HE provision, supported through partnership working with FEIs, ensures a diverse student body has access to study in HE. However, this requires teaching and learning strategies that are flexible and personalised in nature. This chapter proposes that adopting models of PBL and utilising the VLE deepens student engagement with learning through the development of an online learning community in the form of a 'virtual school'.

NOTE

[1] The FurtherHigher Project, https://www.sheffield.ac.uk/furtherhigher/index

REFERENCES

Barber, M., Donnelly, K., & Rizvi, S. (2013). *An avalanche is coming: Higher education and the revolution ahead.* Institute for Public Policy Research.

Barnett, R. (2014). *Conditions of flexibility.* HEA.

Bathmaker, A. (2016). Higher education in further education: The challenges of providing a distinctive contribution that contributes to widening participation. *Research in Post-Compulsory Education, 21*(1–2), 20–32.

Bell, V., & Rothery, A. (2006). *E-sharing: Developing use of e-repositories and e-learning for learning and teaching.* Retrieved from http://eprints.worc.ac.uk/48/

Brown, J., & Duguid, P. (2002). *The social life of information.* Harvard Business School Press.

Brown, S., & Knight, P. (1994). *Assessing learners in higher education.* Kogan Page.

Burch. (2001). Cited in McLinden, M., McCall, S., Hinton, D., & Weston, A. (2006). *Embedding on-line problem-based learning resources in a professional programme for specialist teachers of children with visual impairment.* Retrieved from http://www.education2.bham.ac.uk/documents/research/VICTAR/PBL_phase_2_project_report.pdf

Callan, S., Reed, M., & Smith, S. (2012). A pedagogy for educating 'new professionals': An English perspective. In T. Papatheodorou (Ed.), *Debates on early childhood policies and practices: global snapshots of pedagogical thinking and encounters* (pp. 95–104). Routledge.

Campbell, C., & Norton, L. (Eds.). (2007). *Learning, teaching and assessing in higher education: Developing reflective practice.* Learning Matters.

Curtis, W., & Pettigrew, A. (2009). *Learning in contemporary culture.* Learning Matters.

Davies, P. (2007). HE in FE: The struggle for excellence. *Academy Exchange, 7,* 48–49.

Davies, S., Mullan, J., & Feldman, P. (2017). *Rebooting learning for the digital age: What next for technology-enhanced higher education?* HEPI.

Dearing, R. (1997). *National committee of inquiry into higher education.* HMSO.

Department for Business, Innovation and Skills (DBIS). (2011). *Students at the heart of the system.* DBIS.

Department for Education and Employment (DfEE). (2000). *Foundation degrees.* Department for Education and Employment.

Garrison, D. R. (2009). Implications of online learning for the conceptual development and practice of distance education. *Journal of Distance Education, 23*(2), 93–104.

Gray, C., Swain, J., & Rodway-Dyer, S. (2014). Student voice and engagement: Engaging through partnership. *Tertiary Education and Management, 20*(1), 57–71.

Harwood, J., & Harwood, D. (2010). Higher education in further education: Delivering higher education in further education – A study of five South West colleges. *Journal of Further and Higher Education, 28*(2), 153–164.

Hase, S., & Kenyon, C. (2000). *From andragogy to heutagogy.* ultiBASE.

Husband, C. (2013, October 10). *The importance of outstanding teaching in schools.* University of Worcester.

King, M., Saraswat, A., & Widdowson, J. (2013). *Higher viewpoints: Studying higher education in a further education college. An analysis of student experience.* Retrieved from https://www.aoc.co.uk/sites/default/files/An%20analysis%20of%20college%20HE%20students%20experiences.pdf

Kirkpatrick, D. (2011). Flexibility in the twenty-first century: The challenge of web 2.0. In E. Burge, C. Gibson, & T. Gibson (Eds.), *Flexible pedagogy, flexible practice: Notes from the trenches of distance education* (pp. 19–28). AU Press.

Knowles, M. (1990). *The adult learner: A neglected species* (4th ed.). Gulf Publication.

Littlejohn, A., & Pegler, C. (2007). *Preparing for blended e-learning.* Routledge.

McLinden, M., McCall, S., Hinton, D., & Weston, A. (2006). *Embedding on-line problem-based learning resources in a professional programme for specialist teachers of children with visual impairment.* Retrieved from http://www.education2.bham.ac.uk/documents/research/VICTAR/PBL_phase_2_project_report.pdf

Meyer, J. H. F., & Land, R. (2005). Threshold concepts and troublesome knowledge (2): Epistemological considerations and a conceptual framework for teaching and learning. *Higher Education, 49,* 373–88.

Mezirow, J., & Associates. (2000). *Learning as transformation: Critical perspectives on a theory in progress.* Jossey-Bass.

Moore, M. (2006) Foreword. In B. H. Khan (Ed.), *Flexible learning in an open and distributed environment* (pp. viii–x). IGI Global.

Moore, M. (Ed.). (2012). *The handbook of distance education* (3rd ed.). Routledge.

Parry, G. (2012). Higher education in further education colleges: A primer. *Perspectives, 16*(4), 118–121.

Prensky, M. (2001). Digital natives, digital immigrants. *On the Horizon, 9*(5), 1–6.

The Quality Assurance Agency for Higher Education (QAA). (2010). *Foundation degree qualification benchmark.* Retrieved from http://www.qaa.ac.uk/en/Publications/Documents/Foundation-Degree-qualification-benchmark-May-2010.pdf

The Quality Assurance Agency for Higher Education (QAA). (2015). *Characteristics statement: Foundation degree.* Retrieved from http://www.qaa.ac.uk/en/Publications/Documents/Foundation-Degree-Characteristics-15.pdf

Ryan, A., & Tilbury, D. (2013). *Flexible pedagogies: New pedagogical ideas.* HEA.

Scott, G. (2010). Delivering higher education within further education in England: Issues, tensions and opportunities. *Management in Education, 24*(3), 98–101.

GRAHAM BARTON AND ALEX LUMLEY

9. ACADEMIC SUPPORT ONLINE

Developing an Integrated Academic Support Environment at the University of the Arts London

INTRODUCTION

University of the Arts London (UAL) students are internationally and socially diverse, and aim to succeed in a competitive and volatile global landscape. Anticipating implied needs and expectations, Academic Support responds to a fundamental enhancement aim: to support all students' realisation of their potential through flexible and accessible interactions. The high participatory demands of workshop/studio-based learning, plus pressures of earning whilst studying, affect many students' capacity to engage in academic, preparatory or reflective work, creating a need for 24/7 access to supportive resources.

In recognition of the complex challenges of flexible learning and professional contexts, leadership and investment in Academic Support is committed at UAL at an institutional level. Through interdepartmental collaboration, this has enabled the development of a new online environment: *Academic Support Online* (ASO), launched in September 2015. Being positioned in the transdisciplinary space represented by the University's Library and Academic Support Services, ASO is part of a cross-university offer that complements the curriculum-specific work of the constituent Colleges' Academic Support teams. ASO is designed to facilitate transdisciplinarity, collaborative enquiry into learning, and the development of dialogic space. It offers an integrated approach to the concept and provision of support through co-curricula activities across in-person and online domains.

This chapter reflects on ASO in progress – our initial thinking, influences and intentions, early realisations of experience and responses – and explores synergies and connections with the flexible pedagogies thinking of Ryan and Tilbury (2013), particularly with learner empowerment, social learning, crossing boundaries and transformative capabilities.

UAL comprises six colleges with independent histories and varied creative and cultural disciplinary characters. The Colleges are Camberwell College of Arts, Central Saint Martins, Chelsea College of Arts, London College of Communication, London College of Fashion, and Wimbledon College of Arts, with a total student population of approximately 19,000 (2015–2016). Under the umbrella of 'the Arts' reside a diversity of subjects informing a wide range of pedagogic practices and student support priorities, from FE to PhD levels. Core subjects in art, design, fashion, media, communication and performing arts naturally extend to arts-related business, management, humanities and science subjects.

The UAL Academic Support offer works principally both through the colleges and across them, in liaison with language and library provision. Whilst sharing core values, an overarching strategy and joined up governance, an Academic Support team in each college tunes in to local needs, working closely with courses. Academic support is also offered university-wide both face-to-face and through *Academic Support Online* (ASO) – the focus of this discussion – and draws out the many synergies and commonalities in terms of ways of thinking, knowing and practising across colleges and courses, whilst resisting any suggestion of a one-size-fits-all approach.

ASO is a practical example of a learning environment which represents and interprets flexibility in many interlinked ways: it is a response to the need for flexibility, its content is flexible, it is made flexibly, and its form will always need to be flexible. In this chapter we explore this expanded field of flexibility that we inhabit, and the intersection of our practical work with pedagogic theories that resonate for us, highlighting some of Ryan and Tilbury's (2013) ideas in the HEA work stream on flexibility.

The chapter is structured in three sections, beginning with an explanation of ASO – its features, design philosophy, user experience and responses. We then explore the interlinked ways in which the lenses of social learning, crossing boundaries and transformative capabilities (Ryan & Tilbury, 2013) help articulate the complex, contextual rationale for ASO and its ongoing development. In conclusion, we reflect on three questions generated by the flexible pedagogies literature in relation to our experience of developing ASO, with the aim of contributing to the thinking around flexibility, both conceptually and practically for others. The chapter explores how we think different dimensions of flexibility have positioned and shaped ASO to date, as well as continuing to re-inform it, and suggests further debates.

ACADEMIC SUPPORT ONLINE EXPLAINED

Academic Support Online (ASO) is

- a University-wide extra-curricular learning environment;
- a knowledge base and portal to bespoke and curated resources;
- searchable, and a prompt to further discovery and enquiry;
- an integrated booking system for face-to-face academic support;
- a transdisciplinary space for sharing viewpoints and understandings;
- visually-orientated and mindful of multiple learning preferences;
- flexible in that it allows students to choose means and places of learning;
- informative through its FAQs and links to wider student support;

- designed to be responsive across devices, allowing access across a range of environments.

ASO is integral to a larger institutional strategic initiative: the re-development and expansion of an embedded and explicit, enhancement-based Academic Support offer accessible to all students across UAL. University level endorsement generates a supportive context for ASO, as it has developed from consultation stage through to launch and current ongoing enhancement, in anticipation of positive impacts on student retention, continuation, attainment and satisfaction. Through the objectives of key strategies for Library and Academic Support Services, Research, and Teaching and Learning strategies, ASO responds to institutional aims for transformative education, communication and collaboration, and an inspirational environment. As an initiative within the re-developed Academic Support offer, ASO was very positively reviewed by the University's executive (May 2016), with one Pro-Vice Chancellor helpfully taking to social media: 'UAL students: do you know how [...] brilliant Academic Support Online is?'

From the start, ASO was created as a community for engagement with both the conceptual debates and practical skills surrounding academic support themes at UAL. ASO is distinguished from other online provision within the University – such as the VLE Moodle which is dependent on course structures – as it is designed to provide university-wide access for co-curricular academic support activities. ASO complements *Commonplace,* which is focused on student orientation and student life, and both sites link to each other, and in turn link to Moodle.

Initial scoping indicated that ASO should be developed in phases, drawing on learning from the development of VLEs and online knowledge portals already in use, and from consultations with students and staff (discussed below). The aim was to integrate three domains to promote flexibility of place, pace and mode: a resource repository, a knowledge base, and a booking system. These are cross-referenced and tagged in a way that creates a 'rhizomatic typology' and enable a flexible user experience, while also offering a traditional experience for those who prefer a categorised, menu-based approach to browsing. Figures 9.1 to 9.8 are captioned to describe the way ASO integrates these domains.

ASO's design philosophy is articulated through its architecture. The integration of face-to-face and online resources and knowledge bases is a fundamental design principle: when a student seeks help, s/he will find relevant resources alongside related workshops, tutorials and drop-in advice (Figure 9.4), promoting variation in mode of access. This blended provision reflects our core values of consistency and parity, relevance and timeliness, accessibility and inclusivity, and clarity and visibility. It is an enabling and adaptable pedagogic space, designed from the ground up for meta-level engagement with known, cross-curricula topics of interest – interdisciplinary threshold concepts (Land & Meyer, 2006), practices and understandings. Figure 9.7 shows examples of these: critical thinking, contextual

Figure 9.1. Key features of Academic Support Online; *resources sit under nine topic areas*

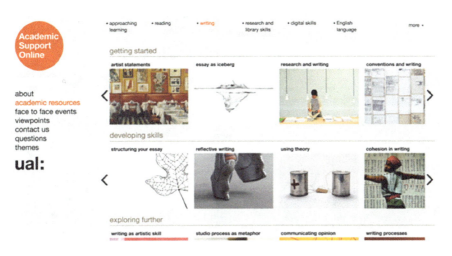

Figure 9.2. Each menu-based topic area ('writing' has been selected in this example) has a range of resources organised under 'getting started', 'developing skills' or 'exploring further'

Figure 9.3. Each individual resource has an introductory page, which is tagged, and shows links to related workshops, tutorials or other events; a click on the image opens the resource

analysis, problem-solving. ASO is not designed for summative assessment or curriculum-specific materials, where course-based sites within the University's VLE (Moodle) are more appropriate, but it is one click away via a high level ASO button on the VLE.

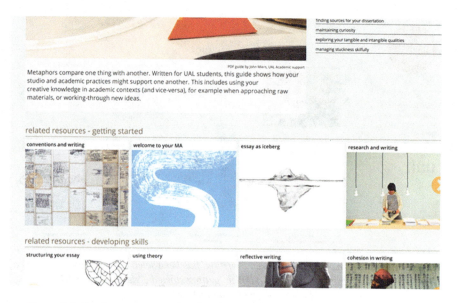

Figure 9.4. Further resources related to the one selected appear under each resource descriptor, extending the visibility of the offer

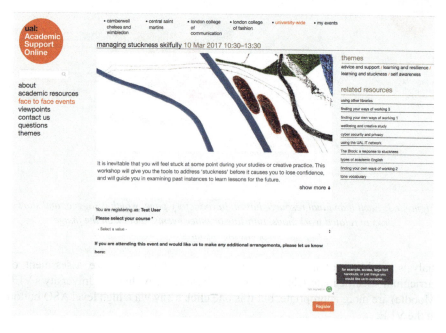

Figure 9.5. Workshop description, with additional screenshot illustrating the one-click registration functionality, and integration of face-to-face and online offer

ACADEMIC SUPPORT ONLINE

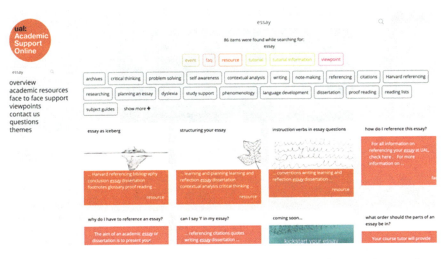

Figure 9.6. Enhanced search functionality and integrated tagging. This example page shows search returns for the term 'essay' – illustrating the ability to search and then browse via ASO content type (event, FAQ, resource, tutorial, viewpoint) and theme

Figure 9.7. Relational tagging, termed 'themes' – users can navigate the site through themed hyperlinks

Alongside the flexibility in searching and tagged browsing, we are also implementing different ways to embed social media. Twitter and Instagram accounts are used to promote any content in the site, from individual resources to events. However, the creation of the 'Viewpoints' resource section (see Figure 9.8 for an example) is a form of an embedded, bespoke media channel that is hosted on the site away from the advertising distractions of external hosting and demonstrates the curated and tailored nature of the site content. 'Viewpoints' aims to offer students a plurality of perspectives (discussed below), promoting variation in mode of delivery and access.

129

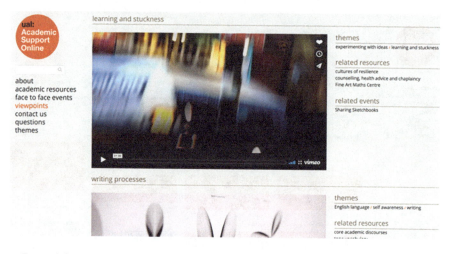

Figure 9.8. A 'Viewpoints' resource within the media channel, illustrating the simplified contextual information

A good variety [...] useful to hear from students and tutors. (Student feedback)

ASO is designed with linked or networked browsing, modularity, multiplicity and plurality in mind. The *Drupal* platform (www.drupal.org) was chosen to build the inter-related functions into one site and allows for agile and anticipatory development. Underpinning this choice is the potential for extensibility – the ability to respond in design and engineering terms to future contexts not known during early iterations of the site, embodying flexibility both in technology and architecture. In summary, flexibility underpins our approach to the development of ASO, and we propose below that it can be seen as an expression of Ryan and Tilbury's (2013) call for a systemic approach to enabling flexible pedagogies, flexible practices and flexible learning. This is also echoed in Ron Barnett's view of the tension and potential between *systems flexibility* and *personal flexibility:*

> Systems flexibility is not an end in itself but more properly becomes a means to assist in helping students to take on personal forms of flexibility so that they may be better equipped to face and, indeed, contribute to a fluid and unstable world. (Barnett, 2014, p. 27)

The additive design underpinning the site architecture gives us in-house flexibility to facilitate learner's choices as these evolve for each person. Our methodology for developing ASO content via a variety of media is also designed to promote engagement. We seek or commission perspectives from our staff and students in order to create an asynchronous dialogue over time. Students and staff who might be reluctant to engage in web 2.0 contexts external to institutional and social media

ACADEMIC SUPPORT ONLINE

platforms are often willing to do so in integrated, curated settings involving, for example, semi-structured interviews and micro-documentaries.

Engagement with ASO has been encouraging. The data analytics for the first year of the site's existence indicate that it is fulfilling its brief to provide inclusive access, with indications of engaged browsing behaviour 24/7. Most students visited ASO from links shared on social media and 20% were from mobile devices. ASO's responsive design, one-click registration for workshops and tutorials, mapping and calendar facilities are being well used. Usage patterns indicate sustained use including overnight, during holiday periods and at weekends. Engagement (see Figure 9.9 for our first year) is increasing year on year, with site use up by 25% in the first quarter of the second year.

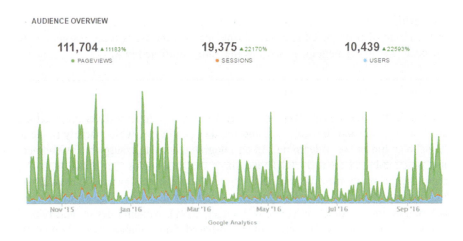

Figure 9.9. Summary analytics data for Academic Support Online *– year 1*[1]

ASO's architecture is paralleled by its interface design, which have evolved together through iterative dialogue. Our awareness of the highly developed visual sensitivity and criticality of UAL users has been paramount, and the creation of a clear, enticing identity for the integrated Academic Support offer across the teams and forms of provision, ensuring continuity between the identity of Academic Support and ASO's interface, was naturally crucial. A product of focused consultation with staff, students and graduates, ASO's style improved recognition of the offer, which has increased enquiry and discovery, in turn raising levels of respect and morale, stimulating interest in contribution of high quality content, and encouraging engagement, which generates ongoing constructive feedback. This generative circle has included a wide range of stakeholders – students, senior managers, course leaders and more. Qualitative feedback has been very encouraging from the outset with a positive reception from students and staff regarding the usefulness, clarity and user-friendliness of ASO.

> Academic Support Online is strong & clear visually with a clear search facility and clear contact details. I see [ASO] as an academic resource, a place to foster collaboration and a place for browsing events across UAL. (Student feedback)
> A joy, basically. (Student feedback)

FLEXIBLE PEDAGOGIES IN PRACTICE

The contextual rationale for ASO weaves together many factors, from the range and nature of creative and cultural disciplines to the diversity of our students, and their current and future conditions/environments. Acknowledging that ASO's main driver is its distinctive and challenging UAL context, we reflect throughout this section on the range of pedagogies that have influenced us, the ways these resonate with aspects of flexible pedagogies, and how they are manifested in ASO.

Flexible Pedagogic Confluences

Situated in the transdisciplinary university-wide space, ASO reflects the teaching and learning values of the colleges, and the theories in use, which largely relate to the scholarship in social learning. As an integrated academic support environment in a practice-based context, ASO recognises the pedagogies that make sense for explorers (primarily the often tacit and intuitive 'experiential learning'), drawing on thinking that promotes open dialogue, revelation and discovery, both of the self and as 'communities of practice' (Lave & Wenger, 1991). Arts and design and related practices are necessarily interactive and team-based if not collaborative – though this is not to say that independence of mind, individual critical thinking, and resilience are therefore less important! Lave and Wenger's work (1991) is probably the most cited in UAL's pedagogic discourse, perhaps together with Kolb's (1984) reflective learning cycle. ASO brings these influences together as a community of academic practice supporting individual enquiry.

In our experience, our students often have an ill-founded but ingrained fear of the so-called 'academic' as something distinct from 'creative' practices. This is often evident in avoidance of research via reading, writing, and thus theoretical course elements. So, in developing ASO we mediate this and bridge between the pedagogic language of study and academe (often found in assessment criteria) such as criticality or evaluative thinking, and practical activities or processes. For example, we encourage 'thinking through drawing', or explain essay structure as storyboarding or composition. Sensitivity to discourse is represented in ASO both through its design and resource base, which speak through a plurality of approaches and choices. In this way, ASO is a 'boundary object' as explored by Wenger (1998, as cited in Kubiak et al., 2015), within a 'boundary orientated pedagogy' in 'a landscape of practice': 'the boundary object supports connection and collaboration but does not force consensus of meaning' (p. 82).

[I now consider how] my online presence ties in with/supports my practice and studying, how could I use it in a more proactive way. (Student feedback)

Learning development, by nature transdisciplinary, provided another research lens that informed ASO's development, linked to enquiry-based approaches adopted to bridge between academic and creative discourses. Further to this linguistic mediation, we ask students to conceive of study as creative practice that interweaves with their own subject, therefore building agency through an enquiry-based approach to their own learning and awareness. Hilsdon (2010) notes the way in which learning development practitioners encourage students to interpret, make sense of and engage critically in HE practices, which moves beyond a deficit model of learning support. This directly aligns with the ideas of transformative capabilities and learner empowerment, in seeking 'to create meaningful ways that learners can influence both their educational and social futures' (Ryan & Tilbury 2013, p. 16).

In addition, we have drawn upon the academic literacies field (e.g. Lea & Street, 1998, 2006) which offers socio-linguistic and linguistic ethnographic (Lillis, 2008) perspectives on the contextual realities of students' multiple learning situations. These are represented in ASO both by the design of the site and its content. The resources are organised into 'Getting started', 'Developing skills' and 'Exploring Further' levels (Figure 9.2), where a plurality of views are presented without pigeon-holing students by assumed levels of study or capability. This influence echoes the connection made by Ryan and Tilbury (2013) in learner empowerment, regarding the positioning of students as peers, respecting different needs, expertise, purposes and ambitions of learners as participation in HE diversifies.

Similarly, the aim to increase learners' influence or agency has been supported by the use of academic research practices in the development of content that involves capturing student voices. Early development of ASO was informed by social research methods, including action research models such as appreciative inquiry, and co-operative and participatory enquiry (Reason & Bradbury, 2001). Phenomenographic approaches (Marton, 1986) also inform our overall enquiry into the variation of study experiences, the outcomes of which inform those dimensions of learning and study selected for content development. These perspectives are represented in ASO by the range of content related to the topic in question, and by the resource types offered, from formal guides and online videos to 'Viewpoints', a social media channel embedded within the site (see Figure 9.8). For example, in order to help students to approach difficult texts, we have produced a resource called 'Reading stories', composed of interviews with many of our creative academics and professional colleagues, including Pro-Vice Chancellors, research leaders, and librarians, who share their experiences, strategies and insights into their own shifts in perspective towards academic reading.

I was quite surprised at how freeing this was. I realised how I approach a creative challenge from storytelling. (Student feedback)

Student Diversity

UAL attracts a highly diverse student population: 51% (2015/16) are from outside the UK, and within that around 40% are from China, Korea or Hong Kong. Of our undergraduate home UK numbers (2015/16), 29% are from a black, Asian or minority ethnic background, 33% from a working class background (SEC 4–7), 17% have a specific learning difficulty, for instance, dyslexia (9% have another disability), and 17% of first years are mature.

For some students, and for many more at certain times, it is valuable to be able to access support discreetly: the availability of extra-curricular support, which ASO particularly affords, is as important as our course-embedded support. In this sense, ASO provides a good example of an online learning community that allows for greater flexibility in terms of the pace, place and mode of delivery and which, as a result, enriches student learning outside formal curriculum settings.

Added to this, the cost of London life is a big issue for students, and travel adds to the challenging conditions for any university-wide provision – UAL's six Colleges are distributed widely, some at several sites, across the capital. Inevitably many students respond to their course and college identity and find the University harder to navigate. Reaching sites across London to access a sharable space or activity takes time, energy and money. Many students commute, have caring responsibilities (not to mention jobs) and are time-poor, as well as managing on very low incomes. Students are also frequently off site on live projects, placements, and research – and do still need support.

In response, ASO is a 24/7 space where students are opened up to multiple views and variation in experiences of learning; alongside this online access to content, the site also offers an opportunity for students to discover a face-to-face offer that they may not have encountered otherwise. An enquiry can arise, a workshop can be stumbled upon through the site, and the student come to be sitting in a workshop or classroom setting interacting with students from other courses or levels, resulting in a valuable learning experience:

Everything I discovered about my own creative process and practice I couldn't have put into words without building a model ... [the workshop encouraged] 'an emphasis on awareness and acceptance. (Student feedback)

This student might not have encountered the workshop without the online space outside the curriculum context and the browsing behaviour that ASO promotes.

In turn, the experiences of the workshop participants are then built on, to inform the creation of resources that bring developments of knowledge and practice back into the ASO knowledge base. For example, workshop improvisations by performance design students have helped them to explore affective dimensions of liminality

(Land, Rattray, & Vivian, 2014) and to participate in short films disseminating this learning via ASO. In these collaborative ways, Academic Support is 'positioning students as peers with valuable contributions to make' (Ryan & Tilbury, 2013, p. 16).

ASO particularly recognises the visual and multisensory tendencies of our students and the plural languages of practices, but does not start with assumptions that arts students are (for example) actually poor writers or struggle with maths, that working class students need academic support, or indeed that students are only interested in support to improve their assessment grades! However, such perceptions are realities presenting a continual challenge: ASO aims to reflect a balance of responsiveness to everyday learning development through an enhancement-based lens of value to all students, as well as a needs-based lens whether self-identified or referred. This is consistent with the diversity of our students, aiming particularly to support the realisation of cultural capital within all individuals' development potential.

We recognise Ryan and Tilbury's (2013) 'need for forms of pedagogic innovation that help develop flexibility' (p. 4), echoed by Barnett (2014) that pedagogic practice should 'provide pedagogic openness' (p.10). We arrived early at the decision to over-ride any classification of content by level or subject of study, recognising that the disciplinary synergies and commonalities previously mentioned also crossed between FE, undergraduate and postgraduate study. Students were just as likely to be 'getting started' at MA level as they were at FE level especially if orientating to UK HE for the first time. 'Developing skills' was a high priority for all throughout, implying enhancement at any level. Given the wide range of prior learning experiences, specialist but transferable material emanating from the disciplines, and links to more scholarly resources, content also began to cluster under 'exploring further'. Despite this openness and sense of plurality, the resources could still feel 'static' in nature. In response, we have introduced the 'Viewpoints' media channel within ASO, where the content is presented in more fluid, broadcast-style format, allowing for greater immediacy, a low-cost production aesthetic and contributions of diverse views of staff and students presented through recorded interviews, podcasts and mini-documentaries.

Crossing Boundaries and Content Development

Since its conception, ASO has set out to cross boundaries (Ryan & Tilbury, 2013) in a way that responds to institutional realities and takes an integrative, systemic approach to knowledge and learning. To ensure that these realities were understood and tested, and prior to the initial site structure being finalised, intensive research and consultation was carried out as part of an agile development process to explore student and staff viewpoints on the content and form of ASO. The methodology included semi-structured discussions/interviews with key stakeholders, scoping workshops, focus groups, and student and staff questionnaires across a range of functions, diverse courses, and daily conversations. The key areas of interest were the 'wants' for resources to be included, identification of existing internal resources suitable for inclusion, issues of best engagement with users through use of language and communication channels, and the practicalities of how ASO could work into and across the colleges and cross disciplinary boundaries.

The consultation was particularly useful for gaining a sense of commonalities and variation in the form, design and priorities for content development. ASO's first phase was focused on the development of a resource base, with 'content' understood as themes and topics and potential forms. Content was conceived as both curated resources and links (continually developing) to offer students opportunities to consider contextualised approaches and interpretations, aiming to support enquiry, not provide solutions. For example, a student searching under the term 'essay' is shown resources and viewpoints from a range of perspectives including 'essay as iceberg', 'design thinking for writing', and 'studio process as metaphor for writing'. In this way, content aims to increase diverse student engagement in 'academic' work drawing on the application of the pedagogic tendencies of arts practices, as discussed above, to de-mystify the 'academic' by identifying study as practice, and surface learning awareness of all kinds.

ASO has been spearheaded by a small team leading the university-wide Academic Support programme, but in a widely collaborative way, from consultation through to the co-creation of content and features of the site. This has involved students, graduates, course-based teaching staff, academic support staff, language tutors and librarians. Content emerging from the contextual awareness of staff leading and delivering Academic Support across the colleges was cross-checked with key questions that students ask, at many stages of their studies. These questions helped to sustain cross-disciplinary development needs, whilst we also anticipated that what students may not be aware of is as important as what they perceived as a 'problem'.

> Discussion of future collaborative opportunities continues – this openness and willingness to learn and work together across departments has been most successful and rewarding. (Academic staff feedback)

ASO content is informed, generated and debated, reflecting the inputs of academic support tutors, who are often inter-disciplinary practitioners themselves. They support an academic portfolio of courses and research projects that reflect post-disciplinary studies such as 'Applied Imagination', 'Innovation Management', and 'Fashion Futures'. Within the wide range of traditional subject areas (e.g. Fine Art, Graphic Design), UAL students often engage directly with global, social and political themes. Added to this, the development of low residency modes and international partnerships form the pedagogic drivers for Academic Support.

The transdisciplinary nature of our students' creative futures combines with the diversity of our student communities, to inform the discovery processes within ASO. Content therefore needs to respond to diverse situations, learning preferences and behaviours. We knew from librarians and student feedback that serendipitous discovery is often as powerful and important as deliberate searching. Realising the plurality of assumptions about ways of thinking and engaging online added to our belief that resources would be best structured thematically as collections using common headings such as 'Approaching learning', 'Reading', 'Presentation skills' and so on.

> Hi, the site looks good. I certainly enjoyed the way it encouraged me to browse around. I found myself learning things I hadn't intended to which must be a good sign. (Academic staff feedback)

Flexibility became enshrined in our approach to ASO's knowledge base as we moved away from the monolithic concept of knowledge to co-constructed collections of knowledges, preferring, as this developed, to think of 'understandings', which suggested less static, more developmental, inclusive and insightful senses of knowing. ASO content presents practical, informative and demonstrative – even empathetic – approaches to gaining learning. This is manifest in the range of forms of content, from book formats to animations, interviews, diagrams, word docs and films which enable students with different learning tendencies or preferences to choose the format that is most accessible (e.g. audio, visual, large text, different backgrounds).

Transformative Capabilities and Uncertain Futures

Our students are mostly aiming to sustain careers in highly creative and competitive arenas and (increasingly) to be people who contribute and impact in contexts wider than arts and design might immediately suggest. Creative practice is self-revealing and requires personal agility and self-efficacy whilst the contexts for professional intercultural creative futures demand sensitivity and collaboration; perhaps most of all, our students need strong senses of enquiry and resilience, or perhaps flexibility. These attributes are helpfully articulated by UAL's Creative Attributes Framework (2016).

Transformative learning theory, whole systems thinking, design thinking and Education for Sustainability (EfS) have all informed the development of ASO. With the relationship between EfS and learning development in mind, Winter, Barton, Allison and Cotton (2015) propose that learning development practice has much in common with EfS pedagogies and context. Sterling's (2010) notion of learning-as-sustainability is important for its values-driven focus, and the purposeful direction towards developing metacognition, and contextual and situational awareness (including system and epistemic cognition). In turn, Sterling draws on foundational understandings of transformative learning such as Bateson's learning levels (1972) – not only learning to learn and learning about learning – but ultimately, learning how to learn about learning (Bawden, 2005; Sterling, 2010).

These influences are represented in ASO by resources and events that explore 'approaching learning' themes and topics, particularly those focused on increasing student awareness of learning processes and purposes applicable to current academic success and uncertain creative/professional futures. As a portal that articulates explicitly the nature of transformative learning – changes in conceptual terrain, values and frames of reference – ASO helps students become aware of multiple dimensions of learning including choosing and decision-making. The site content makes visible supportive elements, such as critical reflection and methods of rational discourse, that can enable students to engage meaningfully with the 'disorienting dilemmas' associated with transformative learning (Mezirow, 1991). This engagement is particularly important given the diversity of prior learning experiences, expectations and aspirations of our students.

Land and Meyer's (2006) and Land, Meyer, and Smith's (2008) work on threshold concepts, practices and understandings, and discipline-specific and interdisciplinary ways of knowing (Allen, 2014; Sandri, 2013), particularly helped course-based staff to help us identify and prioritise troublesome areas to tackle. For example, risk-taking was highlighted as sometimes troublesome in fine art practice as students can find experimental approaches hard to sustain. In response, ASO includes resources designed to support the management of uncertainty and strengthen self-efficacy and personal resilience in relation to assessment.

The development team is in constant iterative processes of reflection, scoping, and informal and formal communications to develop and test ideas. Development and production is coordinated and curated centrally, involving wide-ranging negotiations to adapt existing face-to-face material, the commissioning of new, bespoke material and the sourcing of relevant links. In this way stakeholder engagement has increased and strengthened, and co-creation of content in a blended way – for example, developing online resources from filmed/edited events and workshops – is proving an effective way forward. The transformative capabilities of ASO have extended across the University, drawing out a new, dynamic community of practice.

> A student-friendly, dynamic and exploratory blended site, which challenges traditional concepts of library and academic support, especially important in a creative arts institution. (Academic staff feedback)

CONCLUDING REFLECTIONS

The HEA work stream on flexibility led to a number of further research questions. Below we consider, in summary, (1) how the implementation of ASO responds to the challenges of flexibility; (2) how Web 2.0 technologies have facilitated flexible learning in our context; and (3) what could be learned from the structure and development of ASO in curricula and co-curricular settings.

Responding to the Challenge of Flexibility

Rooted in our institutional context, its signature pedagogies and ways of thinking and practising, ASO is a systemic, holistic, designed response to a range of diverse contexts for a diverse student body. It is limited by its extra-curricula support function, but also liberated by this to take an exploratory approach to the relationships between modes of support. That said, its underpinning thinking, rationale, and approach align with the dimensions of flexibility associated with systems, pedagogy, and students' needs and interests.

The institutional context has demonstrated systems flexibility from a number of perspectives. From the perspective of institutional support for flexible pedagogies, our Academic Support Strategy (UAL, 2013) set out from the start to adopt an integrated and holistic approach. This has been echoed in the architecture, design and technological choices made to develop the online/blended learning community. We propose that these strategic choices align with the notions of *systems* flexibility as well as *pedagogic* flexibility-within-complexity emphasised by Barnett (2014). In particular, our approach to commissioning and curating resources, viewpoints and events that promote plurality and diversity, while at the same time proposing commonalities and synergies, is intended to orientate students towards a 'spirit of flexibility':

> Systems flexibility [...] becomes a means to assist in helping students to take on personal forms of flexibility so that they may be better equipped to face and, indeed, contribute to a fluid and unstable world. (Barnett, 2014, p. 27)

The emphasis here on *assisting in helping students* resonates with the underpinning thinking of ASO – creating learning spaces that develop a broader sense of agency and competence among students, spaces that extend and complement curriculum experiences.

To some extent our students' learning 'needs' have resonance with ways in which those needs are articulated in the flexible pedagogies literature. This is noted in Barnett's (2014) recommendations that institutions should be mindful to 'explore the extent of students' pedagogical isolation', to respond to 'the (possibly limited) scope of students' educational experience and challenge', and 'the (possible) fragmentation of that experience' (p. 69).

Further, the call to respond flexibly to the complexity of student experience is a core strand in our intended user experience of ASO. The relational mapping of 'Viewpoints', resources and events echoes Barnett's (2014) description of contemporary students' contexts: 'It is a world, too, in which connections are crucial (between individuals, institutions and systems)' (p. 24). ASO's 'Viewpoints' resources reflect that, even where there are synergies between disciplines, many concepts and dimensions of study are fluid and not reducible to singular approaches. Pedagogic flexibility suggests that there ought to be a plurality of assumptions about how users think as well as ways in which users are expected to engage with a particular online environment. Seeing this through the lens of systems flexibility, therefore, flexibility in format is arguably an attribute of flexibility in itself – not just in content but in form. What is presented in the site, what it says, and the way in which it says it can also teach. Multiple flexibility is enshrined in the approach to the knowledge base; as such, ASO moves away from the monolithic towards a multiple, co-constructed knowledge base, curated for flexible engagement with collections of answers to any given enquiry. We echo Barnett's (2014) view that 'there can be no freezing of key concepts' (p. 25).

> I am going to take these concepts together to improve my work. (Student feedback)

Facilitating Learning through Web 2.0 Technologies

The next question concerns the way in which web technologies – Web 2.0 and beyond – facilitate flexible learning within our transdisciplinary context and '[improve] the experiences of students to enable [...] connectivity across people, groups and communities' (Ryan & Tilbury, 2014, p. 26). ASO draws on Web 2.0 technologies that underpin the originating open source *Drupal* theme, in order to produce a range of further functionalities, from simple web forms to the potential for embedding micro-sites within ASO pages, demonstrating Barnett's (2014) notion of systems flexibility.

Variety in content has been key to ASO's pedagogic flexibility and its influence on mode of engagement. We use both human intervention (curation) to tag content, as well as the automated linking and tagging across and within content through search returns that are weighted according to relevance. The design of these search returns also reflects or corresponds to the rhizomatic nature of knowledge and plurality of disciplinary views, and the interrelated nature of academic practices. By encouraging discovery through browsing and offering a fair number of support options – downloadable guidance, videos, links, FAQs, bookable workshops and tutorials – ASO enables the user to follow a line of enquiry, find the unexpected, and make choices that suit their learning preferences and circumstances that are not limited to online interaction. The risks that Barnett (2014) alerts us to regarding, for example, 'power browsing' replacing 'authentic' research is important (p. 63), but on balance the learning support enhancements afforded by ASO counter this by raising students' awareness of academically sound research practices.

ASO's development has reached a point where its infrastructure is in place to respond flexibly and in anticipatory ways, as per Barnett's (2014) call for institutions to review the extent to which curricula exhibit 'epistemic flexibility' (p. 11), with students able intellectually to explore knowledge in a relatively open-ended way.

ASO pursues this line of online pedagogic practice by building on the varied forms of content display, in particular through Viewpoints, and a discussion forum cross-linked to discussions at the end of each resource. Plus, by being developed within university systems, there is potential to link resource landing pages within ASO directly to pages within course VLE sites, with contextual information presented to introduce the appropriate context, capitalising on the extensibility of the chosen development platform.

We are working on the potential for personalised learning via learning analytics – a personalised home page to be populated with dashboard-style learning analytics that pull in and display data feeds from each user's engagement. This may also extend to data feeds from other sources (other university systems, such as the VLE, and external sites, e.g. Facebook, Instagram), and to include learning histories, and resources pinned by the student in their interaction within the site (where appropriate permissions granted). The aim of these activities is to continue to promote the development of dialogic community in relation to academic practices and to enhance the student's awareness and ownership of their learning, and their ability to adapt and develop it.

> Not only is flexibility a matter of the ways in which disciplines might open themselves to each other (in transdisciplinarity; in pluridisciplinarity) and of the ways in which researchers are expected to work (in transnational teams, in new forms of 'publication') but it is a matter evident at different levels of knowledge production. (Barnett, 2014, p. 26)

ASO as a Manifestation of Flexible Pedagogies in Practice

Finally, we reflect on our learning from the design and ongoing development of ASO as a manifestation of flexible pedagogies in practice. Although this is an extra-curricula enhancement offer there may be learning from our learning that could inform the development of flexible pedagogic strategies in curricula and co-curricular spaces, because ASO delivers complementary, curricula-related support.

In practical terms, choosing a platform that enables flexibility and extensibility to respond to future opportunities and shifts in student learning behaviours was fundamental. Equally, understanding the current context required adoption of a participatory, inclusive design process, involving more than an objective understanding of audience. The engagement of users (students and staff) as co-creators of form and content has enabled us to design from the diverse user-experience point of view and to build in debate and responsiveness as core values. As a curated portal, ASO provides a situated framework for enquiry by avoiding automated aggregators, thus ensuring that content is tailored, accessible, timely and flexible. This means that as we see and hear of shifts in students' support needs or behaviours, we are able to respond by developing content or improving the user experience.

It was also important to have the support of departments from a range of intersecting perspectives such as IT and Quality infrastructures, internal marketing, the university VLE, library services, student services, careers and more. Approval and reporting through the formal teaching and learning committee structure ensured both rigour in our proposals and recognition of strategic relevance. Combined, these involvements continue to help communicate reflexively the value of a systemic approach.

Transdisciplinary or cross-curricula initiatives can be perceived as challenging to the 'tribes and territories' (Becher & Trowler, 2001) of specific academic programmes, whether individual courses or departments. Acceptance of an online academic support offer has needed critical friends and lead participants from courses, plus the support of the Students' Union. Support for staff in their digital skills and understandings and the establishment of policy regarding, for example, sign off, attribution, and take-down, have been essential in developing participatory confidence. In demonstrating ASO to courses we have promoted its complementary purposes, features that support access to the curriculum-specific and its potential to address students' increasing desire to look beyond disciplinary boundaries.

In conclusion, we surface two key areas of ongoing debate, emerging from both our experience of student and staff feedback to date and the flexible pedagogies literature. First, we are mindful of the need to evidence the value of online support whilst recognising the potential hidden demand it may place on students regarding cognitive load and digital capabilities. Checking assumptions of navigational and decision-making confidence is an ongoing challenge, as we understand that students do not all share the same fluency and intuition in digital environments. Thus we are building in content that helps students to make effective use of digital tools, online technologies and spaces in combination with in-person engagement.

Second, as we have taken an enquiry-based learning approach, particularly of an appreciative and participatory nature, we find that we are actively positioned at the intersection of personal and professional development elements long embedded in practice-based curricula, 'non-academic' support services, and graduate attributes relevant to professional success in the subject driven by employability and self-generated employment. These have the potential to converge holistically, as discussed by Barnett (2014) – the idea that curricula and pedagogies can nurture 'a range of personal dispositions and qualities out of which arise, in turn, capacities for responding flexibly to the world' (p. 62).

Both of these debates surface a common theme within the flexible pedagogies literature – a desire to develop pedagogic spaces (online and 'in real life') that are integrated in a way that allows multiple boundaries and hierarchical systems to become more rhizomatic and permeable. This requires attention to all feedback loops within and between pedagogic spaces and their design – attention to patterns that connect (after Bateson, 1972). In this way, we are mindful of the tension between systems flexibility and personal flexibility referred to by Barnett (2014) – the additive architecture of the platform and its design philosophy increase the opportunities we have to respond and anticipate where systems inflexibility would otherwise prevent personal flexibility. While Web 2.0 technologies afford online collaborations and interconnections between systems, it is perhaps within conceptual domains that feedback loops, although difficult to create, can become pedagogically useful. Appreciative and participatory enquiry into multiple cultures of study, and crucially into the *intersections* of those cultures, creates agency or learner empowerment, additionally informing academic and institutional decision-making. In this way, feedback loops help to surface multiple intersections that can combine to create inter-disciplinary spaces and even future disciplines, in turn leading to pedagogical openness and new spaces as envisaged within the flexible pedagogies literature.

ACKNOWLEDGEMENT

This version of the chapter was written in 2017 and submitted for final proof in January 2019. Since this date, the platform has undergone a substantial upgrade to Drupal 8, which has enabled us to implement intended personalisation functions and other enhancements. However, the principles and approach described in this chapter are still relevant to the new enhanced platform. *Academic Support Online* could not exist without the work, help and support of many colleagues at UAL, in particular Paul Thrippleton (Drupal Developer), Richard Parry (Digital Curator), and the content developers within UAL Academic Support.

NOTE

[1.] In 18/19 academic year, these figures show a substantial increase in site use since the launch period noted in figure 9: 448,989 page views, 69,929 sessions and 20,700 users (Google Analytics).

REFERENCES

Allen, B. (2014). Creativity as threshold: Learning and teaching in a liminal space. In A. O'Mahony, Buchanan, M. O'Rourke, & B. Higgs (Eds.), *Threshold concepts: From personal practice to communities of practice*. Retrieved from https://files.eric.ed.gov/fulltext/ED558533.pdf

Barnett, R. (2014). *Conditions of flexibility*. HEA.

Bateson, G. (1972). *Steps into an ecology of mind*. Ballantine.

Bawden, R. (2005). Systemic development at Hawkesbury: Some personal lessons from experience. *Systems Research and Behavioural Science, 22*(2), 151–164.

Becher, T., & Trowler, P. (2001). *Academic tribes and territories: Intellectual enquiry and the culture of disciplines*. Open University Press.

Hilsdon, J. (2010). What is learning development. In P. Hartley, J. Hilsdon, C. Keenan, S. Sinfield, & M. Verity (Eds.), *Learning development in higher education* (pp. 13–27). Palgrave Macmillan.

Kolb, D. (1984). *Experiential learning: Experience as the source of learning and development*. Prentice-Hall.

Kubiak, C., Fenton-O'Creevy, M., Appleby, K., Kempster, M., Reed, M., Solvason, C., & Thorpe, M. (2015). Brokering boundary encounters. In E. Wenger-Trayner, M. Fenton-O'Creevy, S., Hutchinson, C. Kubiak, & B. Wenger-Trayner (Eds.), *Learning in landscapes of practice* (pp. 81–96). Routledge.

Land, R., & Meyer, E. (Eds.). (2006). *Overcoming barriers to student understanding: Threshold concepts and troublesomeknowledge*. Routledge.

Land, R., Meyer, E., & Smith, J. (Eds.). (2008). *Threshold concepts within the disciplines*. Sense.

Land, R., Rattray, J., & Vivian, P. (2014). Learning in the liminal space: A semiotic approach to threshold concepts. *Higher Education, 67*(2), 199–217.

Lave, J., & Wenger, E. (1991). *Situated learning: Legitimate peripheral participation*. Cambridge University Press.

Lea, M. R., & Street, B. (1998). Student writing in higher education: A academic literacies approach. *Studies in Higher Education, 23*(2), 157–172.

Lea, M. R., & Street, B. (2006). The 'academic literacies' model: Theory and applications. *Theory into Practice, 45*(4), 368–377.

Lillis, T. (2008). Ethnography as method, methodology, and 'deep theorizing': Closing the gap between text and context in academic writing research. *Written Communication, 25*(3), 353–388.

Marton, F. (1986). Phenomenography – A research approach investigating different understandings of reality. *Journal of Thought, 21*(2), 28–49.

Mezirow, J. (1991). *Transformative dimensions of adult learning.* Jossey-Bass.

Reason, P., & Bradbury, H. (Eds.). (2001). *Handbook of action research: Participative inquiry and practice.* Sage.

Ryan, A., & Tilbury, D. (2013). *Flexible pedagogies: New pedagogical ideas.* HEA.

Sandri, O. (2013). Threshold concepts, systems and learning for sustainability. *Environmental Education Research, 19*(6), 810–822.

Sterling, S. (2010). Learning for resilience or the resilient learner? Towards a necessary reconciliation in a paradigm of sustainable education. *Environmental Education Research, 16*(5–6), 511–528.

University of the Arts London. (2013). *Strategy for academic support 2013–16.* Retrieved from http://issuu.com/artslondonlibraries/docs/academic_support-8

University of the Arts London. (2016). *Creative attributes framework.* Retrieved from http://www.arts.ac.uk/about-ual/teaching-and-learning/careers-and-employability/creative-attributes-framework

Winter, J., Barton, G., Allison, J., & Cotton, D. (2015). Learning development and education for sustainability: What are the links? *Journal of Learning Development in Higher Education, 1*(8), 1–23.

SIOBHAN CLAY AND PAUL TABAK

10. COMMONPLACE

A Student-Led Survival Guide to Support Transitions and Belonging at University of the Arts London

INTRODUCTION

This chapter explores a co-created, student-led community web platform at University of the Arts London (UAL) called *Commonplace*. It is framed within the context of an increasingly diversifying UK higher education (HE) landscape and comes at a time when the financial and emotional pressures many students experience are now headlined and take centre stage in the 'Transitions' narrative (Yorke, 2000). With significant increases in tuition fees and the legacy of historic, political, widening participation (WP) agendas to raise the numbers of traditionally underrepresented groups in HE since 2000, the sector has necessarily moved towards a more holistic approach to supporting students to make the transition into HE a more guided and transparent journey. Additionally, the transition discussion acknowledges a heterogeneous student demographic where 'students have multiple identities and all students have aspects of their personal lives that will impact upon the classroom context' (Broughan & Hunt, 2012, p. 182) and thus have different experiences, approaches to learning and needs. It is within this period of educational change, uncertainty and diversification that *Commonplace* is situated. As a resource it embodies concepts of learner empowerment, co-creation, and social learning (Ryan & Tilbury, 2013). As a model, it flips the role of university as knowledge provider, handing ownership to the student experts and, in so doing, contests the university-student hierarchies associated with traditional student advice platforms in what Freire would call problem-posing theory, that which takes the people's history as the starting point for education and knowledge sharing (Freire, 1970, p. 65).

This chapter describes the process of creating *Commonplace* to illuminate the dynamics of student co-creation and social learning that underpin and drive the initiative. Firstly, we discuss the context and rationale for creating *Commonplace* with particular focus on supporting 'transitions' to university. Secondly, we consider the design realisation and process of working collaboratively with a student team to plan, build and maintain *Commonplace*. Thirdly, three *Commonplace* case studies of successfully embedded co-curricular projects explore stakeholder collaborations. These collaborations aim to reach groups who typically feel isolated when transitioning to university, such as international and WP students. Fourthly, the ongoing challenges of maintaining an online community platform and the inherent tensions between ownership, co-creation and sustainability, particularly salient in an increasingly competitive digital world, are discussed. Finally, we consider future developments for *Commonplace* and recommendations to colleagues wishing to support transitions to university through student-led online communities.

CONTEXT

Commonplace is a UAL, co-created student website that launched in the summer of 2011. The aim was to create a friendly and informative online platform where our 19,000 students, located across six colleges and eleven sites, could feel more successfully integrated into the wider university community and London. This was in response to institutional research highlighting a perceived lack of connectedness to the University. *Commonplace* was therefore intended to mitigate the obstacles to students making friends and settling into their course and life in London. This

Figure 10.1. Screen capture of Commonplace homepage

emphasis on student community building is supported by research (Hughes & Smail, 2015) that describes making friends and creating social support networks as being a key importance to students feeling settled and part of their institution, particularly in their first year.

Commonplace is the first cross-university, student-generated platform at UAL and includes pastoral and community-themed articles to provide a flavour of life at the University. The contribution process is open to anyone with a university login and features include a 'Swap Shop' to share skills, flat-sharing posts, stories, reviews, recipes, and general tips and advice that might be useful for other users. *Commonplace* acknowledges that being a student at university is often just one aspect of a student's identity; that they have complex lives managing social, familial and work commitments that influence their expectations and engagement with the institution. Such differences are celebrated by foregrounding students' everyday realities and experiences in an open and friendly online space, to empower them to influence directly their social futures (Ryan & Tilbury, 2013) through story and advice sharing. Furthermore, *Commonplace* is underpinned by a commitment to social justice agendas; to progress student agency and confidence through the democratisation of territory that has historically privileged students with the 'right' cultural capital, particularly salient in art and design institutions (Burke & McManus, 2009).

Commonplace was initiated by the Teaching and Learning Exchange, a department within the University's central Academic, Development & Services. It is a student-Exchange collaboration coordinated by an Educational and Web Developer and is funded by the central WP department. This cross-university approach was important to address students' perceptions of college disconnectedness; it thereby cultivated dialogue across the institution:

> It's a good place to get in touch with other students in London and at ual because it's all spread out, it's hard to create a sense of community, I think it [Commonplace] helps achieve this [6 month questionnaire].

Commonplace enables students to connect virtually across six different colleges and varied subject disciplines to promote a sense of belonging to a wider community that might otherwise be difficult to 'access' or indeed visualise given the University's multiple sites and geographical spread.

TRANSITIONS TO UNIVERSITY

In recent years, there has been increased attention in UK and international HE on supporting students' transition to university. No longer the domain of an elite few, the massification of HE has seen an 11% increase in UK UG student numbers over the last 12 years (HESA, 2014/2015) and a steady increase in those attending university from WP and first in family backgrounds (DfE, 2016). This has necessitated reflection amongst HEIs, including UAL, on the process of going to university from the student perspective, to consider the role played by each element of the journey, from marketing, application and enrolment, through to academic preparedness and social/community building initiatives, in easing the adjustment to university life. Much of this focus has been on acknowledging the barriers faced by some students on entering HE. Such barriers can be exacerbated by limited familial experience of university, entering via vocational routes or from time spent out of education in the workplace. Previously, these barriers were largely located around a lack of transparency around going to university and the academic expectations universities had of their students (Lea & Street, 1998). Bourdieu and Passeron (1977), for example, highlight a perpetuation of a sense of myth and mystery around the university experience underlined by practices that assumed a level of cultural and social capital that would see students naturally transition to the university environment. Additionally, a failure to expose the hidden curriculum (Margolis et al., 2001), the rewarding of certain norms and student behaviours, continues to act as a barrier to both access and academic success for those unfamiliar with the language and 'capital' of HE whilst greatly enabling those with these resources.

Recent research suggests that whilst there has been a rise in underrepresented groups attending university, this is not a straightforward success story. Rather, non-continuation rates are rising: 6% in 2013–2014 (HESA, 2015/2016), with retention figures for students from the most disadvantaged backgrounds at 8.2% (Havergal, 2016). This has precipitated a sector shift to create pre-enrolment online social spaces where students can familiarise themselves with the institution prior to arrival to remediate feelings of isolation and reduce the cultural and academic 'shock' of transitioning into university. Sector research also suggests that successful social transition positively influences academic achievement and supports the development of strong learner identities in the longer term (Chemers et al., 2001; DeAndrea et al., 2012).

As Europe's largest creative arts university and with its six-college structure over 11 London sites – London College of Communication (LCC), London College of Fashion (LCF), Camberwell College of Arts, Chelsea College of Arts, Wimbledon College of Arts, and Central Saint Martins (CSM) – UAL can appear huge and complex, particularly for students new to the city. When the project team was tasked with creating an online community space for students to get to know their peers as well as the University, we needed a better understanding of their expectations, concerns and fears so that we could build a space that would support the journey into and through university in a meaningful and authentic way. DeAndrea et al. (2011) discuss the various benefits of online spaces in supporting students into university life with a focus on social media and closed blogs where students can ask questions on a one-to-one or small group basis. *Commonplace* differentiates itself from the 'closed', individualised focus of online forums and offers instead a broad, open platform for students to browse and contribute content.

In the following section we discuss the design realisation and technical process of creating *Commonplace* as a collaborative student endeavour. Although many of the features discussed are continuously evolving, the following description is of the site's functionality at the time of writing.

DESIGNING COMMONPLACE: LEARNER EMPOWERMENT AND CO-CREATION

The sector and institutional concerns around transition and retention formed the underlying rationale for *Commonplace*. Much of the initial content ideas were informed by institutional research into the first-year experience at Camberwell College of Arts between 2008–2010 (Clay, 2010). Through focus groups and interviews with predominantly WP and first in family to HE students, a picture developed that gave greater clarity into students' perceptions of what undergraduate study would be like and the often challenging reality of degree-level study at UAL. Genuine student collaboration that captured the student voice underpinned this research and acted as the guiding principle as *Commonplace* was developed. We recruited five, third-year students from the Design for Graphic Communication course at London College of Communication (LCC) to work with us as part of their course Live Project unit, thereby engaging the students as co-creators of the website. We worked together for five months, collaborating on all aspects of *Commonplace*, including user and audience research, creating mock-up designs for the website and site taxonomy (how it would be organised, classified and searchable). The general look and feel, and brand elements, including the website's name and logo, were all designed by the students. This emphasis on authentic co-creation was built upon the principle of strong learner autonomy and agency. Additionally, the importance placed on co-design from the outset underpins our understanding that 'early front end co-creation of the design development process can have an impact with positive, long-range consequences' (Sanders & Stappers, 2008, p. 9).

Ownership – Gathering Content

Armed with the first-year experience research findings and guided by the student design team, we put together questions and activities to take to the wider student community for input and feedback. We ran college events gathering short vox pops on topics such as dealing with homesickness, money saving tips, and strategies to managing your first crit (an important art and design pedagogic event where students present work to tutors and peers for feedback). Crits can be stressful, particularly for students not used to the often tacit language, format and rules of taking part (Blythman, Orr, & Blair, 2007). We made a conscious decision to present this information in an authentic way to emphasise ownership with the student body and to demarcate it from the aesthetic of the official university website. This approach had an emphasis on visual content and the design layout of *Commonplace* draws directly from the informal layout of Dazed and Confused, a cutting-edge style and culture magazine aimed at young creatives which our student team were keen to replicate (Dazed Media, n.d.). This focus on the visual – no article can be uploaded without an accompanying high quality image – is a priority for a creative community with 17% of home (UK) students declaring dyslexia and other specific learning difficulties. It also provides a platform to showcase their work as developing artists, writers and designers, and creates a resource that is fit for purpose.

Technical Considerations

Whilst college events provide excellent opportunities to promote *Commonplace* and generate student content quickly, they are impractical to run regularly, led by a small team working on other projects simultaneously. Addressing this draws on the responsive functionality of the open-source platform used to build *Commonplace*, and the ability for students to upload their own content easily was an integral part of the website's open and inclusive aim. As *Commonplace's* content was to be produced by multiple student authors, a dynamic Content Management System (CMS) was essential to facilitate the submission process. *Drupal 7* is an open-source platform which at its basic level provides CMS functionality, user management and an administrative interface. However, to achieve the graphical layout the student design team proposed, bespoke themes were developed. One enabled multiple-sized posts to appear on the front page, displayed in a patchwork fashion, while another allowed the user to scroll through all the published posts on the same page. *Commonplace* was initially designed for personal computers at launch but was developed to be responsive to handheld devices in 2014, whilst maintaining the distinctive patchwork look and feel.

One of the greatest challenges in developing *Commonplace* was to make the submission process straightforward to keep students engaged to the point where they clicked the submit button. We knew that if the site was unappealing or difficult to use we would quickly alienate our audience. This underpinned the rationale for establishing student collaboration from the start so that whatever was created reflected their interests, wants and needs. Although we wanted students to be able to contribute all sorts of articles (e.g. stories, recipes, reviews), we needed a balance between the amount of information we wanted to capture and the brevity of the form to do so. We called these 'content-types' and we created four bespoke themes: 'Recipe', an easy to follow standardised form to list ingredients and directions, whilst 'Student Portrait' and 'Where I live' has fixed questions to create a personal profile or describe a neighbourhood. The most used and flexible content-type, however, is the 'Article' which allows the free contribution of text, photos, video and files. Students can contribute content in the 'Join in' section using these simple content-type forms, while moderators can publish on-the-go from any web enabled device in less than a minute.

As a university-hosted platform there were discussions about how to monitor the quality and content of such an open submission process with some concerns about content that might present the University in a compromising light. The project team were clear that this should be a space for students to share their stories freely and that a rigid or overly formal review process would greatly undermine this principle. Thus our publishing process is democratic and non-hierarchical: the most recent posts sit at the top of the front page and are 'lightly edited'. In practice this means that small grammatical errors or mistakes in syntax are left and content requiring significant revision is given back to the student to amend. This approach has come under scrutiny from colleagues concerned that this undermines the fundamental tenets of good studentship, yet we maintain that for the space to feel student 'owned' this approach works by facilitating students' voices authentically. Additionally, creative work is not 'vetted'; as an HE institution that implicitly embodies high creative standards, we wanted *Commonplace* to be a space where student work is not critiqued or over analysed. Rather we took the approach that if a student wanted to contribute, they could do so unencumbered by the aesthetic preferences of the *Commonplace* or course teams. The intention is to empower students to have agency and control in what can be a demanding working environment. In the first six years since launch we have never received an inappropriate contribution, something that may be attributed to the nature of *Commonplace*'s content in promoting a sense of allegiance and support for peers, which perpetuates similar, friendly content. This echoes sector research into the role online personal profiles play in building a social presence which we believe is evidenced in the student interactions on *Commonplace* (Kear et al., 2014).

CHALLENGES

An early concern when developing *Commonplace* was how to engage students to visit it. We were cognisant of the plethora of digital information students interact with on a daily and sometimes moment-to-moment basis and the challenge of standing out in such an over-crowded virtual space. *Commonplace* needed a Unique Selling Point (USP) to bring students in and three months after going live, we launched a classified section called 'Swap Shop' in response to the many flat-share posters on college noticeboards. 'Swap Shop' also provides an ideal opportunity to bring students together physically and not just virtually.

'Swap Shop' continues to be a consistently visited section of the website connecting students across the University to find flatmates and collaborate on projects and events, with over 100 active advertisements at any one time. These ads are unmoderated and are published instantly with fields for personal information viewable by logging into the site.

Another ongoing challenge has been ensuring that *Commonplace* has regularly changing content. Initially students were commissioned to generate a series of resources, for example video interviews and opinion pieces. These briefs were guided by student focus group feedback on settling in, getting around London and being prepared for academic study. They extend learning beyond the confines of the studio and enable students to draw on skills gained within the formal curriculum as artists, designers and writers, to share academic and pastoral knowledge with their community creatively and informally. This enacts concepts of social learning (Ryan & Tilbury, 2013) in several ways: it connects physically dislocated groups together through a digital space which in turn stretches the traditional educational terrain to create alternative arenas for student collaboration and interaction. Additionally, the potential for user innovation and ownership is greatly enhanced by digital tools that largely sit outside corporate control (Ryan & Tilbury, 2013, p. 26). *Commonplace's* open source CMS *Drupal* is an example which allows for pedagogic 'flex' in response to students' content ideas and requirements of the resource.

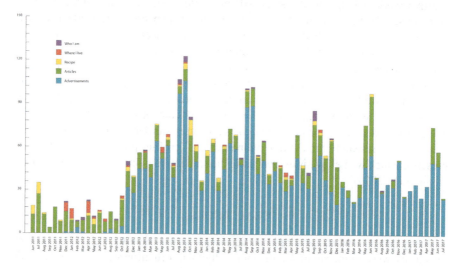

Figure 10.2. Content posted by type 2011–2017

Commonplace went live in July 2011 with 15 student-commissioned articles, growing to 55 within 3 months, with a total of 925 student articles published. Figure 10.2 shows an increase in 'Swap Shop' advertisement activity (blue) between June and September which correlates with students looking for housemates at the end and beginning of the new term. Similarly, spikes in article contributions may be mapped against live project briefings in October, May and June. *Commonplace* was launched to coincide with the new student intake and was included in course, registry and enrolment information, and was featured on the main University website. The site rapidly gained traction among staff and student services departments and was widely praised for its student-centred content and friendly and accessible look and feel. Students were also engaged in the content and understood its support rationale:

[Commonplace] creates a community spirit and find out useful tips about London.
It's an interesting place to get diverse views on how life really is as a student.
It's good for people in the first year or about to start university.

COMMONPLACE

Student feedback also confirmed that the content plugged certain information gaps and spoke to the community:

> nice recipe page as well – it's making me hungry! Also, this is really nice: http://Commonplace.arts.ac.uk/new-arrivals/if-only-someone-had-told-me – I would have liked to have seen this at the beginning of the course. (see Figure 10.4)

Figure 10.3. Screen capture of 'If only someone had told me'

CASE STUDIES

From the outset we were aware that alongside the events-based content gathering, we would need to commission students for some of the more substantial material

153

generation. We worked in collaboration with various student services and university stakeholders to create live briefs that gave students the opportunity to represent information visually in a way that made sense to them, thus integrating project collaborations that crossed boundaries and supported 'genuine forms of stakeholder engagement' (Ryan & Tilbury, 2013, p. 24). These projects were an attempt to demystify some of the more challenging aspects of studying and living independently such as understanding the complicated visa process, joining a doctor's surgery and getting to grips with the language of the art, design and media industry. Our aim is to make accessible processes and hidden pedagogic practices (Margolis et al., 2001) that students told us were barriers to them settling in and approaching life at university with confidence. An example is the 'Jargon Buster', which describes art and design terminology through visual images, and was created by students from the graphic and illustration course at Camberwell.

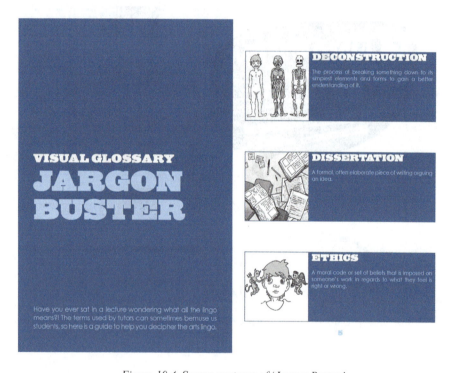

Figure 10.4. Screen captures of 'Jargon Buster'

Commissioning students in this way provides invaluable opportunities to embed *Commonplace* within course curricula and establish it as a source of 'live projects'. As a teaching institution focused on practice-based learning, we embody pedagogic flexibility to prepare students for a creative industry that is ever changing, highly competitive and located across global contexts. UAL has a history of embedding

COMMONPLACE

industry projects within the curriculum; these real-world scenarios give students experience with future employees and experts in the field. Whilst these are invaluable 'ins' to the industry, they can also be selective opportunities open to just a few students. In contrast, *Commonplace's* more open approach to whole-course involvement liberates students from a hierarchical system that can privilege some students whose aesthetic sensibilities conform to those of the tutors.

One example of such a project is 'People and Places', co-written with the BA (Hons) Illustration second-year course team at Camberwell and pitched as a two-week project to illustrate a favourite place in London to share with new students in term 1. Whilst 'People and Places' is assessed as part of a larger unit within the course, not all projects are included within summative assessment. This raises questions around flexible pedagogies in reality; how do we join up innovative and informal types of learning with the formality of assessment and quality processes that dominate contemporary HE?

The 'Student Guide to…' is an annual illustrated guide to the area around Elephant and Castle in London and is a collaboration between UAL's Language Centre, *Commonplace*, and Illustration and Visual Media students at London College of Communication. The brief requires students to illustrate places to eat and socialise around the college site and is created for the more than 400 international students who attend the six-week language summer school each year. The project was

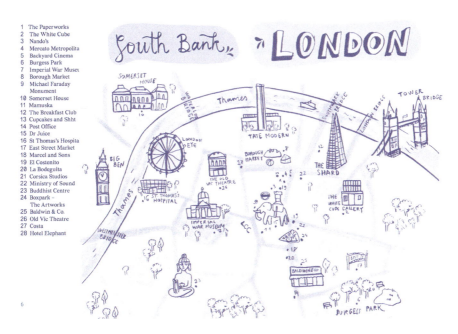

Figure 10.5. Page from 'Student Guide to Elephant & Castle 2017'

155

commissioned in response to student feedback revealing that many were reluctant to explore the area; some were even uneasy and unprepared for the college's urban location. The guide aims to offer a friendly 'in' to parts of London that are likely to be new and possibly daunting for students recently arrived in the UK. Often the students producing the guide are themselves from outside the UK; by sharing their experiences of a new city with communities who may have similar needs, we capitalise on concepts of social learning (Ryan & Tilbury, 2013). This is most clearly articulated by the fact that the 'Student Guide to…' is used as a core learning resource in the first weeks of the course. Its student creators negotiate the territory between informal learning spaces – outside but connected to the curriculum – to influence directly what knowledge is shared with new students to help orientate them to London.

Figure 10.6. Screen capture of 'Cai eats London' article

In addition to established course collaboration projects like these, we have tried different ways to engage individual students in longer-term contributions. An example of this is the 'Departure Lounge', created in response to a frequently articulated student anxiety about what life beyond university would be like. It is easy to find stories of UAL alumni who have been highly successful in the creative sector; these are inspiring reminders that our students go on to work in industry-leading roles and institutions. However, they seldom describe the highly competitive route and often-lengthy timeframes that lead to this success. To shed light on this often forgotten part of the HE journey, we commissioned alumni to write in real-time about life post graduation for the first six months after university. These twice-monthly articles offer insight into the trials, challenges and successes of establishing oneself as a creative practitioner in an increasingly competitive and saturated industry. Our intention is that hearing these stories might reassure others who might be nervous about life post graduation and provide a more realistic and human narrative to what can be a daunting time in a student's life.

In keeping an open, online student community platform active, populated and vibrant, we faced a number of challenges, some of which, such as user engagement, content gathering and promotion, are ongoing. Tackling these issues have prompted the team to contemplate how to future-proof *Commonplace* in order to maintain a sustainable and viable, fit-for-purpose resource for prospective and continuing students at UAL.

SUSTAINING THE ONLINE COMMUNITY

The Human Touch

There are certain (ideal) scenarios and conditions which can greatly support creating a successful online student resource. Allowing the coordinator and web developer time to work almost exclusively on the project for a year permitted us to realise much of the activity described in this chapter and formed firm foundations for *Commonplace* to grow and establish itself in the University eco-system. We also established *Commonplace* 'champions' in the first year, students who were keen to write for *Commonplace*, promote it and be involved in events and activities. We collectively agreed a working plan and 'payment' contract – including number of posts per student, content themes and payment with online vouchers. We also employed a student administrator to manage social media communications and basic technical issues as they arose. These roles underline our commitment to democratic principles of ownership and participation, 'connecting students and educators in collaborative effort to recreate the intellectual commons' (Ryan & Tilbury, 2013, p. 16). Since launching *Commonplace* we have had various iterations of these roles but also periods when none of these were in place. What happens when key staff and student roles are absent from the mix?

There has been a drop in visits to *Commonplace* since its intensive launch year with fewer unmediated article contributions. Whilst not unique for an almost entirely user-generated website, it poses a continual challenge to sustain content and interest when time and competing role demands mean the team are no longer able to oversee the project on a day-to-day basis. We maintain that *Commonplace* can only function as a community if people get involved in it and it is evident that without human care and attention, these online spaces can suffer from their own form of isolation and exclusion. This alludes to what Selwyn (2014) describes as 'the disembodied and dematerialized forms of technology-based education [...] said to involve the experiencing of education on less intimate grounds' (p. 134).

This critique of technology as an ideological salve for the challenges of twenty-first century education offers alternative food for thought and reminds us that whilst online platforms can be successful spaces for students to get to know their community, they rarely entirely replace the human need for face-to-face interaction.

Despite this drop in activity, our CMS means that *Commonplace* functions without our intensive intervention. Students use the 'Swap Shop' and browse the site, but we know that without dedicated people engaging with students, this does not translate into increased content articles. As can be seen in Figure 10.7, a steep rise in page views occurred between its launch in 2011 and October 2013, a period that coincides with the initial, intensive phase of development by the project team. However, there is also a striking drop in activity after this period until July 2017, when the team moved away from regular maintenance and coordination of the site. We put these changes in activity down to the impact a strong team identity can have in encouraging students to contribute. Additionally, advocacy from teaching staff, university departments and official internal and external communications can play a significant and positive role in this process. What is noteworthy is the consistently positive peaks between July and September each year, reminding us that students continue to search for and access support sites like *Commonplace* in the run up to starting (or returning to) university. Yet the question remains, how do we continue to develop *Commonplace* under differing constraints and competing internal agendas?

As a university, UAL has come a long way in understanding the complexity and diversity of our students' needs and experiences. All of our six colleges have some form of online, pre-arrival and transition programme activities and so *Commonplace* sits alongside a much wider suite of resources than when it launched in 2011. One such resource is *Academic Support Online* (ASO), as described elsewhere in this collection, and we make sure *Commonplace* links to it and vice versa. This is undoubtedly positive progress and as the only student-led and generated website we remain uniquely placed to encourage student collaboration, sharing advice across the six colleges.

At the time of writing, we are reviewing *Commonplace* to consider how to maximise its potential going forward, drawing on some of the processes and collaborations that have been successful. This includes working closely with several new student-centred initiatives to bring students more meaningfully into the

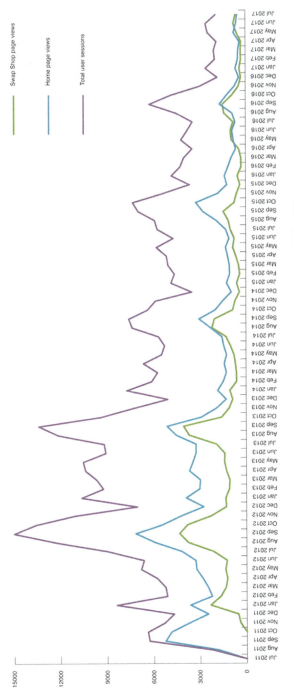

Figure 10.7. User sessions and unique page views 2011–2017

life and governance of the University, and to build on the authentic learning and empowerment that *Commonplace* embodies (Ryan & Tilbury, 2013). We continue course team discussions to embed *Commonplace* projects into the curriculum so that students' work can be included in their portfolio of assessed work. These plans arguably require revisiting how *Commonplace* is resourced while continuing to work towards the project being entirely student-led in the near future. Furthermore, by strategically embedding *Commonplace* within assessed student work, we will move more realistically towards this goal.

CONCLUSION

In this chapter we have discussed the journey, methods, processes and challenges of creating a student-led, user-generated web platform that aims to support belonging and community building at Europe's largest creative arts and media university. We have considered current educational challenges that have precipitated a sector focus on supporting students to have a more informed and engaged experience at university in an attempt to mitigate against the cultural and academic shock that can have significant impact on attrition rates, especially for those from WP and first in family backgrounds.

Our method, to co-create *Commonplace* with students from the very outset and embed projects within and outside the curriculum, embodies Ryan and Tilbury's (2013) notion of social learning. Such an approach encourages learning interactions, collaborations and connections beyond the confines of the classroom. This underpinning ethos has established *Commonplace* as a trusted and friendly student platform. However, we have also identified the challenges that brokering such projects and maintaining engagement with our intended audience can present, especially given time constraints, competing avenues of information, and saturation of the digital and social arena.

Finally, we would like to close by offering some brief recommendations for those considering creating a co-produced student-led platform:

- work early and flexibly with students to shape its content, ethos and direction. Leaving their input to the consultation and user-testing phase will look (and be) disingenuous;
- engage students in fun and quick feedback activities to identify material and resources they want and need;
- build a student project team to manage communications, events and strategy;
- be open and flexible about timelines and be responsive to institutional course cycles and priorities;
- build good relationships early with course teams and departments as they will become your advocates;
- identify channels of communication to promote and disseminate the site;

- connect your project to university strategies and get backing from senior management to secure it is a sustainable, resourced and valued project.

REFERENCES

Blythman, M., Orr, S., & Blair, B. (2007). *Critiquing the crit*. Retrieved from www.adm.heacademy.ac.uk/projects/adm-hea-projects/learning-and-teaching-projects/critiquing-the-crit/

Bourdieu, P., & Passeron, J.-C. (1977). *Reproduction in education, society and culture*. Sage.

Broughan, C., & Hunt, L. (2012). Inclusive Teaching. In D. Chalmers & L. Hunt (Eds.), *University teaching in focus* (pp. 182–198). Routledge.

Burke, P-J., & McManus, J. (2009). *Art for a few: Exclusion and misrecognition in art and design higher education admissions*. NALN Research Report. Retrieved from https://www.heacademy.ac.uk/system/files/naln_art_for_a_few.pdf

Chemers, M. M., Hu, L., & Garcia, B. F. (2001). Academic self-efficacy and first year college performance and adjustment. *Journal of Educational Psychology, 93*, 55–64.

Clay, S. (2010). *Camberwell inclusive induction staff handbook* (Unpublished). University of the Arts, London.

Dazed Media. (n.d.). *Dazed*. Retrieved from http://www.dazeddigital.com

DeAndrea, D., Ellison, N, B., LaRose, R., Steinfield, C., & Fiore, A. (2012). Serious social media: On the use of social media for improving students' adjustment to college. *Internet and Higher Education, 15*, 15–23.

Department for Education (DfE). (2016). *Widening participation in higher education: 2016 report*. Retrieved from https://www.gov.uk/government/statistics/widening-participation-in-higher-education-2016

Freire, P. (1970). *Pedagogy of the oppressed*. Penguin.

Havergal, C. (2016, March 23). Rise in UK university dropout rate 'disappointing'. *Times Higher Education*. Retrieved from https://www.timeshighereducation.com/news/rise-uk-university-dropout-rate-disappointing

Higher Education Statistics Agency (HESA). (2014/2015). *Undergraduate Student numbers 2014/2015*. Retrieved from https://www.hesa.ac.uk/data-and-analysis/students

Higher Education Statistics Agency (HESA). (2015/2016) *UK performance indicators 2015/2016: Non-continuation rates*. Retrieved from https://www.hesa.ac.uk/data-and-analysis/performance-indicators/non-continuation

Hughes, G., & Smail, O. (2015). Which aspects of university life are most and least helpful in the transition to HE? A qualitative snapshot of student perceptions. *Journal of Further and Higher Education, 39*(4), 466–480.

Kear, K., Chetwynd, F., & Jefferis, H. (2014). Social presence in online learning communities: The role of personal profiles. *Research in Learning Technology, 22*. Retrieved from http://oro.open.ac.uk/40771/1/19710-131591-1-PB.pdf

Lea, M., & Street, B. V. (1998). Student writing and staff feedback in higher education: An academic literacies approach. *Studies in Higher Education, 23*(2), 157–72.

Margolis, E., Soldatenko, M., Acker, S., & Gair, M. (2001). Peekaboo: Hiding and outing the curriculum. In E. Margolis (Ed.), *The hidden curriculum in higher education* (pp. 1–20). Routledge.

Ryan, A., & Tilbury, D. (2013). *Flexible pedagogies: New pedagogical ideas*. HEA.

Sanders, E., & Stappers, P.-J. (2008). Co-creation and the new landscapes of design. *CoDesign, 4*(1), 5–18.

Selwyn, N. (2014). *Distrusting educational technology: Critical questions for changing times*. Routledge.

Yorke, M. (2000). Smoothing the transition into higher education: What can be learned from student non-completion. *Journal of Institutional Research, 9*(1), 35–47.

CHRIS DENNIS, STUART ABBOTT AND ROB SELL

11. FLEXIBILITY, SOCIALISATION AND THE USE OF TWITTER BY A UNIVERSITY LIBRARY

Building Community through Social Media in Co-Curricular Settings

INTRODUCTION

The integration of students into an academic community has for long been recognised as a key ingredient of academic success and student persistence in higher education. In setting out his model of student attrition, Vincent Tinto (1975, 1998) distinguished between academic integration, referring to what can be broadly described as a student's academic development, most commonly measured by performance in assessment, and social integration, the extent to which a student is able to interact successfully with other members of the academic community, whether fellow students or members of teaching staff. Integration, particularly in its academic guise, is developed through socialisation processes. In the field of applied linguistics, a number of studies have highlighted such processes at work in academic writing provision, particularly amongst international students or students with English as a second language (for example, Yang & Badger, 2015); in others, these processes have been related to the spoken word (Morita, 2004). Much of this research has been underpinned by Lave and Wenger's (1991) notion of a community of practice, in which socialisation forms part of the process by which a student works towards membership of an academic community through the development of the knowledge, skills and behaviours associated with academic practice. The learning that takes place within such a community is therefore socially situated and the principal challenge for students is to navigate the culture of which the knowledge, skills and behaviours just mentioned form only a part. Indeed, academic socialisation is not something that is applied only in academic contexts; it is a broader process, one that is aimed at inducting new students into both the academic and social elements of university culture (Schofield & Sackville, 2010). It is with its broader applicability in mind that Neil Gordon (2014), in his study of flexibility and technology-enhanced learning, recognised the potential value of flexible pedagogies in offering new ways of achieving academic socialisation. Gordon suggested that Web 2.0 technologies allowed for 'flexible socialisation'; social media, for example, encourages peer interaction amongst students, which allows them to participate in a much larger learning community. The value of these interactions lies in their potential to contribute to the development of flexibility as an attribute of learners, as defined by Ryan and Tilbury (2013) as 'the ability of people to think, act, live and work differently in complex, uncertain and changeable scenarios' (p. 4). In this way, social media can act as a powerful tool for the development of learning experiences geared towards the objective of moulding graduates capable of exercising a meaningful impact on 'a fluid and unstable world' (Barnett, 2014, p. 24). Indeed, it embodies the essence of flexible pedagogies.

This chapter explores Gordon's notion of 'flexible socialisation' from a co-curricular perspective, that of a university library. In particular, it considers the use of social media – specifically, Twitter – in the context of a university library as a means of developing a learning community centred on the library itself. Social media plays an ambiguous role in the world of library services, particularly at a university level: whereas, on the one hand, there is widespread acceptance of its value in engaging users in conversations about library services, on the other, there is uncertainty over how to exploit it fully in pursuing this and related objectives. Much of the ambiguity comes from the way that the role of the academic librarian itself has changed in recent years, as technology has transformed library operations, the services it offers, and, not least, the expectations of users (Chelliah et al., 2015; Ndungu, 2016). The potential impact of the library in contributing to the creation of such a learning community, and therefore its role in cultivating integration amongst students and student persistence, is not always fully appreciated by students or members of academic staff. However, as this case study will show, effective use of social media by library staff can not only position the library closer to the heart of the student learning experience; it can also contribute towards the cultivation of a supportive environment in which this learning might take place, and this in itself has been identified as a key factor in successful academic integration (Severiens & Wolff, 2008).

PARTICIPATION, CONVERSATION AND THE EVOLUTION OF LIBRARY 3.0

Little attention has been given explicitly to the role of flexibility in shaping library-related activities, particularly in a learning and teaching context. A notable exception is the study conducted at Warwick University on the impact of a flexible study space, 'Teaching Grid', located physically in the library, on pedagogical practice. Its purpose is to promote experimental use of space by allowing practitioners to implement imaginative and innovative approaches to teaching that incorporate technological elements; as such, the authors' investigation was concerned with the impact of this project on teaching staff rather than the function of the library *per se* (King et al., 2015). Within library science, aspects of flexibility have crept into key discussions on the nature of service development and the shifting professional identity of the academic librarian. The notion of the 'participatory library' and the importance of engaging users in meaningful conversation about library services in order to drive forward their development provide two notable examples of these discussions; both are linked to a broader debate about the need for libraries – whether operating in public or academic contexts – to create and develop communities of interest, specifically through the use of social media, to foster better conversations between library staff and its users.

The emergence of ideas like participation, conversation and communities of interest as drivers behind more recent developments in service delivery may be attributed to a shift in the expectations of library users towards a demand for immediate access to resources and a more active role in shaping the services offered (Kwanya, Stilwell, & Underwood, 2015). This shift in expectations has been underpinned by fairly rapid advances in technology over the last decade or so, which have dramatically impacted upon library operations, as well as the work of librarians, particularly in terms of facilitating access to a much broader range of digital resources. The focus of these discussions on service delivery and the profession of the librarian is reflected in the attempt to define the different stages in the evolution of the modern library through the application of the 'point oh' labels. To a great extent, these labels allow the integration of technology into library services to be charted whilst, at the same time, illuminating patterns of behaviour amongst library users that affect the way the role of librarian is performed. Within this scheme, Library 0.0 may be described as a traditional library: a collection of books managed by a librarian (Schultz, 2006, as cited in Kwanya, Stilwell, & Underwood, 2015). As its name suggests, Library 1.0 incorporates Web 1.0 technologies in its services (i.e. static websites without interactive features), but its conception of the role of librarian, to act as a custodian of resources, is little different to its precursor's (Maness, 2006; Kwanya, Stilwell, & Underwood, 2015). The emergence of Library 2.0, dated to approximately 2005, dependent, as its name suggests, on the use of Web 2.0 technologies, represented a more significant evolutionary step (Kwanya, Stilwell, & Underwood, 2015; Farkas, 2005). As Jack Maness (2006) has put it, Library 2.0 reflected 'the application of interactive, collaborative, and multi-media web-based technologies to web-based library services and collections' (para. 7). The implications of the concept of Library 2.0, particularly on the professional identity of the librarian, has been significant: whereas in previous iterations of the 'point oh' model the librarian acted as custodian (or even guardian) of information, in Library 2.0, the role is reconceptualised as guide or advisor (Nguyen, 2012). There is a pressing need for librarians to become more adept at employing a variety of web-based media in order to engage more effectively with users who expect to play a greater participatory role in the development of library services. Emphasis is placed on this participation and the interactions – online and face-to-face – involved. A further label, Library 3.0, has come to the fore more recently, in which Library 2.0 is advanced through consideration of the impact of the inter-personal exchanges that occur through Web 2.0 technologies on library services (Kwanya, Stilwell, & Underwood, 2015). In essence, therefore, Library 3.0, even more so than Library 2.0, is beginning to embrace the notion of developing flexibility as an attribute in learners and, in this case, professional librarians.

Several aspects of these discussions are particularly relevant to the way that libraries have created online communities of interest by engaging with social media.

The first is the idea of 'information as conversation', a concept that privileges dialogue between a library's staff and its users as the principal influence on library services, something that has become much easier with the advent of social media (Lankes et al., 2007). Such interactions, as the concept has been applied in this context, have been interpreted through the lens of Gordon Pask's (1976) 'conversation theory', a model built on the notion that it is through conversation that learning might occur. When applied more broadly, beyond just the interactions affecting library services, this idea takes on much greater significance, for the conversations as a whole contribute towards the formation of an environment conducive to the creation and subsequent sharing of knowledge in which an online community of interest might flourish. Such a community is built through participation, and in this sense is intimately related to the second aspect of these discussions that is pertinent to a library's use of social media, the participatory library. This concept refers to a library that is developed through user-driven change; its functions and services are moulded by the interactions taking place within its community of interest (Lankes & Silverstein, 2006; Casey & Savatinuk, 2006). Consequently, participation in such a community requires users 'to think [...] and work differently in complex, uncertain and changeable scenarios' (Ryan & Tilbury, 2013, p. 4); in other words, actively engaging in conversations with others within a community of this type serves to test and enhance a learner's personal flexibility.

The third aspect of these discussions that is worthy of note is the impact of these ideas on the role of the librarian, for the shift in the nature of the responsibilities attached to it reflect the potential of involvement in such communities for developing flexibility as an attribute. Librarians, as a profession, have had to evolve in response to the incorporation of technology into library services, just as libraries, as institutions, have had to adapt to these changes. As a result of the participatory nature of the interactions discussed above, it has become increasingly difficult to distinguish clearly between the librarian and library user, particularly in relation to their respective influence on the development of library services (Nguyen, 2012). Furthermore, much greater emphasis has been placed on librarians acting as advisors in relation to accessing information rather than as its guardians (Lankes et al., 2007). The ability to adapt to this shift in user expectation demonstrates the potential of these interactions in stimulating the growth of personal flexibility even within staff.

THE USE OF SOCIAL MEDIA IN LIBRARY CONTEXTS

The potential of social media to act as a medium through which library services might be developed – based on some of the thematic principles outlined above – has been fairly widely acknowledged by professionals working in academic libraries (Chu & Du, 2013). Twitter, in particular, has been identified as a powerful tool through which library users might be engaged, particularly in relation to community building, because of its potential to facilitate two-way communication (Gunton & Davies, 2012). Studies have shown that it can be particularly effective in developing a quirky and appealing image for the library and its environment, which may then serve to better engage its users (King, 2012, as cited in Smeaton & Davis, 2014).

Yet its value is largely conceived in terms of its suitably for marketing resources and services (Bradley, 2015). In a survey of the use of social media by libraries, promotional activities provided the three most popular uses, with its application in learning and teaching contexts representing 'a much lower priority' (Taylor & Francis, 2014, p. 9). Young and Rossmann (2015) prefaced their own work on the use of social media in building communities by noting that discussion around its use within library science has not really moved on from a focus on what they describe as 'broadcast-driven' (p. 21) notifications related to marketing and promotion. One possible reason for this is that library staff, in their enthusiasm for embracing social media, have treated the integration of platforms like Twitter into library activities as a goal in itself, rather than as an aid in helping to achieve broader objectives (Smeaton & Davis, 2014). Indeed, it may be argued that a pre-occupation with a perceived need to engage in the use of social media has adversely affected understanding of the participatory nature of many aspects of a modern library's online presence. Thus its potential for facilitating socialisation is yet to be fully realised.

TWEETING AT BUTE LIBRARY

Context

At the beginning of the academic year 2011/2012, staff at Bute Library, one of the constituent libraries within the university library service (ULS) at Cardiff University (CU), began a social media initiative. The decision to engage with social media was driven by several factors: first, structural changes within ULS, in which a sharper focus was placed on the delivery of customer service, created a strategic context more conducive to its implementation; second, other departments at CU, as well as some of the academic schools, were beginning to use social media; and third, engagement with social media by libraries at other universities was beginning to demonstrate its potential as a way of communicating with users. A pilot project was undertaken, in which a blog was set up, using a CU-maintained platform, to publicise news relating to Bute Library. This proved popular and it was on the basis of its success that the decision to utilise Twitter was taken. Twitter was the obvious choice of platform at this point, given that it had a virtual monopoly on micro-blogging in 2011. Indeed, in contrast to the situation today, alternatives were few and far between; the library has since used Facebook, Instagram, Vine and a WordPress blog, in addition to Twitter, and the ULS also maintains a YouTube channel, linked to the other platforms. It should be stated that the evolution of the library's use of platforms was not carefully planned in advance; rather, platforms were adopted in response to fluctuations in the popularity of each one, and it is acknowledged that not all of the platforms have fulfilled the potential originally envisaged (e.g. Vine).

Only part of the content posted on Twitter is co-ordinated. Tweets relating to library-related marketing or promotional activities fall under the purview of a ULS working group with a specific responsibility for this aspect of the service. For example, this group would determine a schedule for marketing tweets to be posted during semester time; such tweets would relate to the online library induction at the start of term, for example, or study skills resources (e.g. referencing guides) during assessment periods. The library is asked to post and comment upon information and activities related more broadly to the institution. For this reason, staff monitor quite closely the tweets emanating from other CU-related accounts. Most other content is not planned in this way; it is reactionary, responding to queries or comments tweeted by users as and when they occur. Indeed, Twitter is deliberately used in this spontaneous way, for it is the belief of those who curate the account that the platform is at its most powerful when exchanges are immediate and unfiltered. Taking inspiration from the approach exemplified by several public libraries, notably Cardiff Central, Orkney and Hull, an attempt was made to create a warm, friendly and appealing image for the library through the use of a humorous and engaging tone. Determining which members of staff would be responsible for curating the account was based simply on expressions of interest. Some staff were initially concerned about the possibility of opening up the library to anonymous criticism, but this apprehension was quickly overcome once it was seen not to occur. Academic librarians are instrumental in determining content for scheduled marketing tweets and flagging up aspects of the service, such as drop-in sessions or new books to promote, but responsibility for curating the account has generally fallen to front-line staff.

When the initiative was started it was hoped that Twitter would provide a bridge between the library and its students, in particular; it was conceived as a creative and easily accessible way of showcasing library services and resources. From only a cursory review of the growth of the account, it can be seen to have fulfilled this objective: by 2018, it had just under 3,000 followers and it is estimated that approximately 80% of these Twitterers were students. The account continues to receive much positive feedback. In 2015, it was shortlisted for an 'Enriching Student Life' award at CU and it was longlisted again in the following year. Such recognition illustrates its role in helping to position Bute Library at the centre of university life for the students it serves; the library may be described as something of a 'community hub', one that brings students together, as well as nurturing broader relationships between learners and teachers, and learners and library professionals. This theme may be seen in an analysis of a selection of tweets taken from the account's feed and will be discussed in more detail below.

Investigation

For the purpose of this study, 1,176 tweets, posted between 1 September 2015 and 30 June 2016, have been analysed. The rationale behind the selection of this period may be divided into three points. First, it is roughly coterminous with the academic year at CU, for by including the whole of the months of September and June, induction and examination periods fall within the scope of the study. Second, by the start of this period, the Twitter account was already well established, having acquired 1,968 followers; it therefore follows that the curators had some experience in tweeting and that the approach to using the account would reflect what insights had been gained into good practice. Third, a broad range of data had been collated for this period, which included information about the use of the account before and after it that provided a valuable contextual setting. The analysis proceeded out of a straightforward premise: since the popularity of @ButeLibrary grew significantly during this period, with 369 followers added by the end of June 2016, it follows that the approach taken to tweeting, as evidenced in the tweets, would illuminate some of features and techniques of effective engagement with Twitter by staff in the context provided by an academic library and its activities. It would also provide a suitable moment to assess the extent and nature of the library's impact on the socialisation of students.

The first stage of the analysis involved reading all of the 1,176 tweets in order to identify suitable categories into which the tweets might be sorted. This process was also informed by aspects of a literature review, which had included previous analyses of the use of social media in library settings. Four categories emerged: 'marketing', 'operational', 'engagement', and 'interactions'. Tweets that were categorised as 'marketing' were discrete (i.e. not a retweet or part of an extended conversation) attempts at promoting university-wide initiatives. For example, a series of tweets was posted in November 2015 aimed at promoting security and safety awareness, particularly in relation to bicycles:

> Cyclists! If you're using cycle racks across campus, please get a proper D-lock. They're £17.50 from Security Centre https://t.co/FZABrcPRlA. (4 November 2015)

Another popular subject in this category were study skills sessions and resources:

> For writing tips, research guides, referencing and more – our study skills collection is here for you #CUStudySkills https://t.co/YE6KggYNPz. (10 February 2016)

The second category, 'operational', included tweets related to library operations and facilities. These were mainly concerned with opening hours, particularly as each term ended, and reminders to renew books:

> Don't forget we close at 5pm; will not re-open until 8.45am on Tuesday (when normal term-time hours resume). Get here now for Easter reads! (24 March 2016)

But it would also include any tweets related to the activities of Bute Library itself, as opposed to university-wide campaigns. For example, during exam periods, refreshments were provided outside the library, which were advertised via Twitter:

#RevisionAid Alert! Tea and coffee is being served now! (1st floor landing) https://t.co/VZVsyneHJp (12 January 2016)

The second category, 'engagement', included those spontaneous tweets referred to above, which were often delivered in a witty or engaging way. The range of topics commented upon were broad: David Bowie's birthday appeared on 8 January 2016, with followers invited to complete an online questionnaire (not hosted by the library) about the singer, and several football-themed tweets were posted in June 2016, as Wales performed well at Euro 2016. Even the disturbance caused by a concert taking place in a local park was used to entertain the account's followers:

We're sorry but we're not currently able to control the noise levels of Craig David soundchecking in the park over the road. (3 June 2016)

Some of these tweets blended operational content with current affairs. On the visit of HM Queen Elizabeth II to Cardiff on 7 June 2016, @ButeLibrary tweeted:

If The Queen needs a group study room this afternoon we're quite quiet at the moment. Board markers available from the desk. #CURoyalVisit

And during the exam period in January 2016, students were reminded to be respectful towards others via the following tweet:

If you need us to silence [not in a Sopranos way] people just ask us, or use the text line (see posters). It's our calling and we enjoy it. (7 January 2016)

The final category, 'interactions', was used broadly to categorise tweets that referred to other users. Thus, it included mainly retweets or replies to other Twitter users, many of whom were followers of the account. As noted below, this category provided a huge number of tweets; its importance in building an online community around the activities of the library cannot therefore be underestimated.

Results

Table 11.1 provides a summary of the data collected. It is immediately noticeable that the percentage of operational tweets spikes at the end of terms, in December and June, when opening hours change and students are more likely to be reminded about loan status alterations. Marketing and operational tweets rarely account for more than 30% of the total number of tweets posted (in May and June). When these parts of the data are set aside, a clearer impression of the impact of the engagement and, in particular, the interactive tweets on the popularity of the account may be gained. In Table 11.2, these results may be seen next to the number of new followers.

Allowances may be made for some of the more unusual elements of the data. The number of new followers attracted in September, for example, may be attributed to the atmosphere at the start of term, when students are trying to get their bearings and the level of engagement may be higher. The much smaller number of new followers

Table 11.1. Division of tweets by category

Month	Total number of tweets	Marketing	Operational	Engagement	Interactive
Sep 15	113	6 (5.31%)	17 (15.04%)	32 (28.32%)	58 (51.33%)
Oct 15	87	2 (2.30%)	13 (14.94%)	15 (17.24%)	57 (65.52%)
Nov 15	142	4 (2.82%)	16 (11.27%)	29 (20.42%)	93 (65.49%)
Dec 15	88	2 (2.27%)	21 (23.86%)	13 (14.77%)	52 (59.09%)
Jan 16	113	4 (3.54%)	9 (7.97%)	33 (29.20%)	67 (59.29%)
Feb 16	141	6 (4.26%)	10 (7.09%)	27 (19.15%)	98 (69.50%)
Mar 16	131	4 (3.05%)	21 (16.03%)	33 (25.19%)	73 (55.73%)
Apr 16	158	10 (6.33%)	24 (15.19%)	34 (21.52%)	90 (56.96%)
May 16	127	18 (14.17%)	20 (15.75%)	33 (25.98%)	56 (44.10%)
Jun 16	75	3 (4.00%)	22 (29.33%)	20 (26.67%)	30 (40.00%)

Table 11.2. Percentage of total tweets in the 'Engagement' and 'Interactive' categories next to number of new followers

Month	Total number of tweets	Engagement	Interactive	Number of new followers
Sep 15	113	28.32%	51.33%	78
Oct 15	87	17.24%	65.52%	53
Nov 15	142	20.42%	65.49%	57
Dec 15	88	14.77%	59.09%	62
Jan 16	113	29.20%	59.29%	41
Feb 16	141	19.15%	69.50%	39
Mar 16	131	25.19%	55.73%	37
Apr 16	158	21.52%	56.96%	29
May 16	127	25.98%	44.10%	42
Jun 16	75	26.67%	40.00%	9

in June, which is significantly lower than in any of the other months, is reflective of the drop in student numbers on campus at that time of the year, when many of the examinations have finished. Similarly, the statistics for April coincided with the Easter vacation period, when many students – particularly at levels 4 and 5 – return home and are therefore most likely less engaged with academic affairs. The most striking feature of this data is in the consistency of the number of new followers, particularly between September and January, a period that also coincides with a fairly high (approximately 60%+) proportion of 'interactive' tweets.

Twitter Analytics provide additional data on the popularity of the account, displayed in Table 11.3, which may help to contextualise its development.

Table 11.3. 'Engagement' and 'Interactive' tweets set against tweet impressions, profile visits, mentions and number of new followers

Month	Engagement	Interactive	Tweet impressions (000s)	Profile visits	Mentions	Number of new followers
Sep 15	28.32%	51.33%	72.4	7015	50	78
Oct 15	17.24%	65.52%	51.3	5585	78	53
Nov 15	20.42%	65.49%	76.7	8848	91	57
Dec 15	14.77%	59.09%	101	7298	110	62
Jan 16	29.20%	59.29%	75.8	7454	75	41
Feb 16	19.15%	69.50%	67.6	7757	84	39
Mar 16	25.19%	55.73%	90.6	7644	55	37
Apr 16	21.52%	56.96%	93.5	8003	139	29
May 16	25.98%	44.10%	139	9686	122	42
Jun 16	26.67%	40.00%	30.1	2292	34	9

One point worthy of note here is that the number of tweet impressions (the number of times a tweet has been seen by other users) increases as the percentage of engagement tweets goes up (when it is above 25%), but that the amount of tweet impressions is not necessarily reflected in either the number of profile visits or the number of new followers. Exceptions are provided by December, when the number of impressions reached 101,000, but the percentage of engagement tweets stood at only 14.77, and June, which, as already noted, is exceptional in any case.

To help provide some clarity in relation to the Twitter Analytics data, Table 11.4 offers a breakdown of the most popular tweets posted in December 2015, ranked according to number of impressions. Tweet impressions are useful for this purpose,

Table 11.4. December 2015: most popular tweets, ranked according to total number of tweet impressions

	Tweets	Category	Impressions	Tweet engagements	Retweets
1	Many, many copies of the Daily Mail were harmed in the making of this year's Christmas tree https://t.co/mkg7YtVx4K	E	37,561	2,289	226
2	Here lies lost property man (Sept 2015–Dec 2015) ~forgotten but not gone~ https://t.co/zdDMFkP16L	O	8,028	484	26
3	Still time to pick up last minute gifts at the desk – a classic biro (6p), lined paper (65p) or how about an individual plastic wallet (7p)?	O	3,005	58	11
4	A reminder of our xmas opening hours for those sticking around after the 11th. #feetup #alldaykerplunk https://t.co/wDAO4D8dZV	O	2,584	32	3
5	Library Service xmas jumper day today, in aid of Alzheimer's Research UK (@ARUKnews)! Can someone pls open a window? https://t.co/uU4ZkKIzSC	M	2,400	186	4
6	Good news from today! We now have laptops for you to borrow in the library: https://t.co/Fr5MW0xqKb https://t.co/LlOIv5uR5Y	O	2,055	39	4
7	Use two plastic wallets to wrap a present for a relative who hates surprises (14p)	O	1,819	39	4
8	Internet outages have been affecting most UK education institutions this morning (including us). See @jiscmi for the latest.	O	1,490	52	1
9	Then we're all off down Pryzm for j bombs	E	1,453	76	2
10	A ray of hope for all withdrawn stock. d.Wellington NZ (@wcl_library) 198? ât' Going strong here, 2015. #booksdontdie https://t.co/FPSQPAA5tg	I	1,366	110	1

since they can be used to highlight which tweets are most effective according to their respective 'reach'. The table also includes the figures for tweet engagements – the number of times a user has interacted with the tweet, including retweeting it – and, more specifically, the number of retweets it has received.

As can be seen from these statistics, although operational tweets accounted for only 23.86% of the total number of tweets posted in December, six out of the ten most popular tweets, ranked according to number of mentions, were included in this category. Only one tweet each from the marketing and interactive categories appear in the list, in fifth and tenth positions respectively, and two carry the engagement label. Of these two, the Christmas tree tweet, ranked first, achieved an astonishingly large number of impressions, almost 30,000 more than the tweet in second place. Its popularity may be a reflection of its topical nature – it coincided with Christmas, after all, and it was in vogue at the time for libraries to build trees out of books or stock items – and the reference to the *Daily Mail*, a newspaper that often courts attention. The number of retweets clearly corresponds to the number of impressions, but the level of engagement with a tweet does not appear to reflect either impressions or retweets. The tenth placed tweet, for example, had 110 engagements; only three other tweets had more. The most striking aspect of the top two tweets – which had considerably more impressions than the others in the list – is their humour. The first tweet plays on the reputation of the *Daily Mail*, particularly amongst students, and the second includes a picture of a figure made up of items of lost property. Although it is difficult to do well, humour is important as a way of engaging twitterers, regardless of the nature of the information being disseminated.

DISCUSSION

It is abundantly clear from the thousands of Tweet impressions highlighted above and the number of followers @ButeLibrary has accrued since its inception (2,337 by the end of June 2016 and almost 3,000 at the time of writing) that social media provides a particularly powerful means of building an online community in a co-curricular setting. From the perspective of the library and the role of social media in promoting services and marketing resources, Twitter offers an effective way of broadcasting information. This is supported by the popularity of operational tweets in the top ten list from December 2015, a surprising feature of the data collected that demonstrates the extent to which followers expected and appreciated this type of information to be disseminated via the Twitter account. It also, in a sense, points to the impact of the Twitter account on the socialisation process; although many of the operational tweets are rather mundane, they do clearly familiarise students with the way the library works whilst introducing or reminding users of its broader function in learning by promoting certain services, such as journal subscriptions (e.g. Sight & Sound).

Further evidence of its positive effect on integration may be found in several student tweets that highlight the supportive environment offered by the library in which the Twitter account played a key part. Indeed, in these tweets, the library appears as something of a safe haven for students. For example, one student expressed fears about incurring financial debt but noted that coming to Bute Library relieved the tension (10 November 2015). Another posted a picture of the view of the park from the library with the caption 'Why I love Bute Library' (23 September 2015). A third captured their fondness for the library by tweeting, 'it's a Bute Library kind of day' (10 March 2016). One student, via Instagram, a sister account created on 3

December 2014, on finishing the academic year, lamented, 'it's time to leave this place (Bute Library) for a while' (1 June 2016). Some students felt so comfortable in the surrounding of the library that they even fell asleep! Such affective responses to the library suggest that these students were experiencing a greater sense of social integration, as it was conceived by Tinto (1975).

The heavy bias on 'interaction' in the categorisation of tweets points to role of the library's presence on Twitter in contributing to the development of an environment conducive to the exchange of knowledge between the library and its followers. It is by engaging in these exchanges that students can build a sense of connectedness with a wider learning community. In addition, such 'interaction' tweets provide direct evidence of the vitality of concepts like 'information as conversation' and the 'participatory library', arguably the defining features of Library 2.0 (and 3.0), in building this community. However, whilst these ideas have been discussed in the literature in relation to their impact on the development of library services, the results discussed here suggest that value to the library of conversation with users should be interpreted far more broadly as conversation about almost anything; in other words, Twitter interactions should not be restricted to operational matters. A good example of the role of a seemingly trivial aspect of library life in generating a significant number of Twitter interactions is provided by the Bute Library ducks. Cathays Park, opposite Bute Library, is home to a small family of ducks who are often found sitting outside the library. Consequently, the ducks appear, from time to time, in @ButeLibrary's tweets, and on occasion, students are invited to tweet their photos of the ducks. These tweets, particularly when there is an associated hashtag, have the effect of stimulating interaction between the library and its users, thereby sustaining and even potentially growing the community.

In all of the individual tweets mentioned so far, there is an initiative and willingness to engage and participate in library life on the part of the students or followers that may be directly related to the development of flexibility as an attribute of learners. It is in this independence of thought and proactivity on the part of students that the way in which social media can facilitate socialisation is revealed.

More might have been achieved in terms of locating the library and its activities in a more central position within the learning experience. This may be attributed to the lack of explicit focus on academic activities, which, in turn, is most likely the result of the not having more direct involvement from those members of staff engaged in learning and teaching on behalf of the library. This is not a criticism, for the account, after all, was conceived as a means of engaging users more effectively; but its impact may be developed further by blending in some tweets related to, for example, information literacy sessions. In the period studied, only a few tweets promoting specific journal subscriptions (e.g. Sight & Sound) can be described as academic related.

Finally, it is important to offer some recommendations on the use of Twitter by an academic library to create an online community of interest that can positively impact upon the student learning experience. First, it is vital that those members of staff curating the account prioritise interaction with users. This interaction does not necessarily have to be focused on operational matters or 'serious' content. It can be about almost anything; the significance of each interaction lies in the activity of exchange that takes place, for it is in such exchanges that socialisation is built and students might begin to feel more integrated in the wider learning community. Second, tweets do not necessarily have to be entertaining or humorous; operational tweets proved quite popular, and users clearly expect to receive such information broadcasted through the Twitter account. Marketing tweets – those related to resources or university-wide initiatives – tend to be less popular; but marketing tweets focused on facilities within the library, such as study rooms, did have an impact. Finally, humour forms an important element of successful tweeting – note, the popularity of the *Daily Mail* tweet – but it should not be seen as essential. Hitting the right humorous note is not easy and it can clearly go disastrously wrong if it is misjudged. Of greater importance is the ability to pick up on trivia, incidental details of life in the library that are unique to it, such as the Bute Library ducks. Tweeting about such things not only projects a warm and welcoming image for the library; it also provides the glue with which the online community is bound together. In this way, it is through the interactions that such tweets provoke that the mechanics of building an online community in a co-curricula setting, with a view to fostering the flexible socialisation, can be understood.

REFERENCES

Barnett, R. (2014). *Conditions of flexibility: Securing a more responsive higher education system*. HEA.

Bradley, P. (2015). *Social media for creative libraries*. Facet.

Casey, M., & Savastinuk, L. (2006). Library 2.0: Service for the next generation library. *Library Journal, 131*(14), 40–44.

Chelliah, J., Sood, S., & Scholfield, S. (2015). Realising the strategic value of RFID in academic libraries: A case study of the University of Technology Sydney. *The Australian Library Journal, 64*(2), 113–127.

Chu, K.-W., & Du, H. (2013). Social networking tools for academic libraries. *Journal of Librarianship and Information Science, 45*(1), 64–75.

Farkas, M. (2005). *Web/Library 2.0 backlash*. Retrieved from http://meredith.wolfwater.com/wordpress/index.php/2005/12/01/weblibrary-20-backlash

Gunton, L., & Davis, K. (2012). Beyond broadcasting: Customer service, community and information experience in the Twittersphere. *Reference Services Review, 40*(2), 224–227.

HESA. (n.d.). *Students and graduates*. Retrieved from https://www.hesa.ac.uk/data-and-analysis/students

King, E., Joy, M., Foss, J., Sinclair, J., & Sitthiworachart, J. (2015). Exploring the impact of a flexible, technology-enhanced teaching space on pedagogy. *Innovations in Education and Teaching International, 52*(5), 522–535.

Knight, S. (2009). *Effective practice in a digital age*. Jisc.

Kwanya, T., Stilwell, C., & Underwood, P. G. (2015). *Library 3.0: Intelligent libraries and apomediation*. Chandos.

Lankes, R., & Silverstein, J. (2006). *Participatory networks: The library as conversation*. American Library Association.

Lankes, R., Silverstein, J., & Nicholson, S. (2007). Participatory networks: The library as conversation. *Information Technology and Libraries, 26*(4), 17–33.

Lave, J., & Wenger, E. (1991). *Situated learning: Legitimate peripheral participation*. Cambridge University Press.

Maness, J. (2006). Library 2.0 theory: Web 2.0 and its implications for libraries. *Webology, 3*(2), Article 25. Retrieved from http://www.webology.org/2006/v3n2/a25.html

Morita, N. (2004). Negotiating participation and identity in second language academic communities. *TESOL Quarterly, 38*(4), 573–603.

Ndungu, M. W. (2016). Promotion of electronic resources in academic libraries on a minimal budget. *International Information & Library Review, 48*(2), 94–101.

Nguyen, L., Partridge, H., & Edwards, S. (2012). Towards an understanding of the participatory library. *Library Hi Tech, 30*(2), 335–346.

Pask, G. (1976). *Conversation theory: Applications in education and epistemology*. Elsevier.

Ryan, A., & Tilbury, D. (2013). *Flexible pedagogies: New pedagogical ideas*. HEA.

Schofield, M., & Sackville, A. (2010). Student induction/orientation: from event to entitlement. *The International Journal of Learning, 17*(7), 113–124.

Severiens, S., & Wolff, R. (2008). A comparison of ethnic minority and majority students: Social and academic integration, and quality of learning. *Studies in Higher Education, 33*(3), 253–266.

Smeaton, K., & Davis, K. (2014). Using social media to create a participatory library service: An Australian study. *Library and Information Research, 38*(117), 54–76.

Taylor & Francis. (2014). *Use of social media by the library: Current practices and future opportunities*. Retrieved from http://www.tandf.co.uk/journals/access/white-paper-social-media.pdf

Tinto, V. (1975). Dropout from higher education: A theoretical synthesis of recent research. *Review of Educational Research, 45*(1), 89–125.

Tinto, V. (1998). Colleges as communities: Taking research on student persistence seriously. *The Review of Higher Education, 21*(2), 167–177.

Yang, Y., & Badger, R. (2015). How IELTS preparation courses support students: IELTS and academic socialisation. *Journal of Further and Higher Education, 39*(4), 438–465.

Young, S., & Rossman, D. (2015). Building library community through social media. *Information Technology and Libraries, 34*(1), 20–37.

KAREN FOLEY

12. THE STUDENT HUB LIVE

The Open University's Solution to Facilitating the Development of an Academic Community in Distance Learning through Collaborative Online Interaction

INTRODUCTION

Higher education providers are increasingly concerned with 'community'; it is seen as something important that might enhance the student experience which can – and some propose *should* – be facilitated by higher education (HE) providers (Coates, 2005). Like consciousness is to the body, community can be seen as the ghost in the curriculum machine, the qualia that makes a meaningful and individual contribution to the experience of HE. It is also, however, difficult to measure or correlate with success. It has been widely recognised that integration into an academic community is a key part of student success. The Higher Education Academy report, *What works? Student Retention and Success*, building on a previous report of the same name that identified the importance of belonging and engagement to retention and success, noted that

> [i]t is the human side of higher education that comes first – finding friends, feeling confident and above all feeling part of your course of study and the institution. (Thomas et al., 2012, p. 8)

In addition, this report outlines some of the factors that contribute to the improvement of retention and progression. Most of these involve some kind of relationship building; for example, staff-student relationships, group-based learning, personal tutoring, peer relationships/cohort identity, and belonging to a particular part of the university, all of which are seen to have a positive impact on student success (Thomas et al., 2012). Many of these are facilitated in face-to-face settings and are led by the HE provider, but community is about more than simply bringing together a group of people in a physical setting. Coates (2005), a leading figure in the development of student engagement research (which preceded the focus on community and belonging), argued that community building is more complex than this, with universities also bearing responsibility for developing broader frameworks that can help structure such communities.

If community is predominantly understood in terms of physical and behavioural interactions on a university campus, the question about how it can be facilitated in distance learning environments is important for institutions like the Open University (OU) and the increasing number of traditional 'brick and mortar' universities offering a distance learning option. For the OU, *Student Hub Live* (SHL) delivers online, live and interactive events to facilitate academic community activities in co-curricular settings. This essay outlines how the OU, with its diverse population of students, is using new technologies to scaffold and develop students' sense of belonging through SHL. Furthermore, within the context of community building, it explores how students are able to consider and adjust their future intentions, put their developing academic identities into practice, normalise issues and measure up against their peers, and ultimately gain a sense of empowerment to help them on their HE journey. SHL uses innovative learning designs with existing technologies, such as livestream and the online tutorial platform (Adobe Connect), to provide opportunities for students to interact and connect with the institution, a range of staff, and other students.

NEW TECHNOLOGIES IN HIGHER EDUCATION

Innovations in online learning and social media platforms are increasingly being used to bring learners together, with many involving the grouping of learners, thereby offering the potential for communities to develop. The most notable uses of new technologies in HE settings are livestream[1] services which enable virtual access to live events, such as lectures, making them accessible to remote audiences in real time and to watch at a later date. Whilst this technology can provide a means to access events remotely, it is most commonly used as a delivery channel offering an often inferior alternative to engage with the live event. Many universities are using livestream in this way; however, the OU have taken an approach that places pedagogy before technology, using a learning design that offers an opportunity to provide equity in the experience of all participants, since each learner can access SHL remotely.

In 2014, when SHL was conceptualised, the OU were already using livestream to broadcast their public lectures. These campus-based lectures, which were not linked to the curriculum, were held in a lecture theatre with an audience, but livestream technology meant that they could be viewed remotely in real time and were also available to watch after the event. They were broadcast using an interface called *Stadium* that had been developed by the OU's Knowledge Media Institute, which combined a livestream feed with an avenue for question submissions. Remote participants could pose questions that were included at the end of the lecture with other questions from the audience. The didactic nature of the lecture format lends itself well to the broadcast approach, and the inclusion, as a postscript, of a question and answer session with the audience enables those engaging in real time to contribute. Using this format also makes it easier for the content to be recorded and viewed again. The OU's commitment to inclusivity and distance provision has meant that the streaming of lectures and events has become more prevalent in both student learning and staff development in recent years. Another reason for the growth in popularity of this medium is that it provides greater flexibility in terms of when and where potential audience members might engage with the content.

However, participation in a livestream lecture can deliver a different experience for those who participate in person when compared to those who attend online; in addition, those watching after the event will have another different experience. Remote participation when there is live attendance can be experienced in different ways. While it can be empowering to connect remotely when other options are not possible, the live audience is often viewed as the primary audience. On the other hand, live participation requires more focus and decorum; remote attendance can be undertaken even when the participant is engaged in other activities. Remote participants can also remain anonymous, although they can be listed or named in some instances, such as in webinars. Catching up on the event after it has taken place can be a comparatively passive experience because there are very few opportunities for participants to engage.

In addition to livestream, Webinars are also used in the sector to facilitate real time interaction. This category of live event sometimes includes video; unlike lectures, however, which have live and, if streamed, remote audiences, webinars have an entirely online audience. In a similar way to the live stream of lectures, Webinars often have a didactic approach, while allowing opportunities for questions and discussion from participants; they might also include planned content, either in audio or video format, or both. In many instances, the names of participants are shown; it is therefore possible to gauge attendance figures and in some cases the amount of interaction. Webinars have increased in popularity in recent years, particularly in business-related contexts, but the comparatively high cost of buying into the technology (specifically webinar platform services) can be prohibitive.

Live interaction may also be achieved through synchronous broadcasting platforms. Although some providers charge for premium versions of their service, it is possible to communicate with a remote audience via free-to-use platforms, with little preparation. Social networking sites, such as Google Hangouts, Skype, Twitter, Facebook live and Periscope, are increasingly being applied in educational contexts (Tess, 2013). These sites not only have potential as a means of building a community; educators are also using them to extend the reach of higher education and heighten its accessibility, mirroring their purpose in non-academic settings. The use of forums as a facilitator of peer supported learning within MOOCS provides a good example of this practice (Kellogg, Booth, & Oliver, 2014).

Technology is also used for collaborative learning. There are platforms designed specifically for use in HE as a portal through which students can access material and communicate with each other as well as with tutors on forums, and to teach in real time (and record sessions for catch up). It is the potential of these platforms for live interaction that is most relevant to the development of an online learning community. At the OU, Blackboard Collaborate and Adobe Connect (which are widely available and can be customised) have been used for tutorial delivery. These platforms provide a versatile virtual classroom in which a PowerPoint presentation or a whiteboard might be used, for example, or audio and video content, chat functions or even screen sharing. Like Webinars, the participants' names are shown, and all participants access the event online (Karabulut & Correia, 2008).

These technologies ultimately serve to facilitate remote participation, but the position of the remote viewer and extent to which they can interact varies considerably according to which platform is being used and the way that the educator scaffolds the activity. When considering the potential impact of these technologies on the creation and development of an online community, it is important to think about how they position and present the remote audience. There can be comfort in anonymity (in livestream) and in choosing how and when to interact, but there is also the option to leave or disengage without the consequences that would be present in a physical community setting. This flexibility in terms of engagement poses a question about the extent to which an online audience can be considered a community, a point that will be returned to later.

SHL uses technology, in particular livestream and online tutorial platforms, to facilitate the development of an online community, but the context in which these technologies are being used is distinctive. SHL addresses specific issues related to the unique student population of the OU, many of whom are mature students with varied levels of educational experience, and, in particular, the challenges of open access, part-time study.

THE OU: A UNIQUE OFFERING WITH A DIVERSE STUDENT POPULATION

Flexibility and the use of online technology are fundamental components of distance, online learning. The OU is the UK's largest provider of distance education, offering a range of studying opportunities to a diverse student population. Many are mature students, with a high proportion having protected characteristics; others face challenges, such as being a carer or having a disability, and so many choose to study part-time. The OU's Open Access policy appeals to students who may not have traditional educational qualifications. The diversity of the student population and the mode of distance education present certain challenges for the educator attempting to build a sense of community amongst a specific cohort. Indeed, many students choose to study with the OU because the potential to learn at a distance or in isolation is appealing.

Since its inception in 1970, the OU have developed a variety of effective distance learning designs. In addition to the books and multimedia material available on the virtual learning environment, students routinely have access to optional online tutorials and forums. It is possible for students to succeed without interacting with others, and the fact that interaction is optional can be a challenge in facilitating the development of a community, especially if only a few students in a cohort want to connect with others. Whilst there are some compulsory collaborative activities, often involving contributing to an asynchronous forum, unlike students at other universities who routinely converse with their peers before lectures or who may have spontaneous conversations with their tutors, OU students may not be in regular contact with other students or their tutors. That said, OU students do receive personalised, written feedback on assignments from tutors. Completing and passing the relevant assessment on an individual basis is what is required of a student to gain a qualification.

When faced with challenges that impact on their study, some students may withdraw, interpreting the challenge as a failure on their part, and their inability to continue as something personal and unusual (Butcher, 2015). Yet many students face similar issues and it is ironic that students can acquire a sense of relief when they gain an understanding that they are not alone or unusual by engaging with each other. For this reason, facilitating the development of an academic community is important for students who want to engage actively with other students; it is also important to provide students with an option to reach out for peer support, if they choose to do so.

In addition to tutorials and forums, the OU has Facebook and Twitter accounts, and the OU Students Association (OUSA) arrange physical and virtual events for students. There are also many student-initiated social media groups that are not moderated by the OU. Aside from the face-to-face tutorials and OUSA-facilitated meet ups, all other interaction takes place online. The number of student-initiated groups on social media demonstrates the value of community to some students, but there is an important distinction between groups that have a contribution from the HE provider and those that are set up by students to exist outside that formal education parameter. It will be suggested later that the community linked to SHL has an institutional association and therefore differs from informal networks hosted on social media platforms.

Thus, it is in response to the challenges associated with the diversity of the OU's student population, the distance education mode of learning, and the ease with which a student might limit their interactions with others that SHL has attempted to provide appropriate scaffolding on which a community of learners might be built. As will be discussed below, it is having a positive impact on the student learning experience.

'STUDENT HUB LIVE': THE OU'S ONLINE INTERACTIVE PLATFORM TO DEVELOP COMMUNITY

Launched in 2014, SHL is a livestreamed, interactive online event, originally designed as a platform to welcome new OU students to the academic community. SHL was developed following the 'Student Connections Online' conference, an idea generated within the faculty of Social Science (Foley & Fribbance, 2018). Using a 'breakfast TV' style approach to create engaging content that is both informative and fun, SHL is an extra-curricular and optional event. It was shortlisted in the Times Higher Education awards 2016 in the 'best support for students' category, and also won the UALL (2018) award for innovation.

SHL aims to create a dialogue between students and academics: there is an interaction between the remote audience and the studio panel (guest participants) and whilst sessions (usually a 25-minute discussion, quiz or demonstration) have planned parameters, the contribution from the audience influences the direction of the session. For example, within question and answer sessions, there could be a debate, or it could be that advice is discussed and shared about good study skills. The audience engage exclusively online either live or through the catch-up service. The live audience access the interface via Stadium Live (developed by the OU's Knowledge Media Institute) which showcases the livestream video with a text-based chat function and a range of interactive widgets (voting tools). In addition to the studio panel there is a presenter who anchors the discussion between guest participants and a 'hot desk' moderated by two students or members of staff. The purpose of the hot desk is to collate the points from the live chat discussion with emails, photographs, social media and widget data, and to include these in the live discussion. These points are fed into the live discussion creating a fluid dialogue between onscreen and off-screen participants.

Another important point that differentiates SHL from the traditional lecture is the focus on establishing an equal relationship between teachers and learners, or in this case guest participants in the livestreamed discussion, and participants who are accessing the event online. Guest participants are encouraged to establish the best way to communicate ideas without PowerPoint or scripts, and delivery is visual and interactive. Examples include: Maths and Logic challenges that are demonstrated using children's toys; 'what do a Pina-colada and an Open Degree have in common', which included chemistry experiments to demonstrate how combinations can involve additional components that are greater than the sum of their parts; and the interactive 'Wheel of Ologies Quiz', a multiple-choice general knowledge quiz that would be typical at a Freshers evening, where the online audience compete against two teams in the studio.

There is a catch-up service through which live sessions can be accessed, and there is also a SHL YouTube channel. Despite the lack of interactivity in these formats, the relevance of the content and the value of the remote participants' voice sends a reassuring message to students who want to be part of a community. Over 30,000 students access the studenthublive.open.ac.uk website annually, a figure that is increasing year on year. There have also been over 55,000 views per year on the YouTube channel, demonstrating its considerable reach.

SHL therefore creates engaging events that benefit both the guest participants and the viewers. Another important benefit of the format is that the time spent creating material is significantly less than the amount of time required to make the video content that forms part of the OU learning materials within modules, although these do have different functions. Many members of staff view participation in SHL as part of their ongoing media training, as a unique opportunity to connect with students who are remote in many ways. The creation of time sensitive audio and video assets (which is a core part of the learning design at the OU) can be challenging for a number of reasons, such as the long shelf life of the average module and the limited budget and production resource for peripheral or time sensitive additions. The informal set up of SHL, with a presenter who anchors the session, manages the contribution from the remote audience, and interviews guests, enables academics to engage students with their full attention and without too much preparation time. The format also offers an agile way of responding to time sensitive events, such as the UK referendum in 2016 and Brexit, which have been the focus of several SHL events. The interactive nature of the format can also be used as an opportunity for the institution to consult with students and capture feedback. This has been done in a number of ways by members of staff and even the Vice-Chancellor.

The value of participation, from a student perspective, is neatly summed up by this quote from a student on a general student consultation forum:

> I appreciate the [...] *Student Hub Live*. Although it takes a light hearted approach at times, I really appreciate what SHL is trying to achieve. It is the only place where I can *see and hear* OU staff talking about their work in a meaningful way and giving people a chance to ask questions on the spot. SHL is a great opportunity to allay anxieties about study and provide interesting information about courses. Although it cannot replace the human contact of tutors and tutor groups – I can't emphasize enough how important real, human contact is to learning – but it does provide a window on the OU and OU study which is not otherwise available.

This spontaneous comment expresses the phenomenological value of these events that are difficult to ascertain using other sources of data such as surveys and viewing figures. The richness of the media appears to transcend the audio and visual nature of the livestream and the live nature of discussion, while pointing to the human contact that is so meaningful and difficult to access in distance learning settings.

ONLINE TOGETHER: EMOTIONALLY CONNECTED OR VIRTUALLY CONGREGATED?

As already suggested, communities have different rules of engagement when they are virtual; in addition, the extent to which meaningful relationships can be achieved online, in particular over short time periods, has been questioned. Rheingold (1993, p. 10) defines virtual communities as

> social aggregations that emerge from the Net when enough people carry on those public discussions long enough, with sufficient human feeling, to form webs of personal relationships in cyberspace.

Definitions of community commonly refer to aspects such as belonging and inclusion as defining characteristics of a collective group (e.g. Ashwin & McVitty, 2014). Belonging to a community (even if this is not specifically an academic community) has been identified as a protective factor in student retention, particularly in distance learning environments (Thomas, 2015).

Having conducted a thematic analysis of the chat logs from SHL events, it is possible to see evidence of an emergent online community made up of participants interacting with each over a six-month period. It appears that longevity is important in the creation of community, although it is evident that new members feel connected without necessarily experiencing first hand the interaction over time. The majority of the regular contributors welcomed new participants in a friendly and supportive way. In return, participants, overall, engaged respectfully, creating a nurturing and receptive space, using text-based communication as seen in this example:

> Participant 19: Hello all *hides behind a mug of tea and grins*
> Participant 20 "Hi [Participant 19] you're back!,
> Hotdesk: @[participant 19] Hi *waves back* ☺

Even when there were miscommunications and misunderstandings between participants (e.g. students taking each other's text chat more literally than was intended), in general, participants were able to negotiate relationships and clarify meanings. The online environment and lack of non-verbal cues can limit communication; for example, there have been several students who have disclosed their status as being on the autistic spectrum, which has impacted upon their communication with others at times, particularly when the content was not meant literally. Another example of the potential for miscommunication was when one student specifically asked another student a lot of questions in the context of a general discussion within a group. When the student asked their peer why they were being asked so many questions, in reply, the other student affirmed that it was being done out of interest and that no offence had been intended.

The analysis of the chat logs showed that the function of the chat varied depending on the participant and the nature of the discussion to which it belonged; it was used to resolve technical issues, to share advice, to relate to others, and to ask questions. A sense of community emerged out of these interactions; in-jokes and shared meanings were important in scaffolding these exchanges and empowering participants to engage. For students who have disabilities or are unable to access tutorials (such as international students), the online community created through the platform appeared to offer a unique and highly valued enhancement to the virtual learning experience, as one student explained:

> [Participant 90], unfortunately some people don't actually have the option to do anything but online. In addition to [Participant 28]'s demographics she mentioned, disabled people who might not be physically able to attend a F2F (face-to-face) tutorial.

Thus, there is evidence that SHL has established an academic community, in Rheingold's terms (2017), partly because of the frequency of SHL events, but also because of the evidence that students valued the interaction, came back for more, and included new participants in the discussion.

FUTURE-FACING EDUCATION: THE IMPORTANCE OF FLEXIBILITY ASSOCIATED WITH OPEN ACCESS AND PART-TIME LEARNING

Flexibility is important in shaping the course of study for many students, particularly OU students, most of whom have other commitments alongside study. The Open Degree, one of the OU's largest degree programmes, is unique in offering students choice and variety in the modules that they study. SHL is used to promote the idea of flexibility and demonstrate how this can be applied to OU students. However, while students can receive information about their options through other means, such as a prospectus, at SHL they can meet some of the academics who develop the material first hand. The real benefit in terms of community is the opportunity to explore some of the alternative study scenarios first hand. This can be achieved by listening to other students discussing their experiences as either participants in the studio, or from those participating online.

Flexibility is particularly relevant in part-time learning environments where a degree takes on average six years to complete. Many aspects of student's personal circumstances may change in that time, and for students who have no previous qualifications, there are often challenges in developing the academic skills that are necessary in order to attain a successful outcome at the end of the course. So when anyone can study with the OU due to the open access policy, and when many students study part-time, combining study with other responsibilities, it is easy to see why some students do not progress in the same way as undergraduates in more traditional educational settings. It is therefore important that there are opportunities to explore preferred scenarios when things are not going to plan. SHL also addresses these aspects with timely events that facilitate discussions amongst participants whilst also demonstrating alternatives. An example of this is the resit and resubmissions session of SHL, which has the aim of normalising and removing some of the stigma of failure and enabling students to progress appropriately. This is particularly important in terms of the social mission of the OU, since students are encouraged to succeed when they experience challenges or when they might not have had positive prior experiences of education.

There are other sessions in the SHL programmes that focus on providing spaces to rethink goals, study strategies, and approaches to studying. Each session, students are empowered to share ideas with each other, thereby drawing on the experiences of their peers. While information is available in other formats, the SHL platform and the sense of community it provides appears valuable for some students. Although the OU excels at providing material for students to work through in order to develop behaviours that will enable them to be academically successful, there appears to be something beyond the teaching element of the experience that attracts people to live sessions. This may be defined in humanistic terms, an effect of the SHL to provide the context in which students might be reassured by one another and encouraged to persevere regardless of the perceived challenges met along the way. This element is aptly captured in the feedback of one participant, who wrote:

> It's nice to be active online [...] because it can get lonely studying alone. and it's helpful to bounce ideas so you're not feeling like you're a mile out of where your meant to be.

EMPOWERING STUDENTS: IT'S OK TO BE YOU!

The nature of part-time learning, particularly for mature students, presents challenges to the notion of adopting an identity as a student (Thomas, 2012). It is therefore important to facilitate some space to 'be' a student. Traditionally at the OU, 'being a student' happens at tutorials (whether they are online or face-to-face), but these focus predominantly on the curriculum, or more frequently on assessment, leaving little opportunity for networking or social interaction. At an OU focus group convened in 2017, students talked about the benefits of tutorials; one reported that the most useful thing that happened as a result of attending was the ten minutes beforehand when a student was sharing how they had overcome one particular problem. Offering another perspective to the issue had been very useful. However, when there are time pressures, it can be difficult for a tutor to facilitate this kind of shared experience in a tutorial. In distance learning environments it can also be difficult to raise these questions on forums; an atmosphere needs to be created in which students feel confident and safe to articulate problematic issues. One participant wrote:

> I know that I find processing oral information difficult. I don't know how other people experience it, but I know that I find it hard. I haven't experienced anything but my own experience, but I do know what I experience.

Although the opportunity for a student to develop agency and competence through holistic academic development should be an important aspiration within the student learning experience, it can be difficult to secure a space for this, practically and psychologically, in a distance learning environment. In this sense, the potential to interact with others in a learning community takes on greater significance, offering opportunities for academic identities to be rehearsed and negotiated. The online environment may create a physical barrier between participants, but students still possess the agency to control the level and nature of their interaction within the community. In the absence of physical interaction, textual elements and language take on greater significance; the use of text can actually prompt more interaction, in that it is free from the inhibitions that surround face-to-face contact. Hence, a supportive online space might work towards the greater integration of students into an academic community in a distance-learning environment.

BEING SOCIAL AND BEING A LEARNER DOES NOT EQUAL SOCIAL LEARNING

Although there is a transfer of knowledge at SHL events, participation is unique from other learning formats, such as lectures, videos or reading because of the dialogue that occurs during the dissemination of information in which participants can talk to each other while also asking questions and raising their own thoughts with the panel of speakers. Despite this, unlike in traditional HE settings, distance-learning students are ultimately learning alone, often in a physical sense. While concepts such as Vygotsky's (1978) zone of proximal development, and Lave and Wenger's (1991) communities of practice, can provide useful frameworks for exploring the process of engaging with others, Mezirow's (1991) ideas around transformative learning offer some insight into the combination of acquiring knowledge and sharing experiences as part of the learning process which informed the learning design of SHL.

However, as Hercheui (2011) proposes, there are several motivating factors that can have a positive impact on virtual learning communities. Two of these are evident at SHL events: the transfer of knowledge, in particular regarding experiences as an online learner, which acts a key motivating factor for participation, and emotional support. At first glance, it would be easy to position SHL as a social learning construct because of its social and academic nature, as well as the fact that it is co-curricular. Social learning, as a pedagogic approach, has many positive effects, but implementing it in a distance-learning environment represents a significant challenge, because its effectiveness may be seen to hinge on the face-to-face contact and associated rapport that occurs in physical teaching settings. In distance learning environments, although students may be learning together, they are often fundamentally learning alone. Whilst participants may engage in dialogue during a SHL event, the social nature of the interaction is more closely aligned with notions of community than traditional conceptions of social learning, as outlined by Wenger (1998). It would be more appropriate to align the active learning experiences associated with SHL to Vygotsky's ideas around social development theory (Pardjono, 2016) concerning social environments preceding learning and interaction acting as a means of scaffolding learning. The socially constructed nature of this interaction also means that the community slowly develops reference points and a personality that builds up over time, seen in the chat log analysis with the way that in-jokes are used to engage newcomers and enable them to feel included.

CONCLUSION: ACADEMIC COMMUNITIES AND STUDENT ENGAGEMENT

The main aim of SHL is to establish and develop an academic community. As SHL demonstrates, in relation to promoting belonging and inclusion, there is benefit in providing students with an opportunity to become actively involved in a community. It can provide an option to connect, even if there is no desire to do so frequently, and through externalising issues in more visible ways, students are able to identify with others, even if only passively on occasion, and recognise that many of the issues they are experiencing are 'normal'.

This emotional connection provides a less tangible aspect of student engagement, but it is increasingly being considered within the sector as part of the measurement of student engagement. A key focus in student engagement research and literature emphasises quantitative measurements of engagement such as attendance and success (Trowler, 2010). Indeed, emotional engagement and belonging is perhaps the most challenging aspect to measure. These subjective and individual measures are difficult to quantify, although just because they are difficult to measure does not mean that they should not form part of the student engagement strategy. Proponents of qualitative measurements of student engagement may suggest there is a value in these aspects of experience; at an emotional level, engagement has associations with context and free choice, and if students are not engaged, they may choose to withdraw. The emotional or qualitative aspects of engagement can be seen (even if they are not measured) in the level of activity and depth of involvement of students who are in traditional brick universities, but this emotional relationship can be more difficult to measure in a distance learning environment. SHL offers a platform for emotional engagement, both in terms of academic discussions where students can agree with each other or the academic speaker, and also where they can share concerns, offer advice and support each other.

Whilst all of these aspects are important in the establishment of an online learning community, it is important to recognise that there is some tension between the development of such a community and the needs of the institution to evaluate the effectiveness of SHL. The evaluation of SHL presents an ongoing challenge. The viewing figures and volume of traffic to the website and events are easy to measure, but the impact of participation in this community on student learning is much more difficult to ascertain. A series of interviews has been carried out with a small number of participants as part of the author's doctoral research, and there are plans to measure the progression of students who engage with the events. However, as with so many measures of engagement, it is difficult to know with any certainty whether those who engage in these extracurricular activities are more likely to succeed, or in what ways participation impacts upon success. However, it is evident from reading the chat logs that there is huge value for students in these events:

- Came here for some inspiration
- That is really good, just lovely to meet others.
- This is really cool as I never tried this type of thing before anywhere else
- I wish I could meet other students […] SHL is like the only thing I do with the rest of you guys

Having a space to talk to others and share anxieties can empower students by allowing them to feel that their experiences are both real and valid. Recognising students who return to SHL events and then encourage others provides a very powerful reminder of the potential for online communities to support – in an effective and meaningful way – the academic development of OU students.

NOTE

[1] Live streaming, or streaming, is a term that refers to the real-time, simultaneous online streaming and recording of media. Livestream is a technology but is also a product or service from the company *Livestream*. There are therefore paid for and free versions of the service. Live streaming is a feature of many social media platforms, such as Facebook (Facebook Live) and Twitter (Periscope). The feature is often accompanied by some form of online chat. *Livestream* is one of the most popular commercial services. Whilst the *Student Hub Live* uses both livestream technology and the service from *Livestream*, the term is used interchangeably.

REFERENCES

Ashwin, P., & McVitty, D. (2015). The meanings of student engagement: Implications for policies and practices. In A. Curaj, L. Matei, R. Pricopie, J. Salmi, & P. Scott (Eds.), *The European higher education area* (pp. 343–359). Springer.

Butcher, J. (2015). *'Shoe-horned and side-lined'? Challenges for part-time learners in the new HE landscape*. HEA.

Coates, H. (2005). The value of student engagement for higher education quality assurance. *Quality in Higher Education, 11*(1), 25–36.

Foley, K., & Fribbance, I. (2018). Student connections: Livestreaming and creating community via an annual student conference. In J. Baxter, G. Callaghan, & J. McAvoy (Eds.), *Creativity and critique in online learning* (pp. 169–189). Palgrave Macmillan.

Hercheui, M. D. (2011). A literature review of virtual communities: The relevance of understanding the influence of institutions on online collectives. *Information, Communication & Society, 14*(1), 1–23.

Karabulut, A., & Correia, A. (2008). Skype, Elluminate, Adobe Connect, Ivisit: A comparison of web-based video conferencing systems for learning and teaching. *Society for Information Technology & Teacher Education International Conference*, 481–484.

Kellogg, S., Booth, S., & Oliver, K. (2014). A social network perspective on peer supported learning in MOOCs for educators. *International Review of Research in Open and Distance Learning, 15*(5), 263–289.

Lave, J., & Wenger, E. (1991). *Situated learning: Legitimate peripheral participation*. Cambridge University Press.

Mezirow, J. (1991). *Transformative dimensions of adult learning*. Jossey-Bass.

Pardjono, P. (2016). Active learning: The Dewey, Piaget, Vygotsky, and constructivist theory perspectives. *Jurnal Ilmu Pendidikan, 9*(3), 163–178.

Rheingold, H. (1993). *The virtual community: Homesteading on the electronic frontier*. Addison-Wesley.

Tess, P. (2013). The role of social media in higher education classes (real and virtual): A literature review. *Computers in Human Behavior, 29*(5), A60–A68.

Thomas, L. (2012). *Building student engagement and belonging in higher education at a time of change. Final report from the What Works? Student Retention & Success programme*. HEA.

Thomas, L., Hill, M., O'Mahony, J., & Yorke, M. (2017). *Supporting student success: Strategies for institutional change. What works? Student Retention & Success programme*. HEA.

Trowler, V. (2010). *Student engagement literature review*. HEA.

Vygotsky, L. S. (1978). *Mind in society: The development of higher psychological processes*. Harvard University Press.

Wenger, E. (1998). *Communities of practice: Learning, meaning, and identity*. Cambridge University Press.

CHRIS DENNIS

13. ONLINE LEARNING COMMUNITIES AND FLEXIBILITY IN LEARNING

The essays collected here have explored the potential of technology – specifically, online learning communities – for delivering flexibility in learning. Technology is sometimes treated as something of a panacea for the problems associated with creating a flexible learning experience. Whilst the essays included here have highlighted the potential value of online learning communities in allowing for greater flexibility in the delivery of learning, they have sought to look beyond the practicalities of delivery, along the lines suggested by the HEA work stream (and Ryan and Tilbury's (2013) contribution in particular), to the role of technology in promoting innovation in pedagogy, with a view to developing flexibility as an attribute of both educators and learners. In other words, it is acknowledged here that whilst flexibility is concerned with giving learners greater choice over the pace, place and mode of learning, it is, at the same time, about something more than this, the function of universities as 'beacons of social change' (Ryan & Tilbury, 2013, p. 31) and their responsibility to equip learners with the attributes and characteristics needed for them to make an impact on an ever-changing world.

Online learning communities emerge out of these essays as a particularly effective tool for delivering flexibility in the pace, place and mode of learning. In relation to pace, learning will always be constrained by external factors like the academic calendar; but the existence of learning resources hosted in an online environment, which might be accessed whenever it is convenient for the individual learner, means that online learning communities built around such resources can be highly effective in delivering asynchronous learning, as demonstrated by the use of discussion boards, for example, in Leila Griffiths' study of an online academic skills module. Of greater value, however, is the potential for online learning communities to deliver synchronous learning, through the opportunities afforded by the technology used to provide real-time interactions between educators and learners, and learners with each other. A particularly interesting example of this is provided by Karen Foley's discussion of the *Student Hub Live* initiative in which distance learners might actively participate in discussions as they occur. Here, while the pace of learning may be fixed, the place of learning can vary. Another example, on a smaller scale, is the classroom-based initiative discussed by Chris Little and Matthew Street focused on the use of *Mentimeter* to allow simultaneous engagement with an induction task amongst a group of international students. Flexibility in the mode of teaching is an inherent part of any online learning community. It is perhaps at its most effective when the community forms an element of a blended learning approach, as in Sheila Amici-Dargan, Amber Moorcroft and Stephen Rutherford's example of a shadow module sitting next to a curriculum-based counterpart, or even the use of *Mentimeter* discussed above, in which the community of students participating in the activity is online at the point at which interaction with the task is required, whilst being physically present in the classroom at the same time. However, as Sue Bond-Taylor and Ceryl Teleri Davies remind us in their contribution, flexibility in terms of delivery does not necessarily lead to the development of flexibility as an attribute of learners.

As the essays collected here demonstrate, online learning communities are particularly effective as a means of achieving pedagogical innovation and delivering pedagogies that help to nurture the development of flexibility as an attribute of educators and learners. By offering a virtual space in which learning might take place, sometimes in a way that complements face-to-face learning, and by providing this learning with flexibility in terms of pace, place and mode of delivery, online learning communities immediately allow for the creation of a learning experience that extends beyond formal curriculum-based settings. In addition, the interaction that is usually inherent in their functioning has the potential to add a further dimension to learning. Such interaction may be seen in Griffiths' discussion boards, as noted above, or in the online debate activity discussed by Little and Street. In Amici-Dargan, Moorcoft and Rutherford's example, peer interaction is facilitated through an online community based on a shadow module. Interaction within the community is not always limited to educators and learners; in Bond-Taylor and Davies' youth justice project, interaction occurs with the professionals who are involved, as is also the case in Moira McLoughlin and Wendy Sinclair's discussion of student nurses' use of Twitter to develop awareness of standards in professional practice. Online learning communities also promote interaction in co-curricular settings, as demonstrated in the chapters by Graham Barton and Alex Lumley, Siobhan Clay and Paul Tabak, and Chris Dennis, Stuart Abbott and Rob Sell. Indeed, the online environment appears to make it easier for learners, particularly those who are new to higher education, to share prior experiences and thereby engage in peer interaction, as John Butcher and Liz Marr's study of an 'open box' module demonstrates.

The interaction that occurs within an online learning community can have an empowering effect on the learner. This empowerment may take different forms: in the two examples discussed by Little and Street, in the first, involving an online debate amongst postgraduate students, the empowerment occurs through students adopting different roles and gaining different perspectives on key issues as a result; in the second, involving the international students noted above, learner empowerment is driven by the anonymity provided by *Mentimeter*. Another, particularly powerful example is provided by the shadow module discussed by Amici-Dargan, Rutherford and Moorcroft, which is student-led; as they point out, such an initiative leads to a deeper level of learning, thus empowering learners whilst at the same time building on the principles of social and transformative learning. Online learning communities also facilitate learner empowerment through initiatives based on co-creation. The case studies discussed by Sophie Leslie and Nicola Poole each embrace the notion of 'students as partners', with learners acting as the drivers of change, taking ownership of learning, within the context of quality enhancement. In McLoughlin and Sinclair's Twitter example, learners are again collaborating with educators in achieving the aims of the initiative, while in co-curricular settings, at the design stage, learners are informing the development of content in the examples discussed by Barton and Lumley, and Clay and Tabak. Learner empowerment through co-creation is particularly effective in authentic learning scenarios, as discussed, for example, by Sharon Smith and Ruth Hewston in relation to their 'virtual school'. In some of these examples, learning relationships are challenged: students in Amici-Dargan, Rutherford and Moorcroft's shadow module, for instance, take on the role of educators, while in Foley's chapter, the *Student Hub Live* has an equalising effect on the relationship between educator and learner. Learner empowerment can promote inclusivity. In Butcher and Marr's example, this is inherent in the way that their module values the different pre-university learning experiences students bring with them on entering higher education; it may also be seen in a co-curricular setting in Clay and Tabak's *Commonplace* example, the development of which was in part driven by consideration of the greater diversity of the student body. Reflection and self-monitoring practices can also promote learner empowerment, as Smith and Hewston make clear in the 'virtual school', in which learners are encouraged to reflect on their professional practice, and via its associated assessment, part of which is a peer-assessed presentation. Similarly, in Griffiths' online skills module, quizzes work towards the same end.

Co-creation in particular highlights the transformative potential of such pedagogies. As Butcher and Marr note, a link exists between learner empowerment and transformative learning, the application of knowledge and understanding in alternative contexts, since the former promotes learner agency. Thus, in Smith and Hewston's example, the authenticity of the 'virtual school' scenario and its links to professional practice takes the learning beyond simple knowledge acquisition towards competence and agency, as does the interaction of learners with youth justice practitioners in Bond-Taylor and Davies' example. McLoughlin and Sinclair's Twitter initiative looked beyond knowledge acquisition to the development of competencies associated with professional practice, and in a co-curricular setting, Barton and Lumley's *Academic Support Online* was intended to develop learners' decision-making with an eye on their ability to make a positive impact on the world as graduates. The success of Amici-Dargan, Ruthford and Moorcroft's shadow module initiative has contributed to the creation of a cross-institutional, transformative mindset, in which learning is conceived as being 'lifelong', at their university.

As some of the examples discussed here make clear, online learning communities also allow for learning to move beyond disciplines as points of focus. This is apparent in the module discussed by Butcher and Marr, while in a co-curricular setting,

Barton and Lumley demonstrate how conceptual debates within their community might traverse disciplines, a not unexpected outcome given the number and variety of stakeholders involved in the project. In McLoughlin and Sinclair's Twitter example, learners were interacting with other Twitter users who did not belong to their professional field, and such interactions helped to broaden their perspective on issues related to nursing. Learners in Bond-Taylor and Davies' example also experienced the benefits of such an approach by gaining an understanding of the application of theory in real world settings through an appreciation of different perspectives, including those belonging to practitioners working in the field of study.

Several observations can be made about the circumstances in which online learning communities are at their most effective in terms of allowing for pedagogical innovation and the delivery of pedagogies aimed at the development of flexibility as an attribute. The first is that they work well in socialisation contexts aimed at inducting new students into higher education. This is no doubt due to the interaction involved and the inclusivity inherent in their use. Several of the chapters offered here highlight this feature of their use: Butcher and Marr, for example, point to their effectiveness in what might be described as curriculum-based settings, as do Griffiths and the second case study discussed by Little and Street, while Clay and Tabak, and Dennis, Abbott and Sell do so in co-curricular contexts. Indeed, Clay and Tabak conceived of *Commonplace* as an initiative intended to support learners throughout their higher education journey. Foley's *Student Hub Live* provides a particularly good example of how learners might be integrated into an academic community through a co-curricular initiative. As these references demonstrate, the effectiveness of online learning communities in achieving the objectives set out above is not limited to curriculum-based settings. As Dennis, Abbott and Sell demonstrate by discussing a university library, community building is something that should properly involve stakeholders drawn from across an institution's schools, units or departments; indeed, staff in what might be called professional services are almost uniquely placed to bring about an enrichment of the learning experience through the expertise and know-how that characterises their roles.

The essays offered here have highlighted the need for staff to develop flexibility as an attribute, particularly by being responsive to innovations in technology-enhanced learning, for example, and by engaging in a sustained way with professional development in this area. Pedagogical innovation and the delivery of some of the pedagogical ideas discussed here is driven by the willingness of staff to change the way technology is used. As Smith and Hewston note, staff involved in their 'virtual school' were faced with the challenge of moving away from the habit of treating VLEs as document repositories to using them as tools for delivering an enhanced learning experience. Engagement in such initiatives can in itself form part of a professional development plan, as Foley points out in relation to *Student Hub Live*.

Finally, to different extents, the essays in this collection have also highlighted the need for institutional flexibility as a pre-requisite for pedagogical innovation. Several contributors noted the need for buy-in in relation to their initiatives at an institutional level, notably Butcher and Marr, and Smith and Hewston. Barton and Lumley demonstrated the positive impact of such buy-in when it occurs at a strategic level. It is on the relationship between what Barnett (2014) referred to as 'systems flexibility' and pedagogical innovation that future discussion might focus, for if the latter is to be achieved, and if institutions are to develop graduates who are ready to make an impact on an ever-changing world, greater institutional flexibility is clearly necessary.

REFERENCES

Barnett, R. (2014). *Conditions of flexibility*. HEA.
Ryan, A., & Tilbury, D. (2013). *Flexible pedagogies: New pedagogical ideas*. HEA.

INDEX

A

acculturation into HE, 6, 25, 46, 145
anonymity and online spaces, 42–44, 46, 90, 182, 194
authentic learning scenarios, 40, 43, 140, 160, 195

B

Barnett, R., 3, 4, 18, 20, 115, 130, 135, 139, 140, 142, 197

C

challenging hierarchies of power/
 traditional learning, 7
 relationships, 94
collaborative learning, 26, 79, 80, 83, 87, 94, 181
community of practice, 68, 70, 80, 97, 99, 106, 138, 163
co-creation/students as partners, 8, 13, 24, 39, 49, 58, 59, 61, 70, 74, 101, 114, 136, 138, 145, 146, 149, 195
crossing boundaries, 14, 15, 73, 87, 100, 102, 103, 123, 124, 135

D

debate in online learning community, 6, 39, 40–44, 194
decolonising education, 24, 71, 100, 101, 106
digital professionalism, 7, 68, 70, 74

F

flexible socialisation, 45, 163, 164, 176
flexibility
 and assessment, 4, 17, 30, 33, 105,

and distance learning, 97
and learning design, 1, 14
and personalised learning, 141
and widening participation, 5, 19, 20
as an attribute of learners and, 3, 43, 163, 175, 194
educators, 20, 49, 97, 98, 193, 194
definition, 3
in co-curricular settings, 7, 138, 163
pace, place, mode of learning/time, 1, 49, 97, 134, 193, 194
and place, 2, 193, 194
future-facing learning (or education), 6, 7, 14, 16, 50, 71, 72, 100, 101, 104, 187

I

interdisciplinary learning, 15, 39
integration, into an academic community, 163, 164, 179, 188

L

learner autonomy, 5, 12, 149
learner empowerment, 3, 6, 7, 11, 13, 20, 24, 32, 35, 39, 54, 60, 61, 63, 70, 72, 79, 83, 100, 101, 103, 104, 106, 113, 123, 133, 143, 145, 149, 194, 195

P

Problem-Based Learning (PBL), 7, 79, 109, 112, 113

R

reflective practice, 46, 49, 99
role playing, 7, 18, 29, 36, 40, 41, 43

INDEX

Ryan, A., 4, 6, 7, 11, 15, 23, 24, 30, 32, 35, 39, 40, 65, 67–71, 74, 76, 79, 88, 94, 95, 97, 100, 102, 106, 112–116, 119, 123, 124, 130, 133, 135, 160, 163

S

'shadow module', 7, 82, 83, 88, 90–95, 194, 195
social learning, 3, 6–8, 32, 35, 39, 40, 43, 48, 57, 58, 61, 68, 74, 79–81, 83, 88, 100, 102, 104, 106, 114, 116, 123, 124, 132, 145, 152, 156, 160, 188, 189
social media, 7, 40, 42, 65–69, 71–76, 82, 84, 98, 100, 101, 102 104, 106, 125, 129, 130, 131, 133, 148, 157, 163–167, 169, 174, 175, 180, 183, 184, 191
Student Response System (SRS), 6, 39, 44, 45, 47, 48
systems flexibility, 5, 18, 115, 130, 139, 140, 142, 197

T

Tilbury, D., 4, 6, 7, 11, 12, 15, 23, 24, 30, 32, 35, 39, 40, 54, 65–74, 76, 79, 88, 94, 95, 97, 100, 102, 106, 112–116, 119, 123, 124, 130, 133, 135, 160, 163, 193
technology-enhanced learning, 1, 3–6, 8, 13, 65, 114, 163, 196
temporary online learning communities, 6, 39
transformative learning, 12, 13, 69, 87, 117, 137, 138, 189, 195
Twitter, 6–8, 65–71, 73–76, 103, 104, 129, 163, 164, 166–170, 172, 174–176, 181, 183, 191, 194–196

V

virtual learning environments, 2, 39, 68, 82, 109, 114, 182

W

Web 2.0 technologies, 8, 14, 42, 81, 82, 85, 130, 138, 140, 142, 164, 165
discussion boards, 6, 85, 93

200

Printed in the United States
By Bookmasters